100
TRAILS
5000
IDEAS

100 TRAILS 5000 IDEAS

WHERE TO GO · WHEN TO GO · WHAT TO SEE · WHAT TO DO

JOE YOGERST

NATIONAL GEOGRAPHIC

WASHINGTON, D.C.

Contents

Pages 2–3: Wonderland Trail, in Mount Rainier National Park, lives up to its name, with an enchanting mix of old-growth forests, flower-draped meadows, and snow-capped peaks.

Opposite: Ooh Aah Point on South Kaibab Trail offers sweeping views of the distinctive sedimentary red rocks of Grand Canyon National Park.

INTRODUCTION

The overall number of trails scattered across the United States and Canada is nearly impossible to count. However, it's safe to say it easily runs into the hundreds of thousands.

Hiking for pleasure has been an American passion for centuries. Not long after the Pilgrims landed along the New England shore, adventurous settlers were clambering over the White Mountains of New Hampshire. Henry David Thoreau wrote about his jaunts around Walden Pond and along Cape Cod. John Muir hiked across southern Ontario along a route that conveys the modern Bruce Trail and made a "Thousand-Mile Walk" from his boyhood home in Wisconsin to the Gulf Coast.

Even Edgar Allan Poe got into the act, penning an essay on his forays into Pennsylvania nature with a supplication that "even of this delicious region, the sweeter portions are reached only by bypaths. Indeed, in America generally, the traveller . . . must walk, he must leap ravines, he must risk his neck among precipices, or he must leave unseen the truest, the richest, and most unspeakable glories of the land."

But trails aren't just for the famous and the naturalists. According to the Outdoor Foundation, more than 160 million Americans participated in various forms of outdoor recreation in 2020. That's more than half the entire population.

Three of the top four outdoor activities—hiking, biking, and running—largely revolve around trails of one sort or another. Nearly one out of every five Americans hikes every year. And that figure doesn't consider those who take a casual stroll through their local park or along a beach. Other than nature itself, that makes trails the nation's most important outdoor recreation asset. Given the fact that hiking and biking help improve a person's physical well-being and mental health, trails are also one of the country's paramount health resources.

I largely came to hiking for the latter reason. As a child, walking was among my least favorite activities. I had asthma and was overweight (or "husky" as they politely termed it in those days). Then, as a teenager, I literally hiked my asthma into submission and lost much of my excess weight on treks

to places including the bottom of the Grand Canyon (page 88) and the summit of Yosemite's Half Dome (page 10).

By my early 20s, I was hooked by trails as diverse as the Annapurna Circuit in Nepal, Mount Kilimanjaro in Africa, and Torres del Paine in Patagonia. Researching and writing this book afforded me an opportunity to hike many new routes across the nation, sometimes with good old-fashioned topographic maps and almost always with a GPS app on my phone to show where I was and record my routes for posterity.

With more than 1,300 routes, the National Trails System rambles more than 88,000 miles (142,000 km) across every conceivable landscape in the U.S.; national parks alone boast around 21,000 miles (33,800 km) of footpaths. The AllTrails website lists more than 85,000 hiking and biking trails and adds more each year. Plus, nearly 2,300 rail-to-trail conversions span 25,000 miles (40,000 km).

Although we would love to feature all those routes, *100 Trails, 5,000 Ideas* concentrates on some of the best hiking and biking routes in North America, with a bonus section featuring top trails in other parts of the world.

A few of these paths—like the Appalachian Trail (page 180) and the Pacific Crest (page 34)—are long-distance hiking legends. Some of the others—like the Fiery Gizzard Trail in Tennessee (page 208), the Cape Chignecto route in Nova Scotia (page 272), and the River to River Trail in southern Illinois (page 158)—are largely unknown to those who live outside their regions. Although wilderness is the main focus, our list also includes urban routes for those who want to stretch their legs in the big city, such as the High Line in New York City (page 230), the San Francisco Bay Trail (page 24), and the Paseo del Bosque in Albuquerque (page 110).

The trails throughout offer something for every type of hiker and biker. They include trails that are easy, moderate, and strenuous, as well as those that hikers or bikers can cover in a couple of hours, several weeks, multiple months, and, in one Canadian case, several years.

I hope the book inspires you to many new hiking and biking adventures in spots already on your outdoor adventure bucket list and places you didn't even consider before.

Several suspension bridges soar along the West Coast Trail in British Columbia's Pacific Rim National Park Reserve. This one crosses Logan Creek.

West Coast

Southbound hikers are graced with snowcapped views of towering Mount Rainier as they ascend Elk Pass toward Old Snowy Mountain.

John Muir Trail
California

Inspired by the long-distance walks, outdoor passion, and environmental activism of its namesake, the John Muir Trail offers an incredibly scenic trek across the High Sierra between Yosemite, Kings Canyon, and Sequoia National Parks.

There isn't another hike anywhere on the planet that kicks off in such dramatic fashion. Starting from the east end of **Yosemite Valley,** the first few steps along the **John Muir Trail** (JMT) are literally within the shadow of **Half Dome** and its massive granite face.

The path quickly rises past two spectacular cascades—**Vernal Falls** and **Nevada Fall**—to **Little Yosemite Valley** and what may just be the world's most photogenic outhouse. Hikers can detour up the backside of Half Dome and nudge their chin over the 4,700-foot (1,440-m) summit. Or they can keep tramping along the JMT into the High Sierra that the trail's namesake knew so well.

Born in Scotland in 1838 and raised in Wisconsin after his family immigrated to America, John Muir is known around the globe as one of the founders of the modern

THE BIG PICTURE

Distance: 211 miles (340 km)

Elevation Gain: approx. 46,000 feet (14,000 m)

Time: 2–4 weeks

Difficulty: Strenuous

Best Time: Summer or early fall

More Info: pcta.org/discover -the-trail/john-muir-trail/

environmental movement and his relentless campaign to get Yosemite declared a national park. What a lot of people don't know about Muir is that he was an avid, lifelong hiker.

Long before he ever set eyes on Yosemite, he spent the better part of a year trekking the Niagara Escarpment in Ontario, covering much of what would later become the Bruce Trail. Three years later, he undertook a 1,000-mile (1,600-km) walk from his boyhood home in Wisconsin across the Midwest and south to Florida's Gulf Coast.

Muir never got a chance to thru-hike the trail that bears his name. There was no north-south footpath through the heart of the Sierras at that time. But he certainly would have known many of the routes closer to its Yosemite end, like the leg beyond Little Yosemite Valley, which takes the JMT up **Sunrise Creek** to the **Cathedral Range** and Tuolumne Meadows.

Muir called **Tuolumne Meadows** "a spacious flowery lawn . . . surrounded by magnificent snowy mountains"—a description that holds true more than a century after his death. One of the largest high-altitude grasslands in the Sierra Nevada, Tuolumne harbors a visitors center, restaurant, and large campground, as well as a store that's one of the few places along

Loop the John Muir and Mist Trails to reach more than 600 granite steps beside the spectacular Vernal Falls.

Although famed environmentalist John Muir never thru-hiked the path of his namesake trail, you can now follow in his activist footsteps through the splendor of the High Sierras.

the JMT where hikers can resupply.

Tuolumne is also the last place that thru-hikers will see a road or vehicle on the journey to Mount Whitney at the bottom end of the trail. Joining up with the **Pacific Crest Trail,** the JMT moseys across the huge meadow and into a forest of hemlocks and pines as it follows the Tuolumne River up **Lyell Canyon.** Named for a 19th-century Scottish scientist whose theories on Earth's geological evolution greatly influenced Charles Darwin and others, the canyon offers just a hint of the spectacular scenery that lies ahead.

Climbing past the tree line near the top of the canyon, the trail offers a view of **Lyell** and **McClure,** Yosemite's last glaciers, both of them considerably smaller when John Muir and Galen Clark measured their movement with wooden stakes in 1872. The glaciers

drape the slopes of 13,114-foot (3,997-m) **Mount Lyell,** the highest peak completely inside Yosemite National Park.

Exiting the park via **Donohue Pass**—the first of six passes along the route that rise more than 11,000 feet (3,350 m)—the trail rambles into the

OTHER GREAT TRAILS

Theodore Solomons Trail

There's another way of walking between Yosemite, Kings Canyon, and Sequoia National Parks. Cobbled together in the 1970s from existing routes, the **Theodore Solomons Trail** (TST) offers a little-used alternative to the John Muir via the lower-altitude "middle" rather than the sky-high Sierra Crest.

The 271-mile (436-km) path runs between Glacier Point in Yosemite and Horseshoe Meadow in Sequoia, with historic Buck Camp, Mono Hot Springs, Lakeshore, Cedar Grove, and Mineral King along the way.

Although the John Muir Trail owes

its existence to numerous people, teenager Theodore Solomons first suggested the idea of a north-south trail along the Sierra Crest while working on his uncle's ranch near Fresno in the 1880s.

By the 1890s, Solomons and his hiking companions were scouting routes through the High Sierra that would later become part of the JMT. It was Solomons who named the Evolution Basin and its biographical peaks, as well as other landmarks.

Trailblazing by Solomons and others convinced the Sierra Club to petition the California legislature for $10,000 to start construction of the trail in 1915.

remote **Ansel Adams Wilderness** in **Sierra National Forest.** The route passes one of the famed photographer's favorite subjects: **Thousand Island Lake** with jagged **Banner Peak** in the background.

The wilderness area spills over into **Devils Postpile National Monument** and its oddball volcanic formations. **Reds Meadow** offers the possibility of two detours off the main route, a short hike to **Rainbow Falls** or a longer (15 miles/24 km) walk into **Mammoth Lakes** with its myriad hotels, shops, and restaurants.

A 40-mile (64-km) trek across the aptly named **John Muir Wilderness** takes the trail over **Selden Pass** and into the northern tip of **Kings Canyon National Park.** Descending into the **San Joaquin River** watershed, hikers soon reach **Muir Trail Ranch** with its rustic restaurant, hot springs, general store, and backpacker resupply service.

Having rested their weary bones, trekkers carry on through the gorgeous **Evolution Basin,** its alpine lakes framed by peaks named for **Charles Darwin, Alfred Russel Wallace, Thomas Huxley,** and other early evolutionists. That old stone hut at the top of **Muir Pass** is the **John Muir Memorial Shelter,** erected during the final stage of trail construction in the 1930s as a tribute to the man.

The track along the western edge of the Sierra Crest continues through **Le Conte Canyon** and past the granite pinnacles of the **Palisade Crest** (one of the holy grails of American mountain climbing). A series of

A 200-mile (320-km) track of the John Muir Trail passes through Le Conte Canyon to Muir Pass via the Sierra High Route in Kings Canyon National Park.

The John Muir Memorial Shelter, also called Muir Hut, can be found on Muir Pass and was built in 1933 in honor of Muir's conservation efforts.

wicked switchbacks called the **Golden Staircase** takes the route across a rocky and often snowbound high-altitude desert through **Mather Pass.**

Having conquered the dreaded staircase, there's a welcome downhill walk into the **Upper Basin** of the **Kings River** and a meander through the lovely **Rae Lakes.** Just south of **Glen Pass,** the JMT intersects with several other major trekking routes. The **Kearsarge Pass Trail** enables a seven-mile (11-km) hike to **Onion Valley** on the eastern side of the

Sierra. Heading in the other direction, the 12-mile (19-km) **Bubbs Creek Trail** drops down to **Roads End** and **Cedar Grove** deep in the bottom of **Kings Canyon.**

For those continuing along the JMT, **Forester Pass** is both the highest pass along the route (13,117 feet/3,998 m) and the lofty segue from Kings Canyon into **Sequoia National Park.** Reaching **Crabtree Meadows** in the upper reaches of the **Kern River** watershed, the John Muir finally bids adieu to the Pacific Crest Trail after 170 miles (273 km) of traveling together and turns sharply to the east.

Mount Whitney looms ahead, an 8.4-mile (13.5-km) uphill hike to the summit of the highest point in the lower 48 states (14,505 feet/4,421 m), along the nation's highest maintained trail. The easiest way to round off the thru-hike is descending to **Whitney Portal** on the eastern side of the Sierra, although hikers can also backtrack to Crabtree and trek west to the trailheads and visitors hubs of Sequoia National Park. ■

High Sierra Camps

Although glamping is considered a modern phenomenon, "glamorous camping" traces its roots to the fashionable Adirondack camps of the 1800s, the posh African safaris of the early 20th century, and Yosemite's High Sierra Camps.

Established in the 1920s to make the wilderness more accessible to greenhorns, tenderfoots, and city slickers, the camps offered comfy tents and dining facilities at remote spots beyond Yosemite Valley. Guests could hike between camps or travel by mule.

A century later, the circuit remains true to its original mission.

The modern-day circuit features five tent camps along a 49-mile (79-km) loop around Tuolumne Meadows, Tenaya Lake, and the Cathedral Range. And mules remain an option for those who don't (or can't) walk.

With no need to cook or backpack, those who undertake the High Sierra circuit can explore the wilderness with little more than a daypack and a water bottle. The camps are booked through an annual lottery that opens October 1 at travelyosemite.com.

Lost Coast Trail
California

California's Lost Coast offers two totally different trekking adventures along the longest stretch of undeveloped shore in the Golden State.

THE BIG PICTURE

Distances: North, 25.3 miles (40.7 km); South, 27.9 miles (44.9 km)

Elevation Gains: North, approx. 1,580 feet (480 m); South, approx. 6,620 feet (2,020 m)

Times: North, 3–4 days; South, 2–3 days

Difficulty: Moderate to strenuous

Best Time: Summer and fall

More Info: blm.gov/visit/lost-coast-trail

Located around 230 miles (370 km) north of the Golden Gate Bridge, the **Lost Coast Trail** offers an exhilarating glimpse of what the entire California coast must have been like before European settlement.

The area gained its cryptic name after the Great Depression, when the local logging and mining industries collapsed and the population plummeted. Aiding and abetting the downturn was a decision by state engineers that the region's steep coastal topography was too extreme even for vertiginous **Highway 1,** which turns inland just south of the Lost Coast. As human civilization vanished, the region found its way back to nature.

More or less evenly split between **King Range National Conservation Area** and **Sinkyone Wilderness State Park,** the Lost Coast has evolved into the largest slice of undeveloped shoreline between Baja and British Columbia.

Lost Coast Trail North flows across driftwood-strewn beaches for most of its length between **Mattole** and **Shelter Cove.** Tramping across sand, pebbles, and wet boulders makes for slow going, so plan on at least three days. Hikers should carry a tide chart and camp above the high-tide line.

The payoff is unfettered California coastal nature: black-sand beaches, a blend of swarthy sandstone and shale rather than volcanic sand; seaside mountains draped in wild grasses and evergreen trees; sea lions and elephant seals lazing along the shore and on offshore rocks. And the only thing human-made—other than rusty shipwreck relics—is the abandoned **Punta Gorda Lighthouse** (built in 1911).

Reaching Shelter Cove comes as a shock to many hikers. Oceanfront inns and vacation rentals offer beds, showers, and central heating. **Gyppo Ale Mill** cooks up hearty meals complemented by craft beers, wines, and ciders. Those doing the full trek rather than just the north half can resupply at **Shelter Cove General Store.**

Hikers can hop onto Lost Coast

Certain sections of the Lost Coast Trail, like this rocky one between Sea Lion Gulch and Spanish Flat in the King Range National Conservation Area, are passable only at low tide.

The Lost Coast Trail leads hikers to stunning coastal views and the remains of the Punta Gorda lighthouse.

Trail South at either **Hidden Valley** or **Nadelos Campground** on the south side of Shelter Cove. Instead of treading the beach, the Sinkyone segment meanders through oak and evergreen forest, coastal prairie and scrub, and even the occasional old-growth redwood grove.

About eight miles (13 km) out, **Needle Rock** features several good campsites and a state park visitors center. Reachable by car, Needle Rock also offers another spot to start or bail on the Lost Coast Trail. The final stretch rambles across cliff tops and woodland and coastal chaparral on footpaths and dirt roads left over from the region's ranching and timber days.

Once again, there are few remnants of the days when humans rather than Mother Nature ruled this coast. **Bear Harbor** once had a wharf for shipping wood products to the coast on a short-lived railroad line. **Little Jackass Gulch** once boasted a wire shoot that conveyed lumber to waiting schooners. At the tail end of the trail, **Usal Creek** was a thriving company town with a sawmill, school, hotel, and other structures. ■

OTHER GREAT TRAILS

• **James Irvine Trail to Fern Canyon Loop:** This 12-mile (19-km) trek at Prairie Creek includes old-growth redwoods, Gold Bluffs Beach, and primeval Fern Canyon, where scenes from *Jurassic Park 2* and *Walking with Dinosaurs* were filmed.

• **Tall Trees Grove:** Only 50 parties a day are allowed on a remote four-mile (6.4-km) loop in Redwood National Park that meanders through many of the world's tallest trees. The drawback is 1,600 feet (488 m) of elevation change.

• **Clear Creek National Recreation Trail:** Keep an eye out for Sasquatch on a 42-mile (68-km) backpacking route through a remote corner of Klamath National Forest that meanders through prime Bigfoot country.

Historic Columbia River Highway State Trail

Oregon

Explore the south side of the Columbia River Gorge on a unique road-to-trail conversion along the old Oregon Trail and one of the nation's first scenic highways.

THE BIG PICTURE

Distance: 15.9 miles (25 km)

Elevation Gain: approx. 1,800 feet (550 m)

Time: 3 days

Difficulty: Easy

Best Time: Spring, summer, or fall

More Info: oregon.gov/ODOT/ Regions/Pages/State-Trail.aspx

Few trails anywhere in the nation travel across such storied ground. Native Americans blazed the original path through the **Columbia Gorge** thousands of years ago. Lewis and Clark passed this way, as did thousands of immigrants following the **Oregon Trail.**

Pulled by mules rather than steam, the first railroad on the West Coast rumbled through the gorge in 1851. Just five years after Ford's Model T debut, the state began construction of the **Columbia River Highway.** When it opened in 1922, the road was considered one of the engineering marvels of the time.

By the 1960s, an interstate had superseded the highway. Decades later, some of the remaining sections of the old road were converted into a nonmotorized path called the **Historic Columbia River Highway State Trail.** Stretching almost 16 miles (26 km) along the Oregon shore, the path is paved and divided into three segments.

Around an hour's drive east of Portland, **John B. Yeon State Park** kicks off the **Bonneville segment.** Landmarks along the 5.6-mile (9-km) trail include **Elowah Falls, Bonneville Dam,** and **Eagle Creek Campground**'s famous **"Big John"** restroom (the first flush toilet in the national forest system!) before reaching the **Bridge of the Gods** near **Cascade Locks.**

The middle **Mitchell Point segment** links **Wyeth Campground** and **Viento State Park** along a 5.8-mile (9.3-km) corridor that includes the high-flying **Summit Creek Viaduct** and **Starvation Creek State Park,** which gained its ominous name in the 1880s, when a passenger train became stranded there during a blizzard.

Bringing up the rear, the 4.5-mile (7.2-km) **Twin Tunnels segment** between **Hood River** and **Mosier** offers great Columbia River views

The golden heads of balsamroot (*Balsamorhiza deltoidea*) blanket Tom McCall Preserve in the Columbia River Gorge National Scenic Area.

Winding along 16 miles (26 km) of Oregon's shorelines, the Historic Columbia River Highway State Trail treats hikers to expansive views from Rowena Crest Viewpoint.

and passage through the **Mosier Twin Tunnels,** another remnant of the 1920s highway.

Hikers seeking a more challenging passage through the illustrious gap can trek **Gorge 400 Trail,** which meanders over the wooded ridges and waterfall-filled canyons between the highway trail and the gorge walls. Stretching between **Angel's Rest** and **Wyeth,** the 35-mile (56-km) route is more rugged, often more remote, and entails far more elevation gain and loss.

After a quick rise to Angel's Rest with its bird's-eye view of the gorge, 400 flits across the bottom of **Multnomah Falls** and **Horseshoe Falls,** with the option of ascending to **Rock of Ages Arch** and another incredible view.

Ainsworth State Park offers camping before a second day that includes **Wahclella Falls** and **Cascade Salmon Hatchery,** then camping at **Eagle Creek** or **Cascade Locks Marine Park.** On the third day, Gorge 400 joins four miles (6.4 km) of the **Pacific Crest Trail** before sauntering into **Wyeth State Park.** ∎

OTHER GREAT TRAILS

• **Timberline Trail:** Circumnavigate Oregon's highest peak—11,249-foot (3,429-m) Mount Hood—on a rugged 40-mile (64-km) trail that follows the tree line around the huge stratovolcano.

• **Wildwood Trail:** Rambling through Forest Park on Portland's northwest side, this woodsy 30-mile (48-km) route brings wilderness hiking to the big city.

• **Blue Mountains Trail:** Completed in 2021, one of the nation's newest long-distance hiking trails wanders 530 miles (853 km) through three national forests, seven wilderness areas, and Hells Canyon in the remote highlands of eastern Oregon.

• **Trail of Ten Falls:** A 7.2-mile (11.5-km) loop route connects the many ribbons of water in Silver Falls State Park along the eastern edge of the Willamette Valley near Salem.

• **Big Indian Gorge Trail:** This 16-mile (26-km) out-and-back or 10-mile (16-km) point-to-point hike probes an impressive U-shaped gorge in the Steens Mountain Wilderness of arid southeast Oregon.

The mystical Multnomah Falls is a photogenic stop on the Historic Columbia River Highway and the most visited natural recreation site in the Pacific Northwest.

Rogue River Trail
Oregon

A legendary white-water river through Oregon's Coast Range provides a liquid backdrop for a trail through a region that flourishes with Wild West history and tales of Hollywood's golden age.

THE BIG PICTURE

Distance: 40 miles (64 km)

Elevation Gain: approx. 4,420 feet (1,350 m)

Time: 3–5 days

Difficulty: Strenuous

Best Time: Spring or fall

More Info: blm.gov/visit/rogue-river-national-recreation-trail

A designated wild and scenic river, the Rogue is well known for rafting, paddling, and fly-fishing. What's far less known is the fact that the wilderness watershed also boasts a hiking route that's just as challenging as its famed white water.

Although the river flows 215 miles (346 km) from **Crater Lake National Park** into the Pacific Ocean, the trail covers just a 40-mile (64-km) portion through **Rogue River-Siskiyou National Forest,** the **Wild Rogue Wilderness,** and a pristine wild and scenic river corridor supervised by the Bureau of Land Management (BLM).

The Rogue has a long, colorful, and sometimes violent history that includes the Rogue River War of the 1850s between settlers and Native Americans (it didn't end well for the latter) to the 1930s, when stars like Clark Gable, Bing Crosby, and Ginger Rogers and authors William Faulkner and Zane Grey frequented the watershed.

By the late 20th century, the Rogue had evolved into one of the nation's premier wilderness recreation rivers, as well as the front line in an ongoing environmental struggle to remove dams and restore salmon habitat.

The **Rogue River Trail** runs along the waterway's north side, a sometimes precipitous route with narrow segments high above the river. For the most part, the bird's-eye views easily outweigh any vertigo. Thru-hikers best avoid the high temperatures of summer and the messy blend of rain, sleet, and intermittent snow that descends upon the region in winter. Hikers and boaters share the same campgrounds along the route.

Most folks follow the trail east to west, starting from **Grave Creek Boat Ramp** around a 40-minute drive from **Grants Pass.** From there it's downstream past the **Rainie Falls** rapids to **Whisky Creek,** with its historic **gold miner's cabin** (built in 1880) and the first of numerous primitive campsites along the river.

Rogue River Ranch National Historic Site is home to more than 9,000 years of Native American history in what is now Rogue River-Siskiyou National Forest.

Moss-draped rocks line the meandering Tate Creek on the Rogue River Trail.

Another six miles (9.6 km) down the river is **Black Bar,** a campsite on the north side of the river, a rustic lodge on the opposite bank. Beyond are **Jenny Creek** and **Battle Bar,** where the Takelma people skirmished with would-be settlers. **Zane Grey's Cabin**—where the celebrated Western author wrote *Rogue River Feud* in 1929—is the next landmark along the river.

Farther downstream, the trail passes through historic **Rogue River Ranch,** founded in 1903 and later owned by dancer Ginger Rogers for half a century. **Marial** hamlet provides a brief respite from the wilderness before the big S-curve in the river below **Paradise Bar** and a final leg down to **Foster Bar,** where the trail ends.

The most comfortable way to walk the Rogue River Trail is a raft-supported hiking trip through outfitters like **Morrisons Rogue Wilderness Adventures** or **Momentum River Expeditions.** The boats pace hikers along the route, arrange overnights at riverside campsites or lodges, and provide all meals. ∎

LAY YOUR HEAD

• **Black Bar Lodge:** Founded in 1934 and owned by the same family since the 1960s, this rustic abode lies on the south bank but provides a ferry service to hikers with reservations; from $175; blackbarlodge.com.

• **Marial Lodge:** Hot showers and awesome meals await hikers in overnight digs that were once the home of a pioneer family whose daughter Marial gave the riverside town its name; from $150; facebook.com/MarialLodgeInc.

• **Paradise Lodge:** Popular with rafters, anglers, and hikers, this vintage 1950s inn serves what's arguably the best grub along the entire Rogue; from $175; paradise-lodge.com.

• **Clay Hill Lodge:** Homesteaded by legendary Rogue River storyteller Hathaway Jones, the remote lodge is only reachable by foot or boat; from $175; clayhilllodge.com.

• **Illahe Lodge:** Near the western end of the trail, Illahe offers private rooms, shared living spaces, and communal dining in two farmhouse-style buildings; from $165; illahelodge.com.

Tahoe Rim Trail
California & Nevada

THE BIG PICTURE

Distance: 165 miles (265 km)

Elevation Gain: approx. 27,920 feet (8,510 m)

Time: 10–14 days

Difficulty: Strenuous

Best Time: Summer and fall

More Info: tahoerimtrail.org

Sierra wilderness and stunning views of "Big Blue" are the lures of a rugged 165-mile (265-km) route around the Lake Tahoe Basin that enables hiking and biking in summer and Nordic skiing and snowshoeing in winter.

Completed in 2001, after two decades of development, the **Tahoe Rim Trail** (TRT) offers a rugged, two-state journey around one of the world's deepest and most beautiful lakes. The first thing that any would-be walkers should know is that, rather than hugging the shoreline, the trail follows a roller-coaster route through the highlands along the California-Nevada frontier.

Eight designated trailheads with parking offer quick and easy access to the TRT. Users can also trek spur trails from lakeside locations like **Emerald Bay State Park** or **Sugar Pine Point** on the California side and **Incline Village** on the Nevada shore. The only place the trail comes close to the waterfront is **Tahoe City,** beside a transit center with public buses serving the north shore.

From Tahoe City, the TRT quickly climbs into the heights above **Truckee River Canyon** past an ancient cinder cone, lava cliffs, and other evidence of the long-ago volcanic activity that formed the Tahoe Basin. The **Lava Cliffs** offer especially stunning lake views. Crossing the state line high above **Crystal Bay,** the trail reaches its highest point at **Relay Peak** (10,338 feet/3,151 m) before descending into **Mt. Rose ski area.**

Bending around to the south, the trail dances across peaks on the Nevada side to a short spur called **Christopher's Loop** that renders what many TRT veterans consider the most stunning views along the entire route. Meandering through mixed woods and over granite outcrops, the next segment offers views of both Tahoe and broad **Carson Valley** before crossing back into

Open year-round, the Tahoe Rim Trail traverses a range of landscapes, from lush conifer forests and flowering meadows to snowcapped vistas.

The Lake Tahoe Basin provides a breathtaking backdrop to sky-high hiking and biking trails on the Tahoe Rim Trail.

California above **Heavenly ski area** and the neon-studded casinos of **Stateline.**

The trail blazes a wide berth around the bottom end of heavily populated **South Lake Tahoe** before intersecting with the **Pacific Crest Trail** (PCT) at **Meiss Meadow** in the **Upper Truckee River Valley.** Joined at the hip, the two trails head north across a glacially carved region spangled with small alpine lakes. The watery terrain offers a brief respite from climbing, but dead ahead are the high peaks of **Desolation Wilderness.** One of the nation's oldest federally protected wilderness areas (established in 1931) carries 17 miles (27 km) of the TRT through conifer forest, flower-filled meadows, and lofty granite summits with more sky-high views of Lake Tahoe. A final

segment that starts at **Barker Pass** takes the trail back into Tahoe City to complete the epic loop.

The Tahoe Rim Trail is open throughout the year. However, the region's typically heavy snowfall can make some portions difficult or nearly impassible even for trekkers equipped with cross-country skis or snowshoes. Although much of the TRT is open to mountain bikers, Desolation Wilderness, Christopher's Loop, and the westside portion shared with the Pacific Crest Trail are open only to hikers.

For those who want company trekking the loop, the **Tahoe Rim Trail Association** offers guided hikes ranging from educational day trips and four-day overnights to weeklong backpacking trips and two-week journeys along the entire length. ◼

APRÈS HIKE

• **Vikingsholm:** This extravagant, Scandinavian-style mansion in Emerald Bay State Park was constructed in the 1920s as the summer home of wealthy philanthropist Lora Knight.

• **Sand Harbor Amphitheater:** On the lakeshore near Incline Village, the open-air stage provides a starry venue for the annual Lake Tahoe Shakespeare Festival, as well as performances by the Sierra Nevada Ballet, Reno Jazz Orchestra, and Reno Philharmonic.

• **Donner Memorial State Park:** Memorials and museum exhibits highlight the Wild West immigrant experience, the native Washoe people, the Chinese workers who helped build the transcontinental railroad, and the Donner party of 1846–47.

San Francisco Bay Trail
California

Hike or bike around California's largest bay on a meandering shoreline trail that runs across city parks, legendary bridges, and wildlife refuges, and through cities that continue to impact culture and technology around the globe.

THE BIG PICTURE

Distance: 354 miles (570 km)

Elevation Gain: Negligible (except bridges)

Time: 2–3 weeks

Difficulty: Easy

Best Time: Year-round

More Info: baytrail.org

Few American water bodies are as celebrated as **San Francisco Bay.** Crossed by famed bridges, complemented by an iconic skyline, and flanked by lush national and state parks, it's one of the world's most photogenic bays. And witness to all that history—from the California gold rush and 1906 earthquake to liberty ships, flower power, and Silicon Valley.

It's always been a great place to walk (assuming you don't have an aversion to hills). But only recently, the bayside itself has become a great place to hike and bike, thanks to an epic and still evolving trail that will one day run along the entire shore. Around 70 percent of the proposed 500-mile (800-km) route is currently open, with the remaining 150 miles (240 km) slated for completion in the near future.

When finished, the **San Francisco Bay Trail** (SFBT) will traverse the waterfront of nine counties and 47 cities, including San Francisco, Oakland, and San Jose. It will cross seven major spans, including the Golden Gate and Bay Bridge. It will meander through much of **Golden Gate National Recreation Area** (the most visited unit of the entire National Park System), skirt the southern edge of the Napa-Sonoma wine country, and thread several national wildlife refuges.

The SFBT is divided into 25 numbered sections starting from the San Francisco waterfront and running counterclockwise around the bay. It intersects with a lot of other trails, especially in the San Jose/Santa Clara Valley area, the Oakland-Berkeley Hills, and Marin County.

A thru-hike is possible for users willing to shell out for hotel accommodations (there's only one campground along the route), trek surface streets across portions that are yet to be completed, or migrate between finished sections via rideshare or public transport.

Section 1 along the San Francisco waterfront is far and away the most popular, especially during the summer or weekends throughout the year. That's because it runs along the **Embarcadero, Fisherman's Wharf, Fort Mason,** and **Crissy Field** on its way between the **Oracle Park** home of the San Francisco Giants and

Opened in 1883, this waterfront saloon was the first—and last—opportunity for arriving and departing sailors to imbibe before setting sail.

The San Francisco Bay Trail meanders past verdant wine country and several wildlife refuges as it winds counterclockwise around San Francisco Bay.

Fort Point beneath the **Golden Gate Bridge.** The SFBT will eventually run all the way south along the San Francisco waterfront, a route that will curl around the old shipyards at **Hunter's Point** to the shore where **Candlestick Park** stadium once stood.

After crossing the Golden Gate to **Marin County,** the trail offers a gentle amble along a bay shore spangled with very expensive homes to **Sausalito** with its popular waterfront restaurants, art galleries, and craft shops of just about every ilk. You can shop until you drop or keep chugging along the SFBT to **Bothin Marsh Preserve** and

• **Back Ranch Meadows:** The trail runs through the middle of this China Camp State Park campground and its 33 walk-in, tent-only sites; $35 per site; friendsofchina camp.org/visit-the-park/camping.

• **Union Hotel:** Established in 1882, this historic abode along the Carquinez Strait segment of the SFBT lies near the old California State Capitol in downtown Benicia; from $119; unionhotelbenicia.com.

• **East Brother Light Station:** An active lighthouse since 1873, this islandbound Victorian landmark offers five B&B rooms with views across the bay to the city, Marin, and a future portion of the SFBT on Point San Pablo; from $475; ebls.org.

• **Waterfront Hotel:** This chic little boutique on the Oakland Estuary is just steps away from the Bay Trail, Jack London Square, and the San Francisco Bay Ferry landing; from $179; jdvhotels.com.

• **HI San Francisco Fisherman's Wharf:** Vintage army barracks at Fort Mason are the venue for a Hostelling International hangout with both private and dorm rooms astride a San Francisco northern waterfront walk; from $42; hiusa.org.

Strawberry Point in **Mill Valley.** A sidewalk hike or street bike along Strawberry Drive leads to **Tiburon Linear Park** and an easy run down to the **Tiburon** docks and a ferry back to San Francisco.

Farther north in Marin, users have an opportunity to cross the **Richmond-San Rafael Bridge** to the East Bay via a dedicated bicycle and pedestrian lane. Or they can continue along the San Rafael waterfront to **China Camp State Park,** which preserves the site of a shrimping village that immigrants from southern China founded in the 1880s. With resident deer, coyotes, foxes, and copious birdlife, China Camp is one of the best places along the SFBT to watch for wildlife.

The trail remains sketchy around the north end of **San Pablo Bay,** with long stretches where users must use streets or sidewalks. The landscape at this bottom end of the **Sonoma-Napa** wine country remains largely rural, a mosaic of pastures and grassy hills smothered in wildflowers come spring, tidal creeks and marshes, and soggy mudflats. This far north, the only long portions of the SFBT that are completed are found in the **Sears Point Restoration Area** and along the **Napa River** estuary.

Reaching the bay's northeast corner, the trail detours inland along the **Carquinez Strait** at the mouth of the Sacramento River, the route passing through historic towns like **Vallejo, Benicia** (California's capital city in 1853–54), and **Martinez** (birthplace of Joltin' Joe DiMaggio).

At some point in the near future, hikers and bikers will be able to glide across that other huge span, the **San Francisco-Oakland Bay Bridge.** The bridge's west span remains vehicle-only, but plans are under way to create a dedicated bicycle and pedestrian path. However, the new east span—constructed after the Loma Prieta earthquake of 1989—offers a new

Cyclists and pedestrians alike enjoy a picturesque day on the San Francisco Bay Trail beside the Fort Point U.S. Coast Guard Station.

hike/bike lane that links **Yerba Buena Island** and the East Bay.

Coming down from the Bay Bridge, users have two choices. They can hang a left onto a bayside trail that runs along the **Emeryville** and **Berkeley** waterfronts to **Albany.** Or they can turn right into **Oakland** on a route that follows Maritime Street through a huge container terminal and **West Oakland** residential streets to reach **Jack London Square.**

Although most of the buildings are modern, the square does preserve the cabin where author Jack London lived during his gold mining days in the Klondike, as well as the historic **First and Last Chance Saloon** that appeared in several of his novels. More important, the portion of the SFBT along the **Oakland Embarcadero** is refreshingly vehicle free.

From Oakland, trail users can hop a ferry back to San Francisco. Or continue south along the SFBT to **San Leandro Bay** and **Oyster Bay Regional Shoreline.** This stretch of the trail also lends itself to detours along the surface streets of **Bay Farm Island** and **Alameda,** including a jaunt through an old U.S. Navy air station that now hosts **craft breweries, boutique distilleries,** and **wine-tasting cellars**.

South of San Francisco International Airport, **Bayfront Park** in **Millbrae** marks the start of a long, largely nonmotorized portion of the SFBT down the shoreline of the **San Francisco Peninsula.** Beyond the canals of **Foster City,** the route glides into a series of bayside burgs—**Redwood City, Menlo Park, Palo Alto, Mountain View,** and **Sunnyvale**—that form the heart of **Silicon Valley.**

As it nears the bottom end of the bay, the trail skirts past the

China Camp State Park is host to some of the most pristine tidal salt marshes in the San Francisco Bay Estuary, making it an ideal home for birds such as the great egret.

Googleplex, Facebook headquarters, and other high-tech holy grails on a stretch that also includes organic marvels like **Palo Alto Baylands Nature Preserve** and **Don Edwards San Francisco Bay National Wildlife Refuge.**

Alviso Historic District in **San Jose** marks the southernmost point of the Bay Trail with Victorian and Mission Revival structures and a vintage Chinese gambling hall. From there, the route starts a long run up the tidelands along the bay's southeast shore, a segment that features **Coyote Hills Regional Park** in **Fremont** and **Eden Landing Ecological Reserve** in **Hayward** before the SFBT completes the loop in Oakland. ◼

OTHER GREAT TRAILS

Bay Area Ridge Trail

The trail around the bay complements the **Bay Area Ridge Trail,** a much more challenging hiking, biking, and equestrian route that rambles across many of the highest peaks and ridges in the nine counties that surround the bay.

Nearly 400 miles (640 km) of the proposed 550-mile (890-km) route are open, including segments through the Presidio, Golden Gate Park, the Marin Headlands, the Santa Cruz Mountains, the Santa Clara Valley, the Oakland-Berkeley Hills, Napa Valley, and Bolinas Ridge.

The Bay Area Ridge Trail Council offers a selection of curated adventures and three-day hike/bike base camp suggestions on its website.

Among the many possibilities are dog-friendly, family-friendly, and wheelchair-accessible trails; lunar new year, solstice, and redwood hikes; swim-and-hike and dine-and-hike adventures; and portions of the trail that flaunt the best wildflowers.

Kalalau Trail
Hawaii

The remote Nāpali Coast along the north shore of Kauai provides an iconic setting for a trail that blends jungle valleys, remote beaches, and lost-in-paradise camping.

THE BIG PICTURE

Distance: 22 miles (35 km) out and back

Elevation Gain: approx. 6,180 feet (1,880 m)

Time: 2–3 days

Difficulty: Strenuous

Best Time: Year-round

More Info: kalalautrail.com and dlnr.hawaii.gov/dsp/hiking/kauai/kalalau-trai

This epic route along the **Nāpali Coast** isn't just the most renowned walk in Hawaii. Its fame has spread around the globe. And for good reason. The scenery is simply stunning: rust-colored cliffs rising thousands of feet above the shore, remote rainforest valleys with jungle streams and waterfalls,secluded beaches, and the deep-blue sea stretching as far as the eye can see.

Yet beauty can be deceiving. Despite its short length (11 miles/ 18 km out and back), the **Kalalau Trail** is not to be trifled with. *Nāpali* means "cliffs" in Hawaiian, and the route's steep terrain and sheer drop-offs present a real challenge. *Backpacker* magazine rates the Kalalau as one of the nation's 10 most dangerous hikes.

Weather can also cause problems.

Given the fact that it's perched on the edge of one of the rainiest spots on Earth, the trail often experiences washouts, landslides, and flash floods. As a result, it can be closed for months at a time while the Hawaii Division of State Parks undertakes repairs.

Another issue that hikers must address before they set off is how to reach the trailhead at the end of the **Kuhio Highway** (State Route 560). There's no parking at the trailhead itself, and overnight parking is extremely limited at nearby **Ha'ena Beach** and **Ke'e Beach.** However, there is a shuttle service from **Hanalei** and **Princeville**.

The initial leg of the Kalalau Trail is a relatively easy two-mile (3.2-km) walk through tropical forest and along a sheer slope with dreamy ocean views to the **Hanakapi'ai Valley** in **Nāpali Coast State Wilderness Park.** The valley's offshore waters are too rough for swimming or snorkeling, but the beach is ripe for picnics or just lazing around. A steep and often rocky spur trail meanders up the narrow valley to 300-foot (90-m) **Hanakapi'ai Falls.**

Day-trippers can visit Hanakapi'ai Valley without a permit. But anyone who ventures beyond that point—even those who are not

A two-mile (3.2-km) hike through tropical rainforest and a narrow valley leads to the 300-foot (90-m) Hanakapi'ai Falls, an impressive stop on the Kalalau Trail.

Verdant sea cliffs capture the sunrise on the Nāpali coastline of Kokee State Park on Kauai, Hawaii.

camping—must obtain an overnight permit from Hawaii State Parks. Permits are available 30 days in advance and sell out quickly.

Beyond Hanakapi'ai, the trail quickly climbs from sea level to 800 feet (240 m) as it traverses the **Hono O Nā Pali Natural Area Reserve.** Those making the trek as a multiday rather than single-day hike can overnight in the **Hanakoa Valley** at primitive campsites perched on ancient stone agricultural terraces.

Anyone who's afraid of heights probably shouldn't attempt the next leg, because it includes a narrow passage called **Crawler's Ledge** that hugs a cliffside around 300 feet (90 m) above the waves. Hikers who master that challenge find the rest of the trail pretty easygoing, a little

more than three miles (4.8 km) across a series of volcanic ridges to the **Kalalau Valley.**

More than a mile wide and framed by 2,000-foot (610-m) cliffs, Kalalau Valley offers shaded

campsites, a composite toilet, and several freshwater sources. Having reached paradise, many hikers are tempted to stay forever. However, five nights is the maximum the state allows. ■

APRÈS HIKE

- **Hanalei:** The nearest town to the trailhead offers bikini shops, Asian fusion food, and the famous Wishing Well Shave Ice stall.

- **Limahuli Garden and Preserve:** Guided and self-guided tours meander through a 900-acre (364-ha) wonderland of tropical plants, including species introduced by ancient Polynesian immigrants.

- **Polihale State Park:** The crown jewel of Kauai's west shore is

celebrated for dramatic sunsets that include a silhouette of Ni'ihau Island on the horizon.

- **Waimea Canyon:** The "Grand Canyon of the Pacific" (often lauded as the wettest place on Earth with an average 450 inches [1,140 cm] of rain a year) is truly spectacular, a deep multicolored chasm draped in waterfalls plunging down the side of Mount Wai'ale'ale volcano.

The lush cliffs of the island of Kauai plunge into the Pacific.

Eklutna Traverse
Alaska

Rambling across Chugach State Park, this hard-core trek over high mountain passes and imposing glaciers offers a quick study in the forces that have shaped the Alaska landscape.

You don't have to travel to the Arctic to get the full-on Alaska wilderness experience. Starting and ending little more than an hour outside Anchorage, the **Eklutna Traverse** takes winter skiers and summer hikers on an adventurous journey up remote river valleys, past alpine lakes, and across four glaciers in the rugged **Chugach Range.**

There's also historic significance:

The southern half of the traverse traces part of the original **Iditarod** route between Seward and Nome. Blazed in the early 20th century to supply the Nome goldfields and isolated settlements in the Alaskan Interior, the route inspired the modern Iditarod Trail Sled Dog Race. The Eklutna Traverse also shares half its path with the slightly less daunting **Crow Pass Trail.**

THE BIG PICTURE

Distance: 38 miles (61 km)

Elevation Gain: Unknown

Time: 4–5 days

Difficulty: Strenuous

Best Time: Year-round

More Info: dnr.alaska.gov/parks/aspunits/chugach/chugachindex.htm

Although the southern and northern sections of the traverse are fairly well marked, the middle part requires the glacier equivalent of bushwhacking across the ice fields. Anyone attempting the thru-hike should have winter backcountry camping and survival experience, and come equipped with a compass, map, and GPS device.

During winter, the traverse is really only doable with backcountry-rated Nordic skis and a good pair of ski touring boots. During summer, a good pair of hiking boots, crampons, and trekking poles should get you through. Four overnight huts or cabins are available throughout the year.

Which end you choose to start from largely depends on whether you want a gentle slope over the first few days (north to south) or to get the steepest part behind you on the first day (south to north). Our description follows the latter.

The traditional southern start is a parking lot in **Glacier Gulch,** seven miles (11 km) north of **Girdwood.** It's just under two miles (3.2 km) from the trailhead to **Crystal Lake** and **Crow Pass Cabin,** but with an elevation gain of more than 1,600 feet (488 m), it can be slow going. Rather than overnight so close to the start, many trekkers prefer to push on.

After breaching the pass, the trail splits, the Crow Pass Trail to **Eagle**

Nimble billy goats climb the mountainside near Crow Pass in Chugach State Park, Alaska.

The old Iditarod Trail provides a point-to-point route along Eagle River and Crow Pass Trail in Chugach State Park, with the Raven Glacier looking on in the distance.

River Nature Center veering off to the left, the Eklutna Traverse hanging a sharp right that takes you across **Raven Glacier** and the welcome sight of **Rosie's Roost.** Surrounded by the jagged peaks of the Chugach Range, the sturdy A-frame cabin is perched along the south edge of **Eagle Glacier.**

The route continues across Eagle Glacier and over the southern tongue of **Whiteout Glacier** to bright red **Han's Hut** and another overnight. Day three or four is a relatively easy glide over **Whiteout Pass** and across gently sloping **Eklutna Glacier.** Trekkers can overnight at **Pichler's Perch** cabin beside the glacier or descend along the West Fork of the **Eklutna River**

to **Serenity Falls Hut** with its big picture windows.

Having come down from the high country, the last day entails a 12-mile (19-km) hike along the

north shore of **Eklutna Lake** to the state park visitors center and campground. From there it is a quick zip down Alaska Highway 1 to Anchorage. ◼

APRÈS HIKE

• **Alyeska Resort:** Alaska's summer mountain biking hub offers rentals, downhill lessons, guided rides, and a full-blown bike park; come winter, it's the state's largest and most popular ski resort. alyeskaresort.com.

• **MICA Guides:** Guided hikes, ice climbing, and overnight camping on Matanuska Glacier, plus zip line and ATV adventures on the Chugach Range's north side are available. micaguides.com.

• **Alaska Helicopter Tours:** Flight-seeing, chopper landings, and dogsled tours on Knik Glacier in the central Chugach are offered from a base at Knik River Lodge. alaskahelicoptertours.com.

• **Iditarod HQ:** A combined museum and shop in Wasilla offers everything you ever wanted to know about the legendary dogsled race, as well as dog cart rides. iditarod.com.

Pacific Crest Trail
California, Oregon & Washington

Meandering more than 2,600 miles (4,200 km), the Pacific Crest crosses deserts, foothills, majestic river valleys, and two mighty mountain ranges on its journey between Canada and Mexico.

The **Pacific Crest Trail** (PCT) may be the youngest of America's "triple crown" of long-distance thru-hikes—and it may stretch across just three states—but in several respects it's more spectacular than the Appalachian or Continental Divide Trails.

Consider the fact that it runs across seven national parks—Sequoia, Kings Canyon, Yosemite, Lassen Volcanic, Crater Lake, Mount Rainier, and North Cascades—during a journey that takes most hikers at least half a year to complete.

Beyond the national parks, the trail also threads its way through 48 federal wilderness areas, 25 national forests, six state parks, and four national monuments. Its geographical variety is also astounding: a trek that embraces parts of the Colorado and Mojave Deserts, the Sierra Nevada and Cascade Ranges, Lake Tahoe, and the Columbia River Gorge.

No doubt inspired by construction of the Appalachian Trail between the world wars, Catherine Montgomery first proposed the idea of a trail through the Pacific Crest wilderness in 1926. During an interview that year, the "mother of the Pacific Crest Trail," who was an avid hiker, suffragist, and teacher at the Washington State Normal School in Bellingham, envisioned "a high winding trail down the heights of our western mountains with mile markers and shelter huts."

Six years later, Los Angeles theater impresario Clinton C. Clarke ("father of the PCT") formed a committee to put Montgomery's proposal into action. Clarke's committee began a plan to create the route. Among those who joined the group were photographer Ansel Adams, as well as the Boy Scouts of America and the YMCA. Between 1935 and 1938, teams of YMCA "Relay Boys" mapped the route and members of the Civilian Conservation Corps began to undertake much of the construction.

Although the PCT was declared a national scenic trail in 1968, the entire route wasn't completed until 1993, when the route's golden spike

THE BIG PICTURE

Distance: 2,650 miles (4,265 km)

Elevation Gain: approx. 429,830 feet (131,010 m)

Time: 5–7 months

Difficulty: Strenuous

Best Time: Spring, summer, or fall

More Info: pcta.org

The Pacific Crest Trail's northern terminus, in the Pasayten Wilderness, lies on the U.S.-Canada border and is a celebratory marker for those who reach it.

A gnarled tree clings to the rocky cliff face at Inspiration Point in the Angeles Mountains, accessed via the Pacific Crest Trail with views of Mount Baldy and San Gabriel Canyon.

was driven in Soledad Canyon in **Angeles National Forest.**

Trekking the PCT has inspired several epic books. After completing the first known thru-hike along the entire route in 1971, Eric Ryback wrote *The High Adventure of Eric Ryback: Canada to Mexico on Foot.* But the most famous tale of hiking the trail is *Wild: From Lost to Found on the Pacific Crest Trail* by Cheryl Strayed, a 2012 book recounting her emotional, life-changing trek that was later made into a hit movie.

Whether you start the Pacific Crest from north or south can be a totally random decision. Ryback started from the Canadian border in Washington State, Strayed from the Mexican border in southern California.

Unless you're a veteran walker who can reel off 30 to 50 miles (48 to 80 km) a day with a fully laden backpack, it's probably best to start from the south. Given the usual snow cover in the North Cascades, the trek is difficult to start until May and sometimes even June or early July. However, the relatively low mountains to the east of San Diego expedite quick and easy passage for those who set off as early as April.

SHORT CIRCUITS

These sections of the PCT are ideal for day hikes:

• **San Bernardino National Forest:** This 12-mile (19-km) segment of the PCT rambles across the mountains north of Big Bear Lake between Polique Canyon trailhead and mile 266.1 on Highway 18.

• **Yosemite National Park:** With 70 miles (110 km) of the PCT, including relatively flat sections north and south of Tuolumne Meadows, the park offers hikes of anywhere from half an hour to a full day.

• **Lassen Volcanic National Park:** A 20-mile (32-km) stretch of the PCT goes from Warner Valley to Old Station right through the heart of the park.

• **Crater Lake National Park:** A six-mile (9.6-km) section that wraps around the western rim of the crater between Rim Village and Merriam Point is one of the most spectacular sections of the PCT.

• **North Cascades National Park:** Those who hop the ferry across Lake Chelan can hike short sections of the PCT up Agnes Creek or the Stehekin River from High Bridge Campground.

The PCT starts its northward journey at a marker beside a barbed-wire fence and metal border wall near **Campo,** California, in the San Diego backcountry. The elevation is only 2,915 feet (888 m) at this point, one of the lowest along the entire trail. But after moving through chaparral foothills, the trail quickly climbs into pine-studded heights of **Mount Laguna** in **Cleveland National Forest.**

Dipping down into **Anza-Borrego Desert State Park,** the trail cuts across aptly named **Earthquake Valley** and the old **Butterfield Stage** route before rambling up the south side of **Mount San Jacinto** (10,834 feet/3,302 m). The nation's sixth most prominent peak affords incredible views of the **Coachella Valley,** especially from terraces around the top of the **Palm Springs Aerial Tramway.**

Tumbling down into the lowlands again, the PCT crosses beneath Interstate 10 near **Cabazon,** a quirky little desert community renowned for its casino, outlet mall,

Signage helps guide nature lovers in the right direction.

At 14,494 feet (4,418 m), Mount Whitney is the tallest mountain in the lower 48. Reach the crest via a steep spur trail in Sequoia National Park.

and full-size dinosaur statues. Dead ahead are the lofty **San Bernardino Mountains** and **Big Bear Lake,** and a brief flirtation with the **Mojave Desert.**

Kayaking on **Lake Isabella** and rafting the **Lower Kern River** provide a watery sideshow before the trail ascends into the **Sierra Nevada.** After entering **Sequoia National**

Park, a steep spur trail climbs to the crest of **Mount Whitney,** tallest mountain in the lower 48 states at 14,494 feet (4,418 m). Continuing through **Kings Canyon National Park, Ansel Adams Wilderness,** and the volcanic wonders of **Devils Postpile National Monument,** the PCT shares its route with the **John Muir Trail** (JMT).

LAY YOUR HEAD

• **Warner Springs Ranch Resort:** This historic cattle ranch (established in 1844) was transformed into a rustic resort around large mineral springs pools in the San Diego backcountry; restaurants, bar, spa, general store, tennis, golf, bikes, horseback riding; from $74; warnerspringsranchresort.com.

• **Railroad Park Resort:** Overnight in converted vintage cabooses, rustic cabins, or the campground at this quirky retreat near Mount Shasta;

dining car restaurant, outdoor pool, game room, internet; from $135; rrpark.com.

• **Drakesbad Guest Ranch:** Book a dude ranch astride the PCT in Lassen Volcanic National Park; restaurant, bar, hot springs, horseback riding, laundry service; from $162; drakesbad.com.

• **Olallie Lake Resort:** Unplug at this remote camp in Oregon's Mount Hood National Forest with self-catering yurts, cabins, and campground; general store, boat rental, picnic area;

from $70; olallielakeresort.com.

• **Timberline Lodge:** This classic wilderness lodge (opened in the 1930s) below Mount Hood caters to winter and summer sports; restaurant, bar, fitness center, outdoor pool, laundry service; from $155; timberlinelodge.com.

• **Stevens Lodge:** This friendly backpacker hostel beside the PCT in Stevens Pass, Washington, has dining room, showers, laundry facilities; from $60; mountaineers.org/locations -lodges/stevens-lodge.

For a change of pace, explore the expansive Pacific Crest Trail on horseback.

Donohue Pass takes the trail into **Yosemite National Park,** a heavily trekked portion that runs down **Lyell Canyon** to **Tuolumne Meadows.** Many hikers sojourn in the Yosemite high country for a couple of days before heading north into **Stanislaus National Forest** and the **Lake Tahoe** region. The PCT follows the **Tahoe Rim Trail** around the western edge of "Big Blue" past the **Squaw Valley** snow sports area, which hosted the 1960 Winter Olympics, and then through **Donner Pass** (named for much earlier trekkers, the ill-fated Donner party of 1846).

Making the transition from the Sierra Nevada into the Cascade Range, the trail meanders through **Lassen Volcanic National Park,** perpetually snowcapped **Mount Shasta,** and through **Klamath National Forest** (renowned for its Bigfoot sightings) on its final leg in California.

The rustic towns of southern Oregon provide other respites from trail routine, especially **Ashland** with its annual **Oregon Shakespeare Festival** (February to October). The PCT traverses ecologically diverse **Cascade-Siskiyou National Monument** before ascending into **Sky Lakes Wilderness** and **Crater Lake National Park.** Whether you take a dip in one of the world's top 10 deepest lakes (1,949 feet/594 m) or simply gaze at its amazing deep blue color, the Oregon landmark offers another great chance to take a break from walking.

Between Crater Lake and **Mount Hood,** the PCT follows the path of an even older hiking route called the **Skyline Trail,** cobbled together by the U.S. Forest Service in the early 1920s from old Native American, pioneer, trapper, prospector, and mountain men trails through the Cascades of central Oregon. Along the way are five wilderness areas, scores of alpine lakes, and the historic **Dee Wright Observatory,** lava-stone towers built in 1935.

Skirting the western edge of Mount Hood, the trail descends into the incredible **Columbia River**

LOCAL FLAVOR

• **Pie for the People:** Get hand-tossed, New York–style pizza just off the PCT in the Cascades of central Washington; 741 Highway 906, Snoqualmie Pass, WA; (425) 518-7799.

• **Thunder Island Brewing:** Easy Climb, Ornery Goat, and Remember the Forest are a few of the suds on tap at this gastro-brewery beside the Columbia River; 515 NW Portage Road, Cascade Locks, OR; thunderislandbrewing.com.

• **Wildwood Tavern:** Deep in the heart of Bigfoot country, this backwoods eatery specializes in local free-range Rainey beef, wild berry cheesecake, and other homemade delights; 45200 Highway 96, Seiad Valley, CA; wildwoodtavernand lodge.com.

• **PlumpJack Cafe:** Find this gastronomic landmark with the finest dining along the entire PCT near Lake Tahoe; 1920 Squaw Valley Road, Olympic Valley, CA; plump jackcafe.com.

• **Reyes Winery:** A tasty detour beside the trail in southern California serves cabernet, muscat, rosé, and other fine wines; 10262 Sierra Hwy, Agua Dulce, CA; reyeswinery .com.

• **Pine House Cafe:** Burgers, sandwiches, salads, and incredible broccoli-and-salmon mac and cheese flavor this vintage mountain-top restaurant (established 1942) near the southern end of the PCT; 9849 Sunrise Highway, Mount Laguna, CA; pinehousecafe.com.

Gorge, an 80-mile-long (130 km) canyon that carves a 4,000-foot (1,200-m) furrow through the Cascade Range. Descending to the riverside town of **Cascade Locks,** the PCT crosses the Columbia River on the **Bridge of the Gods** (completed in 1926) before crawling back into the mountains.

Diving into south-central Washington State, the trail makes a beeline for **Mount Adams**, a giant snow-covered stratovolcano spotted in 1805 by Lewis and Clark, who thought it might be "the highest pinnacle in America." Turns out it's the second highest peak in the Pacific Northwest, surpassed only by the next lofty landmark along the trail: **Mount Rainier** (14,410 feet/4,392 m).

The trail continues along the Cascades through **Mount Baker-Snoqualmie National Forest,** a stretch that features four wilderness areas and the **Kendall Katwalk,** a narrow cliffside section perched along a sheer granite face. The northern branch of the transcontinental railroad was constructed through **Stevens Pass** in the 1890s, but nowadays trains bound for **Seattle** chug through a tunnel burrowed deep beneath the PCT.

Continuing its roller-coaster ride across the Cascades, the trail cuts across the upper part of **Lake Chelan National Recreation Area.** Perched at the lake's north end, the bucolic **Stehekin Valley** affords another great place to rest and recuperate before the final push to Canada. Besides exploring the valley's historic pioneer district and browsing the **Golden West,** hikers might even consider a voyage on the *Lady of the Lake* across the fjord-like water body.

Beyond the vale, the trail runs through the Bridge Creek section of **North Cascades National Park** into **Okanogan-Wenatchee National Forest** and a rendezvous with the **Pacific Northwest National Scenic Trail** at Holman Pass. The PCT finally reaches the international frontier at **Monument 78** (the 78th boundary marker west of the Pacific Ocean along the 49th parallel). The marked path continues eight miles (13 km) into **Manning Provincial Park** in **British Columbia,** but anyone undertaking that portion must carry their passport and written permission from the Canada Border Services Agency. ■

Home to numerous volcanoes, including one of the largest plug dome volcanoes in the world, Lassen Volcanic National Park is one of the oldest national parks in the United States.

San Juan Islands
Washington

Floating in the Salish Sea between Vancouver Island and Puget Sound, the exquisite San Juan Islands offer a smorgasbord of short scenic trails and a gnarly mountain route.

THE BIG PICTURE

Distances: Various

Elevation Gains: Various

Time: 1 hour to half day

Difficulty: Easy to strenuous

Best Time: Late spring, summer, or fall

More Info: nps.gov/sajh and parks.state.wa.us/547/Moran

Washington's San Juan Islands may be more renowned for boating, but the woodsy archipelago offers an enticing variety of hiking routes through national and state parks on San Juan and Orcas Islands, the two largest landmasses.

SAN JUAN ISLAND

Great Britain and the United States nearly came to blows in 1859, when an American farmer killed a pig owned by an Irishman working for the local branch of the British Hudson's Bay Company. Both nations dispatched troops and warships to the island. But the "Pig War" was settled peacefully, leading to a mutual 12-year occupation recalled nowadays in the two units of **San Juan Island National Historical Park**.

Near the island's north end, the whitewashed blockhouse and barracks at **English Camp** mark the start of **Bell Point Trail** that meanders through the woods along the edge of **Garrison Bay** (where the British anchored their gunships) and **Westcott Bay.** Starting from the parking lot, the full loop is around two miles (3.2 km). Hikers can extend the walk—and savor an organic, sea-to-table lunch—on a short spur trail to **Wescott Bay Shellfish Company** just outside the park boundary.

The Yanks dug in at **American Camp** on the island's south shore. A new **visitors center** marks the start of several trails. The short, easy **History Walk** includes the Officers' Quarters, Parade Ground, and an earthen redoubt overlooking the **Strait of Juan de Fuca.** From the redoubt, hikers can set off along a cliff-top route to **Grandma's Cove** or the **South Beach Trail** along the rocky shore to a meadow popular with red foxes.

ORCAS ISLAND

Named after a Spanish viceroy of Mexico rather than the black-and-white whale, Orcas Island harbors the archipelago's largest nature preserve—5,252-acre (2,125-ha) **Moran State Park.** Hikers can choose from 15 marked routes that total more than 38 miles (61 km) of trail through a wildlife-rich forest comprising lodgepole pines, Douglas

The white-tipped red fox *(Vulpes vulpes)* is the unofficial mascot of the San Juan Islands.

The Patos Island Lighthouse was established in 1893 at the edge of Patos Island.

firs, hemlocks, and red cedars.

One of the easier, more popular routes, the **Cascade Lake Loop** runs 2.7 miles (4.3 km) around the shore of its namesake lake. While the trail runs through lush forest and cliff tops along the western shore, it parallels the main park road for much of its run along the lake's west coast. On the way are the **Sugar Shack** ice-cream stand and a dock where hikers can rent canoes, kayaks, and paddleboards from **Orcas Adventures.**

Hard-core hikers can conquer the **Mount Constitution Loop,** a 6.7-mile (10.7-km) trail that starts on the west side of the park's **Mountain Lake.** Climbing quickly through the woods, the route skirts little **Summit Lake** on to the summit of the tallest peak in the San Juans. The view from 2,409-foot (734-m) Constitution is sublime, a panorama that spans Vancouver's skyscrapers, Mount Baker, Puget Sound, and Vancouver Island. The vista is even better from the peak's historic stone **observation tower** (built in 1935). ∎

LAY YOUR HEAD

• **LeanTo Glamping:** These comfy tents beside Cascade Lake in Moran State Park are outfitted with queen beds, indoor table and chairs, outdoor picnic table, fire ring, and Coleman stove; available June to September; from $200; stayleanto .com.

• **Rosario Resort & Spa:** Created in 1905 for Seattle shipbuilder Robert Moran, the waterfront estate has morphed into a modern resort with restaurant, spa, marina, and museum a short drive from Moran State Park; from $139; rosarioresort.com.

• **Lakedale Resort at Three Lakes:** With everything from lodge rooms and log cabins to camping, yurts, and RV hookups, this San Juan Island resort offers a full range of overnight choices in various price ranges; lakedale.com.

• **Saltwater Farm:** Modern, designer-savvy cabins in the woods near Friday Harbor make a great base for hiking San Juan Island National Historical Park; from $349; saltwater farmsji.com.

Tony Knowles Coastal Trail
Alaska

Urban nature is the theme of a multiuse trail along the Anchorage waterfront that combines wildlife and wilderness with aviation and panoramic skyline views.

THE BIG PICTURE

Distance: 22 miles (35 km) out and back

Elevation Gain: approx. 1,220 feet (370 m)

Time: 1 day

Difficulty: Easy

Best Time: Spring, summer, and fall

More Info: alaska.org/detail/tony-knowles-coastal-trail

Anyone who treks the **Tony Knowles Coastal Trail** between downtown **Anchorage** and Kincaid Park can expect close encounters with nature, whether beluga whales cruising offshore or a moose stepping from the woods.

Paved from start to finish, the trail welcomes hikers, bikers, skaters, and strollers during the warmer months, and Nordic skiers and snowshoers during the long Alaska winter.

Although you can hop onto the Tony Knowles in numerous spots, the most popular trailhead is **Elderberry Park** at the bottom of 5th Avenue in downtown Anchorage. That old mustard-colored structure beside the trail is the **Oscar Anderson House,** built in 1915, when Anchorage was little more than a tent city, and now a museum dedicated to the city's pioneer days.

After ducking beneath the railroad tracks, the trail runs along **Cook Inlet,** named after the celebrated British mariner who explored the bay in 1778. The inlet is renowned for extreme tides (second only to the Bay of Fundy) that expose vast mudflats along the shore. Around high tide, keep a lookout for the bright white beluga whales that frequent the inlet home.

Westchester Lagoon, Bootlegger Cove, and **Fish Creek** offer opportunities to spot some of the feathered friends who visit during summer, including sandhill cranes, arctic terns, the short-billed dowitcher, and both the greater and lesser yellowleg.

Dense forest on both sides of the trail marks the start of **Earthquake Park,** where history boards describe the Good Friday quake of 1964 that rocked Anchorage. Measuring a literal earth-shattering 9.2 on the Richter scale and lasting four minutes, the tremor devastated much of downtown Anchorage and caused landslides that destroyed 75 homes in the Turnagain neighborhood where the park now stands.

Reaching **Point Woronzof,**

You may spot bull moose while trekking the 11-mile (18-km) Tony Knowles Coastal Trail into Kincaid Park.

An Alaskan husky leads bicyclists along the Tony Knowles Coastal Trail in Anchorage, Alaska.

hikers and bikers should take in a view that includes the downtown skyline, snowy peaks beyond the north shore of Cook Inlet, and jets coming in low to land at nearby **Anchorage International Airport.**

Around the other side of the airport is **Kincaid Park,** one of the city's largest green spaces and the spot where users are most likely to encounter a moose, bear, and other wild things along the route. Sprawling across 1,400 acres (566 ha) of forest, meadow, and shoreline—and with more than 37 miles (60 km) of interconnecting trails—the park offers plenty of scope to extend your hike or bike off the Tony Knowles. During winter, it's a huge Nordic skiing hub.

Those who want to cycle the route can pick up a ride at **Pablo's Bike Rentals** near the start of the trail in downtown Anchorage. The selection includes electric bikes, as well as tandems, cruisers, adult trikes, and kids' bikes. ∎

OTHER GREAT TRAILS

• **Chitistone Goat Trail:** Trekkers hop a 20-minute bush flight from McCarthy to the start of this route through the remote wilderness in Wrangell-St. Elias National Park. The trail is often steep, but the payoff is glaciers, peaks, and wildlife along a route originally blazed by Dall sheep rather than humans.

• **Triple Lakes Trail:** The longest maintained trail in Denali National Park offers an undulating 9.5-mile (15-km) trek between the main visitors center and Denali Park Village.

• **Harding Icefield Trail:** Kenai Fjords National Park offers a single hiking trail—a spectacular 8.2-mile (13-km) out-and-back through coastal forest and tundra to an overlook of the frozen behemoth that feeds the park's glaciers.

• **Hatcher Pass:** History and nature are the dual focus of a route that combines a self-guided tour of Independence Mine ghost town and the Gold Cord Lake Trail to an alpine tarn in the rugged mountains above Palmer.

Wonderland Trail
Washington

Hikers can circumnavigate glacier-draped Mount Rainier, the highest peak in the Cascades Range, on a trail that varies from lush old-growth forest to sparse, snow-covered heights in one of the nation's oldest national parks.

THE BIG PICTURE

Distance: 93 miles (150 km)

Elevation Gain: approx. 22,000 feet (6,700 m)

Time: 10–14 days

Difficulty: Strenuous

Best Time: Summer or early fall

More Info: nps.gov/mora/planyourvisit/the-wonderland-trail.htm

You won't run into Alice, but you'll find plenty of other astonishing sights along the Wonderland Trail—especially when the clouds clear and hikers get their first glimpse of glacier- and snow-covered **Mount Rainier** against a deep blue Pacific Northwest sky.

With only 93 miles (150 km) of distance to cover, the **Wonderland Trail** doesn't seem like much of a challenge. Yet with multiple ridges and valleys, segments that top 6,000 feet (1,830 m) in altitude, and the possibility of snow, sleet, or heavy rain even at the height of summer, the trail is far more challenging than it seems at first glance.

Blazed during the early 20th century after Mount Rainier was declared one of the first national parks, the trail was used mainly for ranger patrols and guided horseback trips during its formative years. Nowadays, horses, bikes, and pets are forbidden on the trail.

The Wonderland offers an intimate journey through the park's diverse highland landscapes and ecosystems. At lower elevations, the trail meanders through thick, old-growth forest dominated by cedar, hemlock, spruce, and Douglas fir trees. The trail leaps major water bodies (like the **Tahoma Creek** and the **Carbon River**) on sturdy wooden suspension bridges; lesser streams are crossed on narrow log bridges that may or may not be there after a major rain.

Reaching 5,000 feet (1,500 m), the terrain transitions into subalpine parkland with flower-filled meadows, berry bushes, heather, sedge, and stunted trees. On the hike through **Panhandle Gap**—Wonderland's highest point at 6,750 feet (2,060 m)—the route breaks through the tree line into an alpine zone typified by rocky scree, sparse grass, and snow patches that can sometimes outlast the summer.

Although the trail doesn't cross any permanent ice fields, it does skirt many of the park's 25 named glaciers. **Emmons** and **Winthrop** on the mountain's northeast face are the largest and most impressive. Sinuous, snakelike **Carbon Glacier** on Rainier's north face is the longest, plunging deep into the **Carbon River Valley,** where it runs parallel

The northwest section of the Wonderland Trail leads to a waterfall at Cataract Creek beside the Carbon River campsite.

Once busy with activity from boats and a storefront, Reflection Lakes now make for a serene backdrop to a relaxing portion of the Wonderland Trail.

to the Wonderland Trail. Carbon is also the lowest-altitude glacier in the lower 48 states.

Scattered along the trail are 18 primitive campgrounds and three rustic mountain huts built by the Civilian Conservation Corps during the Great Depression. Most of these camps can accommodate anyone from solo hikers to small trekking groups (6 to 12 people). The backcountry digs are complemented by three developed (drive-in) campgrounds near the **Cougar Rock, Mowich Lake,** and **White River** trailheads.

With its grassy wide-open spaces and tiny alpine lake, **Klapatche Park** campground offers the trail's best sunsets. On the mountain's opposite side, **Summerland** campground and **Indian Bar** shelter offer

two of the highest overnight spots as well as a chance to catch sunrise over central Washington.

Wilderness permits are required to overnight along the Wonderland

throughout the year. But during the busy summer trekking season—to prevent overuse of the trail—the Park Service has a daily quota dispersed through a lottery system. ■

SHORT CIRCUITS

These sections of the Wonderland Trail are ideal for day hikes:

- **Reflection Lakes:** For those who want to hike just a portion of the Wonderland, the easiest segment is a dead-flat stretch along the south shore of the Reflection Lakes.

- **Longmire-Cougar Rock:** Another relatively easy section is the 1.7-mile (2.7-km) hike through thick woods from historic Longmire village to the Cougar Rock overlook on Paradise Road.

- **Mowich Lake-Spray Park:** This three-mile (4.8-km) section of the Wonderland climbs from the lakeshore to an alpine meadow on the mountain's northwest face, a strenuous out-and-back trail that includes a short spur to towering Spray Falls.

- **Glacier Basin Trail:** Starting from White River Campground, this 6.5-mile (10.5-km) round-trip hike ascends the rocky river valley to Glacier Base Camp with a steep spur to Emmons Moraine.

Spray Park Trail is an offshoot of the Wonderland Trail's northwest section with views of Mother Mountain.

Olympic Discovery Trail
Washington

Explore the backwoods and byways of the lush Olympic Peninsula on a multiuse hiking, biking, and horseback trail that stretches from Puget Sound to the Pacific Ocean.

The idea for developing the **Olympic Discovery Trail** (ODT) sprang from the minds of three young cyclists who in the late 1980s envisioned a vehicle-free route through some of their favorite terrain. More than 30 years later, the trail offers a super-scenic journey across the North Olympic Peninsula.

Much of the 135-mile (217-km) route follows former railroad lines that once transported timber to Port Angeles and Port Townsend. Around a quarter of the trail shares the right-of-way with highways and country roads, a factor that makes a thru-

THE BIG PICTURE

Distance: 135 miles (217 km)

Elevation Gain: approx. 6,170 feet (1,880 m)

Time: 5–8 days

Difficulty: Moderate

Best Time: Spring, summer, or fall

More Info: olympicdiscoverytrail .org

journey easier for bikers than hikers or horse riders.

In addition to the aforementioned coastal cities, the ODT also runs through Olympic National Park, several state and local parks, the traditional homelands of the S'Klallam, Quileute, and other Indigenous people, and a region renowned for Sasquatch sightings and the *Twilight* vampire books and movie series.

Port Townsend Boat Haven marks the eastern end of the trail, a gentle bayside stretch that soon veers inland through the mixed forest and farmland of the **Quimper Peninsula.** Beyond **Discovery Bay,** run beside Highway 101 to **7 Cedars resort** with its collection of three dozen Jamestown S'Klallam totem poles before rolling into **Sequim Bay State Park** and a campground that features dedicated hiker/biker sites.

Veering away from the busy highway, the ODT passes through the lavender-growing countryside on either side of **Sequim,** a stretch that includes **Carrie Blake Park, Dungeness River Audubon Center,** and **Robin Hill Farm County Park.** The trail eventually follows **Morse Creek** to the **Strait of Juan de Fuca** and a lovely coastal section that runs along the **Port Angeles** waterfront. Crossing the **Elwha River,** the

This vehicle-free trail winds 135 miles (217 km) through lush forests, coastlines, and farmlands.

Catch movie-worthy sunsets at James Island off of First Beach in the village of La Push, the conclusion of the Olympic Discovery Trail.

route follows Highway 112 to Joyce, where the **Blackberry Café** offers Sasquatch burgers and other roadside diner dishes to hungry hikers and bikers. A left turn at Crescent School takes the journey down into **Olympic National Park** and the most scenic stretch of the entire ODT. The **Log Cabin Resort** on **Lake Crescent** makes a great place to chill for a couple of days before following the **Spruce Railroad Trail** along the heavily forested shoreline to the lake's western end.

The ODT follows a nonmotorized route through much of the **Sol Duc Valley,** but eventually links up with Highway 101 again about a dozen miles (20 km) north of **Forks.** Surrounded by the Olympic rainforest, the town averages more than eight feet (2.4 m) of rain each year. The **Forks Timber Museum** now competes with the girl-meets-vampire

Twilight saga as the local claim to fame.

From Forks, it's about a 14-mile (22.5-km) hike or bike down Highway 110 through the **Quillayute Valley** to the western end of the Olympic Discovery Trail. The route finally peters out beside **First Beach**

in the middle of **La Push** village on the **Quileute Reservation.** Several seafood restaurants offer a great place to celebrate completing the trail. The rugged, remote coast flanking La Push is part of Olympic National Park. ∎

Seattle Waterfront Trails
Washington

Seattle has transformed its hardworking industrial waterfront into nirvana for urban hikers, with a pair of trails that render astonishing views of Puget Sound and the city's visionary skyline as well as clear-day peeks at Mount Rainier and the Olympic Range.

The Emerald City was born and raised on a hilly isthmus between Lake Washington and Puget Sound. To facilitate maritime passage between these two water bodies, the city constructed the Lake Washington Ship Canal and the Ballard Locks.

In bygone days the shoreline was a forest of sailing ships, fishing boats, and Klondike steamer masts.

The vessels of old have been replaced by modern cruise ships and the ubiquitous Washington State Ferries that ply to the outer islands. Meanwhile, the waterfront has taken on new life as Seattle's favorite hiking, biking, and running spot.

ELLIOTT BAY TRAIL

This six-mile (9.6-km) route along the downtown waterfront

THE BIG PICTURE

Distance: Elliott Bay, 6 miles (10 km); Burke-Gilman, 19.8 miles (32 km)

Elevation Gains: Elliott Bay, approx. 130 feet (40 m); Burke-Gilman, approx. 400 feet (120 m)

Time: Half a day

Difficulty: Easy

Best Time: Late spring, summer, or fall

More Info: wta.org

runs past many of Seattle's landmark attractions, as well as some of the best shoreline benches, picnic lawns, and people-watching spots.

Starting near **T-Mobile Park** (home to the Seattle Mariners of major league baseball) and **Lumen Field** (home of the Seattle Seahawks of the NFL), the **Elliott Bay Trail** heads north along **Alaskan Way.** Off to the right is the city's oldest neighborhood, the **Pioneer Square-Skid Road Historic District.** Seattle started here in 1852, when the first lumber mill opened. **Yesler Way,** a street leading down to the waterfront, earned the nickname "Skid Road" because logs were literally skidded down the muddy thoroughfare to be loaded onto ships.

Just past the always-busy **Seattle ferry terminal** is Pier 54 and a vintage novelty store called **Ye Olde Curiosity Shop** that's been around since 1899. Strange artifacts from around the world are exhibited in the shop museum, while the merchandise runs a wide gamut from Bigfoot keepsakes and Native American art to a wide variety of flasks and totemic T-shirts.

Pier 57 hosts two modern attractions. Soaring 175 feet (53 m), the **Seattle Great Wheel** is the tallest

The glass-sided fishing ladder at Ballard Locks provides an intriguing up close look at salmon as they swim upstream.

The Elliott Bay Trail weaves among downtown Seattle's waterfront landmarks for six miles (10 km).

Ferris wheel on the American West Coast. Lit at night by half a million LED bulbs, the wheel carries passengers in 42 pods on a three-revolution ride that extends out over Elliott Bay. The pier's other pull is **Wings Over Washington,** a blend of IMAX theater and theme park ride that features "flying" seats and bird's-eye views of Washington State landscapes and landmarks.

Opposite the excellent **Seattle Aquarium** on Pier 58, the Pike Street Hill Climb stairs rise to legendary **Pike Place Fish Market.** Founded in 1903, it's one of the nation's oldest continuously operated public markets. Fresh-off-the-boat seafood is the main event, but hundreds of stalls also dispense flowers, fruits and vegetables, clothing, arts and crafts, souvenirs—you name it.

The Elliott Bay Trail tags along to **Pier 70,** where it finally breaks away from road traffic to carve its own

path along the shoreline. Part of the **Olympic Sculpture Park** tumbles down the grassy hill to the trail, including the **Father and Son**

fountain by Louise Bourgeois and the huge white **Echo** head by Jaume Plensa.

Up ahead are a couple of

LOCAL FLAVOR

• **Ray's Boathouse:** Sablefish (black cod), Alaskan king salmon, black cherry margaritas, and honey lavender crème brûlée highlight this shoreline eatery along the BGT near Golden Gardens Park; 6049 Seaview Avenue NW; rays.com/boathouse.

• **Westward:** "All the creatures of the sea" is the motto of a canalside restaurant just off the BGT in Northlake with an expansive outdoor deck and a maritime menu that ranges from classic crab rolls to Baja shrimp with polenta; 2501 N. Northlake Way; westwardseattle.com.

• **AQUA by El Gaucho:** Surf and turf are the specialty at a classic seafood restaurant on Pier 70

opposite the Olympic Sculpture Park; 2801 Alaskan Way, Pier 70; elgaucho.com/aquabyelgaucho.

• **Old Stove:** Perched above Alaskan Way and the Elliott Bay Trail, this microbrewery in the modern Pike Place Fish Market extension complements its suds with shellfish, chowders, and salmon BLT sandwiches; 1901 Western Avenue; oldstove.com/restaurant.

• **Ben Paris:** Inspired by a pool hall that occupied the same space 100 years ago, this hip joint in the State Hotel is renowned for its weekend brunch and wicked cocktail creations conjured by celebrity mixologist Abigail Gullo; 130 Pike Street; benparis.com.

driftwood-strewn pocket beaches where hearty swimmers can slip into Puget Sound, and then picnic-friendly **Myrtle Edwards Park.** That giant rooftop sphere over on the right is the famous **P-I Globe,** erected in 1948 as the neon emblem of the *Post-Intelligencer* newspaper and now an official city landmark.

The trail continues past the towering grain silos of **Pier 86** and the new **Expedia** corporation complex, and then makes a huge inland loop around **Smith Cove** before a final stretch along the **Seattle Yacht Club** to a small rocky beach at the end of West Marina Place.

BURKE-GILMAN TRAIL

Popular with locals, the **Burke-Gilman Trail** (BGT) runs roughly 20 miles (32 km) between **Golden Gardens Park** on **Puget Sound** and Blyth Park in suburban Bothell. The route rambles along the north shore of the **Lake Washington Ship Canal** and then makes a huge fishhook bend over the north end of Lake Washington.

Much of the trail follows the disused bed of the old Seattle, Lake Shore and Eastern Railway, founded in 1885 by Daniel Gilman, Thomas Burke, and other local entrepreneurs. The first section of the hike/bike trails opened just a few years after the railroad line was abandoned in the early 1970s.

From Golden Gardens, the BGT makes its way past the huge **Shilshole Bay Marina** to the **Ballard Locks.** Constructed between 1911 and 1917, the nation's single busiest shipping locks provide passage for more than 50,000 vessels

The Great Wheel—a Ferris wheel with half a million LED bulbs—offers a stunning waterside view.

OTHER GREAT TRAILS

• **Sammamish River Trail:** From the northern end of the BGT, this wine-tasting route runs 10 miles (16 km) through the vineyard-infused Sammamish Valley between Bothell and Redmond.

• **Blake Island:** A fast ferry connects downtown Seattle to a marine state park in Puget Sound with eight miles (13 km) of trail along the shore and across the island.

• **Discovery Park:** Seattle's biggest city park offers numerous hiking options through the woods and along the sound, including the 2.8-mile (4.5-km) Discovery Park Loop National Recreation Trail.

• **Lake Sammamish Loop:** Circumnavigate this big lake on the city's east side on a 22.4-mile (36-km) route through forests, fields, wetlands, and semirural residential areas.

• **Duwamish Trail:** This offbeat hike through a heavily industrialized area links the Duwamish Longhouse and Cultural Center with several new shoreline parks and West Duwamish Greenbelt.

each year. The national historic landmark also has a glass-sided **fish ladder** where visitors can view salmon swimming upstream (between June and September), an **Army Corps of Engineers** visitors center, and the leafy **Carl S. English Jr. Botanical Garden.**

East of the locks, hikers and bikers must cross a 1.5-mile (2.4-km) "missing link" through **Ballard,** where the trail runs along busy surface streets rather than its own path. Despite years of planning and promises by the city, this missing section of the BGT is years away from fruition. However, the missing link

does have a major trailside attraction—the **National Nordic Museum**—reflecting the fact that Ballard was once a Scandinavian immigrant community.

The nonmotorized trail picks up again at 45th Street and 11th Avenue, the start of a segment that includes **Fremont Canal Park** with its topiary dinosaurs, the deep-blue **Fremont drawbridge** (built in 1917), and wonderful skyline views from **Kite Hill** in steampunk-flavored **Gas Works Park.**

Huskies dominate the next leg of the BGT. Not the dogs, mind you, but students at the **University of Washington** (UW). The trail makes a big bend through the campus as it transitions from the ship canal to **Lake Washington.** Trekkers can detour across **Montlake Bridge** to the university's **Washington Park Arboretum,** wander through the UW **Union Bay wetlands preserve,** and mingle with students at **University Village** shopping mall.

Tacking to the north, the Burke-Gilman undertakes another remarkable mood change as it traverses upscale residential areas like **Laurelhurst** and **Hawthorne Hills** before reaching the lakeshore near **Matthews Beach.** The latter was once home base for the legendary Pan Am "Clippers"—huge flying boats that provided the world's first transoceanic passenger service.

The BGT traces the lakeshore through **Cedar Park, Sheridan Beach,** and **Kenmore** at the north end of Lake Washington, before a short homestretch along the **Sammamish River** to suburban **Bothell.** Hikers can return to downtown Seattle by hopping Metro Bus no. 522 from a stop at 96th Avenue and Bothell Way near **Blyth Park.** ∎

Coast to Crest Trail
California

This recently created San Diego County route connects the Coast Range with the chaparral foothills and some of the region's most celebrated beaches.

THE BIG PICTURE

Distance: 71 miles (114 km)

Elevation Change: approx. 6,000 feet (1,830 m)

Time: 3–4 days

Difficulty: Easy to moderate

Best Time: Year-round

More Info: sdrp.org

The **San Dieguito River Valley** provides a natural pathway between the mountains and ocean on the outskirts of **San Diego,** a transition from oak and pine forest at the higher altitudes to aromatic coastal chaparral and lush riverside vegetation.

Awaiting those who trek the route from east to west are two sandy strands where the Southern California beach lifestyle plays out every day. But the main reason for hiking the **Coast to Crest Trail** is nature.

More than 120 bird species have been sighted along the route, and the valley is home to a wide variety of critters, ranging from mountain lions, bobcats, and coyotes to mule deer, ringtail cats, rattlesnakes, and even the occasional octopus.

Around 48 miles (77 km) of the trail is currently nonmotorized, open only to hikers, bikers, and horseback riders. Road and sidewalk sections provide a transition for thru-hikers, although most users seem to complete the trail over time rather than all at once.

The upper (eastern) starting point is **Volcan Mountain Wilderness Preserve** in **Cleveland National Forest** near the historic gold mining town of **Julian.** A telescope at the summit affords views of the far-off coast before you set off along the trail.

The route quickly drops into the **Santa Ysabel Valley,** where Spanish padres established a small mission in 1818 that became a private rancho after Mexican independence. The valley's **Volcan Mountain Nature Center** stages everything from bird counts and wildcrafting workshops to historic dinners and wine and cheese tastings.

Hugging the north shore of **Lake Sutherland,** the trail makes its way into the **San Pasqual Valley,** where the U.S. Army of the West battled Mexican lancers in 1846 during the Mexican-American War. Nowadays it's better known for its small wineries and as home of the **San Diego Zoo Safari Park.**

Slipping around **Escondido,** the route passes **Sikes Adobe** (built in the 1880s) and along the north

Once completed, the San Dieguito River Park Coast to Crest Trail will stretch from the coast of Del Mar to Volcan Mountain, with views of Lake Hodges.

The San Dieguito River Park Trail takes horseback riders past the Lake Hodges Dam.

shore of **Lake Hodges** before a steep descent through narrow **Del Dios Gorge** to the **Santa Fe Valley** with its lush country clubs and Thoroughbred horse ranches. Just past the **Del Mar Polo Fields** (normally busy with youth soccer games), **San Dieguito Lagoon** comes into view.

After ducking beneath Interstate 5, the trail edges past the **Del Mar Fairgrounds,** home to the annual county fair in June and July and the **Del Mar Thoroughbred Club,** one of the nation's premier horse-racing facilities.

The Coast to Crest officially ends beside the roundabout on **Jimmy Durante Boulevard.** But hikers and bikers can continue along a dirt path beside the lagoon and across

the railroad tracks (look both ways!) to the ocean. The river finally empties into the sea between super-hip

Del Mar Beach to the south and **Dog Beach** with its sand volleyball courts to the north. ■

LOCAL FLAVOR

• **Julian Beer Company:** Located just over two miles (3.2 km) from the Volcan Mountain trailhead, this craft brewery offers pub grub and great suds brewed on the site of the town's first home (built in 1869); 2307 Main Street, Julian, CA; julianbeerco.com.

• **Julian Pie Company:** Caramel, Dutch apple, boysenberry, apple crumb, strawberry rhubarb, and pecan are just a few of the flavors at the county's most famous pie emporium; 21976 Highway 79, Santa Ysabel, CA; julianpie.com.

• **Hernandez Hideaway:** Sunday brunch with margaritas is the local favorite, but this eatery beside the trail near Lake Hodges offers traditional California Mexican cuisine six days a week; 19320 Lake Drive, Escondido, CA; facebook.com/MargaritasByTheLake.

• **El Pueblo:** This strip-mall restaurant may look unassuming from the outside, but it's where local surfers head for delicious 99-cent fish tacos after hanging ten at Del Mar Beach; 2673 Via de la Valle, San Diego, CA; delmarmexicanfood.com.

California Riding & Hiking Trail

California

Despite its grandiose name, this backcountry trail wanders across just a small section of the Golden State, a meander through the Joshua trees and giant boulders of the Mojave Desert.

"Riding" referred to horses when this trail was blazed across **Joshua Tree** in the late 1940s. Mountain bikes wouldn't become a thing for 30 years, and the **Mojave Desert** outpost was an obscure national monument in those days rather than one of the nation's most visited national parks.

The trail's rather generic name comes from the fact that it was originally part of a grand scheme to blaze an epic horseback and hiking route that would have stretched the entire length of the Golden State. By the 1970s, that incredibly ambitious plan had been abandoned and all except one already built portion of the **California Riding and Hiking Trail** (CRHT)—the one across Joshua Tree—had been absorbed into other trails.

But the noble idea lives on across 37-odd miles (60 km) of high desert spangled with giant rust-colored boulders and the outstretched arms of the park's namesake *Yucca brevifolia*.

The route is easy to follow—marked with etched-metal signs—and not all that rugged. But the remote location and extreme weather that can vary from snow in winter to triple-digit temperatures throughout the summer—make this no trail to trifle with. Thru-hikers should cache water at road-accessible waypoints.

Veteran hikers like to start from **Black Rock Campground** at the trail's west end because you get most of the uphill climb over within the first five miles (8 km) and it's either flat or downhill after that.

Black Rock also affords a chance to camp the night before and hit the trail in the crisp, clean dawn air with the sun coming up over the cloudless Mojave. The route kicks off with a slow but steady ascent into the park's highest region, a leg that culminates at 5,170 feet (1,575 m) below **Eagle Peak.**

From there, it's a welcome downhill walk into the Joshua tree–filled **Upper Covington Flats** and around the south side of **Quail Mountain**

More than 250 species of birds thrive in Joshua Tree National Park, including seven different types of hummingbirds.

The 35-mile (56-km) California Riding and Hiking Trail traverses moderately difficult terrain near the Juniper Flats trailhead in Joshua Tree National Park.

into the heart of the park. With plenty of space for dispersed camping, **Juniper Flats** is a good place to break for the night. Look for spots on the leeward side of boulders to shield yourself from the fierce desert winds that often blow through Joshua Tree.

You'll pass a hint of civilization the following morning through **Ryan Campground** before wandering off into the roadless desert again. As the trail crosses Geology Tour Road, hikers can snatch a glimpse of the famous **Jumbo Rocks** to the northeast and might even be tempted into a detour that includes a selfie at **Skull Rock.**

Most thru-hikers shun those often crowded spots and continue along the CRHT to **Queen Valley** and the possibility of a second overnight.

East of **Pinto Basin Road,** the trail slips between **White Tank** and **Belle Campgrounds,** although the area's boulder clusters offer a far more picturesque place to pitch your tent.

From Queen Valley, it's about an eight-mile (13-km) hike on day three via the **Pinto Wye** area to the end of the trail at the park's **North Entrance Station.** ∎

OTHER GREAT TRAILS

• **Goat Canyon Trestle:** Starting from Mortero Palms, this 5.8-mile (9.3-km) loop meanders through the rocky wilderness of Anza-Borrego Desert State Park to the world's longest curved wooden railroad trestle.

• **Golden Canyon/Zabriskie Point:** Starting from either the Golden Canyon or Zabriskie Point parking lots, this 5.8-mile (9.3-km) loop traverses some of Death Valley's most intriguing geology, including the Red Cathedral.

• **Kelso Dunes:** Mojave National Preserve presents a Sahara-like setting for a strenuous three-mile (4.8-km) out-and-back path that ascends the park's spectacular 600-foot (180-m)-tall sand dunes.

• **Palm Canyon:** An easy grade, plenty of shade, a cool stream, and an interesting Native American backstory make this two-mile (3.2-km) oasis trail one of the highlights of visiting Palm Springs.

Haleakalā-Kaupō Hike
Hawaii

The summit-to-sea hike across Haleakalā National Park to historic Kaupō Market on Maui's south shore segues from volcanic desert and cinder cones to grasslands and tropical forest.

THE BIG PICTURE

Distance: 17.8 miles (28.6 km)

Elevation Loss: approx. 9,490 feet (2,890 m)

Time: 2 days

Difficulty: Strenuous

Best Time: Any season

More Info: nps.gov/hale

*H*aleakalā means "house of the sun" in Hawaiian—the lofty summit where legendary chief Maui captured the solar orb and held it captive until the sun pledged to give Earth more daylight. Yet these days, the hike across Haleakalā feels more like walking on the moon.

Much of the **Haleakalā-Kaupō Hike** crosses rugged lava rocks and loose cinder ejected from the massive shield volcano during various eruptions over the past 30,000 years. Although the last one occurred around 500 years ago, geologists still classify Haleakalā as a dormant, rather than extinct, volcano that could spring to life again.

The trek from summit to sea entails two trails with very different personalities. The **Keonehe'ehe'e "Sliding Sands" Trail** crosses the desertlike main crater to the Palikū overnight area. From there, the **Kaupō Trail** passes through a gap on the crater's southeast side and downhill through progressively thick vegetation to Highway 31 near the Maui coast.

Hard-core hikers can walk the entire route in a single day or undertake a tough out-and-back with a turnaround at Palikū—but those who do miss out on the extraordinary experience of spending a night in the bottom of a volcanic crater.

The downhill version of the route kicks off on the west rim beside **Haleakalā Visitor Center.** Take in the view from the highest point (10,023 feet/3,055 m) before diving into the belly of the beast on a long descent to the crater floor. The high-altitude desert is almost devoid of organic life. Yet here and there are hearty plants. Like the rare silversword, which can survive up to 90 years in the harsh volcanic environment.

Around 3.9 miles (6.3 km) from the start, a secondary trail veers off to the north to a chain of cinder cones and **Halemau'u.** But the Sliding Sands continues east, the desert terrain gradually giving way to grasses and shrubs. Along the way is Kapalaoa Cabin, where hikers can take a bathroom break, eat

The Haleakalā silversword thrives in hot, dry climates like that of the Haleakalā Crater on the island of Maui.

The Halemauʻu Trail in Haleakalā National Park, Maui, grants hikers a peek at stunning mountaintops draped in clouds.

lunch, and refill their water containers (be sure to treat it before drinking).

Located near the eastern end of the main crater, Palikū features a primitive campground and another rustic cabin. Reservations are required for both. Campers have access to a pit toilet, firewood, and non-potable water, and should be prepared for the possibility of wet and/or cold overnight weather.

Day two involves a southbound trek on the **Kaupō Trail** that starts with a massive gap in the crater wall and a gate that marks the national park boundary. The remainder of the route is through private land that hikers have permission to cross.

Although it's along an old, double-track ranch road, the trail is often overgrown, sometimes difficult to follow, and more often marked by colored ribbons than mileage or direction signs. The route eventually reaches the **Piʻilani Highway** (Route 31) just east of the historic **Kaupō General Store** (founded in 1925). ■

OTHER GREAT TRAILS

• **Kalaupapa Trail:** Spectacular views and Hawaiian history are the payoffs on a jungle trail that drops 2,000 feet (610 m) down a sheer cliff on the north side of Molokai to Kalaupapa National Historical Park.

• **Shipwreck Beach:** Coral shelves combined with sandy footpaths through the shoreline undergrowth make for an eight-mile (13-km) hike along Lanai's north shore that features a rusty World War II wreck and ancient Hawaiian petroglyphs.

• **Mauna Loa Summit:** The lofty summit of the world's largest volcano (13,678 feet/4,170 m) is most often reached via a 7.5-mile (12-km) trail from the end of Mauna Loa Road in Hawaiʻi Volcanoes National Park.

• **Diamond Head Summit:** Starting from the crater of the extinct volcano, a steep trail leads to an old U.S. Navy observation station with bird's-eye views of Waikiki Beach and Honolulu.

Sliding Sands Trail is a challenging 11-mile (18-km) out-and-back trail near Kula, Maui.

Giant Forest Loop
California

The world's biggest living things soar high above a route that rambles through the largest and most beloved stand of arboreal giants in Sequoia National Park.

THE BIG PICTURE

Distance: 7 miles (11 km)

Elevation Gain: approx. 1,270 feet (390 m)

Time: 2–3 hours

Difficulty: Easy

Best Time: Year-round

More Info: nps.gov/seki

What's nearly as tall as the Statue of Liberty, has been alive since the pharaohs ruled ancient Egypt, and continues to grow? The answer to this riddle is easy for anyone acquainted with arboreal wonders or California icons—it's *Sequoiadendron giganteum.*

Although not quite the oldest living things at more than 3,200 years, giant sequoias are certainly the largest, some of them rising to more than 300 feet (90 m) and weighing as much as 2.7 million pounds (1.2 million kg). Their natural habitat is between 4,000 and 8,000 feet (1,220 and 2,440 m) on the western slopes of the Sierra Nevada, a region that includes the adjacent **Sequoia and Kings Canyon National Parks.**

Sequoia harbors the world's largest unlogged sequoia grove, around 2,000 in Giant Forest, famously saved during the 2021 KNP Complex fire by wrapping the trunks in burn-resistant aluminum sheets.

Although visitors can drive to within steps of several landmark trees, the best way to experience the magic of the sequoia wilderness is along trails like the **Giant Forest Loop.**

The loop is an easy seven-mile (11-km) hike through woodland that also nurtures four different species of pine trees and both red and white firs, plus all the wildlife that lives amid the ruddy behemoths. With immense trunks and branches hovering above, much of the trail is shaded, with slivers of sunlight slipping through arboreal nooks and crannies.

The route kicks off at the General Sherman Tree parking lot and shuttle stop, a gentle downhill hike along a paved path and steps with plenty of benches along the way. Soon you're staring up at the massive **General Sherman Tree,** the world's largest living thing with an estimated wood volume of 52,508 cubic feet (1,487 m³). How big is that? Consider the fact that one branch of the General Sherman is bigger than most trees east of the Rocky Mountains and that it weighs around 30 times more than a blue whale (the world's largest animal).

Both branches of the **Congress Trail** lead south to an even larger cluster of giant sequoias that includes the **Senate Grove, House**

Take in the awesome splendor of California's sequoias by hiking the seven-mile (11-km) Giant Forest Loop Trail.

The 2.7-mile (4.3-km) Congress Trail is a gentle lollipop-shaped trek that starts near the grand General Sherman Tree, the largest living tree on Earth.

Grove, **McKinley Tree,** and **Chief Sequoyah Tree** among its leafy patriarchs. A short walk down the **Alta Trail** you'll find two presidential giants. The **Lincoln Tree** is the world's fourth largest, while the **Washington Tree**—once the world's second largest—lost much of its height after a 2003 lightning strike.

From the Congress Grove, hop onto the western branch of the **Circle Meadow Trail** as it ducks through the **Founders' Grove** to a pioneer-era shack called the **Cattle Cabin** built in 1916. Up ahead are more goliaths: the twin **Pillars of Hercules,** the fire-scarred **Black Arch Tree,** and the **Three Amigos.**

The loop eventually curves around to **Crescent Meadow** and **Tharp's Log**—a hollowed-out sequoia transformed into a cabin in 1861 by pioneer Hale Tharp—before a 2.8-mile (4.5-km) leg along the **Trail of the Sequoias** that takes the route back to the Congress Grove and General Sherman Tree. ∎

OTHER GREAT TRAILS

- **Moro Rock Trail:** On the southern edge of Giant Forest, this short (0.5 mile/0.8 km) but steep trail climbs to the summit of a granite dome with awesome views across Sequoia National Park and California's hazy Central Valley.

- **Mount Whitney Trail:** Starting from Whitney Portal on the eastern side of the Sierra, hikers summit the highest peak in the lower 48 states via an ultra-steep 21-mile (34-km) out-and-back trail.

- **Zumwalt Meadow Trail:** Short but sweet, this easy 1.3-mile (2-km) riverside hike affords incredible views of Kings Canyon in the park's Cedar Grove area.

- **Crystal Lake Trail:** Sample the High Sierra on an 8.8-mile (14-km) out-and-back route that rambles above the tree line to a pristine alpine tarn perched at around 10,000 feet (3,050 m).

Rocky Mountains
& Southwest

Mist skims the surface of Little Redfish Lake, accessible via a challenging leg of the Idaho Centennial Trail through the Sawtooth Wilderness.

Pacific Northwest Trail

Montana, Idaho & Washington

The least trekked of America's epic long-distance hiking trails meanders through the remote backwoods on a journey from the Rocky Mountains to the Pacific coast.

There are lots of cool things about the **Pacific Northwest Trail** (PNT), a 1,248-mile (2,008-km) ramble through Montana, Idaho, and Washington State. But maybe the coolest is the fact

THE BIG PICTURE

Distance: 1,248 miles (2,008 km)

Elevation Gain: approx. 230,000 feet (70,100 m)

Time: 2–3 months

Difficulty: Strenuous

Best Time: Midsummer and early fall

More Info: pnt.org

that it's the only U.S. route where you can start hiking in the Rocky Mountains and finish on a Pacific Ocean beach.

Along the way, the PNT passes through three national parks, seven national forests, and six federal wilderness areas. It crawls up and over nine mountain ranges, crosses five major rivers, and runs along countless lakeshores.

What the trail doesn't include is many towns or other signs of civilization. And for most of the route, you won't come across a lot of other people on the trail. The **Pacific Northwest Trail Association**—which helps maintain and manage the route with federal, state, and local partners— estimates that only 65 to 75 people a year attempt the complete thru-hike. For hikers who relish wilderness with as few human beings as possible, the PNT is paradise.

That paucity of people combined with extreme wilderness equals lots of wildlife. Nearly all the big North American mammals inhabit portions of the PNT, including grizzlies and black bears, moose, elk, and deer, mountain goats and bighorn sheep, cougars and lynx, coyotes and wolves. And if they're lucky, hikers might even spot orcas, dolphins, or seals on the route's ferry crossing of Puget Sound.

Like all long-distance trails, timing

Hikers in search of lush forests will find their bliss in Olympic National Park along the Bogachiel Rain Forest Trail.

As Washington's most visited state park, Deception Pass delights visitors with 3,854 acres (1,559 ha) of forests and bluffs, beaches and lakes.

is critical, and even more so on the PNT because it runs east to west rather than north-south (in other words, no desert segments to knock off in winter). You can't really launch from Glacier in the east or the Olympics in the west until early summer when snow melts.

The trail association suggests an early July start for those hiking east to west, which means covering the entire route from the Rockies to the Pacific in two to three months, a span that necessitates a pace of 14 to 21 miles (22 to 34 km) a day through very rough terrain with tons of elevation gain. Thus, it comes as no surprise that so few people elect to complete the thru-hike in a single calendar year.

There is help along the way. Twenty places on the path are official trail towns where hikers can rest and resupply, glean information about weather and trail conditions, and generally mellow out for a few days before recommencing the trek.

The Montana end of the PNT kicks off in the extreme northeast corner of **Glacier National Park,** a trailhead beside State Highway 17 near the **Chief Mountain** international border station. The 55 miles (88 km) of the trail through

LOCAL FLAVOR

• **Northern Lights Saloon:** Perched on the west side of Glacier National Park, this historic log-cabin restaurant (opened in 1916) offers the first hot meals and ice-cold drinks along the PNT; 255 Polebridge Loop, Polebridge, MT; thenorthernlights saloon.com.

• **Yaak River Tavern & Mercantile:** Take in live music, pub grub, full bar, general store, and Sasquatch

sightings in Kootenai National Forest; 29238 Yaak River Road, Troy, MT; facebook.com/yaaktavern.

• **Farmhouse Café:** Maple pecan French toast, avocado toast, homemade banana bread, and honeybee lattes beckon hikers to breakfast at this northeast Washington eatery; 221 East 5th Avenue, Metaline Falls, WA; facebook.com/farmhousecafe221.

Glacier include a brief section along the **Waterton River** that it shares with the **Continental Divide Trail,** as well as a steep climb over **Stoney Indian Pass,** where snow can sometimes stick until late summer.

A pleasant stroll along the north shore of **Bowman Lake** leads into **Polebridge** village and a historic mercantile store that's been serving residents of the remote upper **Flathead Valley** since 1914. A circuit through **Flathead National Forest** heads over the **Whitefish Range** and the highest point along the entire trek to the sea—**Tuchuck Mountain** (7,755 feet/2,364 m)—where you peek across the border into Canada.

After crossing **Lake Koocanusa** on the longest and tallest bridge in Montana, the PNT continues its rough-and-tumble circuit through the **Purcell Range** of **Kootenai National Forest.** Hikers should keep an eye out for moose, bear, and wolves while passing through the **Yaak River Valley.**

Given the fact that the **Idaho Panhandle** is only 50 miles (80 km) wide, the trail doesn't spend much time in the Gem State. The route fords the **Kootenai River** at **Copeland** and then rises into the majestic **Selkirks**—the most formidable of the half dozen ranges between the Rockies and the Cascades, as well what was once the last refuge

of the woodland caribou in the lower 48 states.

Scooting past the picturesque **Priest Lakes,** the PNT sneaks into eastern Washington via the **Salmo-Priest Wilderness,** which safeguards the region's largest old-growth forest. The town of **Metaline Falls**—which may have been the model for Twin Peaks in the creepy 1990s TV series—expedites resupply before the trail leaps across the mighty **Columbia River** at **Northport.**

Making a huge U-bend through the **Okanogan Highlands,** the route rises over the **Kettle River Range** and through the **Grand Canyon of the Sanpoil River.** There's another close encounter of the

With striking panoramas of forests, snowcapped mountain peaks, and crystal blue lakes, North Cascades National Park is as rugged as it is beautiful.

urban kind in **Oroville**—the traditional halfway point of the Pacific Northwest Trail—before a long and often lonely stretch of more than 150 miles (240 km) through the massive **Pasayten Wilderness.** Near **Castle Pass,** the PNT shares 13 miles (21 km) of terra firma with the **Pacific Crest Trail** and offers a chance to swap stories with folks on another epic journey.

Ross Lake National Recreation Area offers a gateway into **North Cascades National Park** with its manifold glaciers, alpine lakes, and snowcapped peaks. Many trekkers consider this the most visually stunning section of the entire hike, especially the segments along the **Chilliwack River** and **Swift Creek.** Trekkers can chill out (or rather, heat up) at **Baker Hot Springs** before skirting around **Mount Baker** and down the **Skagit River Valley** to **Puget Sound.**

South of **Anacortes,** the historic **Deception Pass Bridge** takes the trail over to **Whidbey Island** and a coastal walk that includes the possibility of spotting whales along the **Bluff Trail** at **Ebey's Landing National Historical Reserve.** Near **Fort Casey State Park,** hikers hop the **Keystone Ferry** across the sound to the **Olympic Peninsula.**

Port Townsend offers a last chance to resupply—and admire its pristine Victorian architecture—before a rugged and extremely remote trek across more than 100 miles (160 km) through **Olympic National Park** and its eponymous mountains. The PNT summits **Hurricane Ridge** with its drop-jaw views of the **Olympic Range** and traverses the lovely **Seven Lakes region** before a long descent through the **Bogachiel Rain Forest.**

At almost a million acres, Olympic National Park is a hiker's dream, with more than 95 percent designated as protected wilderness by Congress in 1988.

The short leg along the **Hoh River** takes the trail to its long-awaited rendezvous with the **Pacific Ocean.** But the trek isn't over yet, because the homestretch of the PNT is a 44-mile (70-km) hike up the coast to **La Push** and **Ozette** along the nation's longest stretch of wilderness coast outside of Alaska. ∎

SHORT CIRCUIT

These sections of the Pacific Northwest Trail are great for day hikes:

• **Bowman Lake Trail:** A 26.2-mile (42.2-km) out-and-back trail, this popular route in Glacier National Park takes about 10 hours to complete but is worth the longer day for the epic views. It is particularly popular with birders.

• **Little Divide Loop:** While this 14.1-mile (22.7 km) loop trail in Olympic National Park will take you off the PNT, it's a great day hike if you just want a flavor of what the thru-hike has to offer, boasting beautiful lakes, meadows, and waterfalls, too.

• **Larry Scott Trail:** Near Port Townsend, Washington, this 14.7-mile (23.7-km) out-and-back trail takes about five hours to complete, or take it one way to its terminus at Port Townsend Bay, where you can catch a ferry to Coupeville on Whidbey Island, Washington State's second oldest community.

• **Highline Trail:** Tackling 14 miles (22.5 km) one way, this route through the heart of the Ten Lakes Scenic Area in the Kootenai National Forest ends at the U.S.-Canada border and offers mountain vistas (including views of the Canadian Rockies and Whitefish Range), alpine lakes, and dozens of potential campsites.

Hayduke Trail
Arizona & Utah

One of the nation's most remote and rugged trails was inspired by an iconic outdoor writer and the fictional ecowarrior that he created for his best known book.

THE BIG PICTURE

Distance: 812 miles (1,307 km)

Elevation Gain: approx. 101,850 feet (31,040 m)

Time: 1–3 months

Difficulty: Strenuous

Best Time: Winter, spring, or fall

More Info: hayduketrail.org

Author and environmental activist Edward Abbey would be proud to know that his work inspired a hiking route across Utah and Arizona that embodies the ideals and landscapes that he fought so hard to preserve during his life.

The **Hayduke Trail** (HDT) takes its name from George Washington Hayduke III, a fictional character in *The Monkey Wrench Gang,* Abbey's novel about a group of radical environmentalists who plot to blow up the Glen Canyon Dam so the Colorado River can flow freely again.

As Abbey writes in the book, "There are some places so beautiful they can make a grown man break down and weep." From the Grand Canyon and Zion to Bryce Canyon and Capitol Reef, you'll find plenty of those spots along the Hayduke.

Split into 14 sections, the Hayduke flows along existing trails, dirt roads, game trails, slickrock, and streambeds through extremely remote terrain. The route is rarely marked. Maps, compass, a GPS device, and a detailed guidebook—like *The Hayduke Trail* by Joe Mitchell and Mike Coronella—are essential tools.

Making the trek even more daunting, the trail strays well away from anything that might be deemed civilization. There are few places to resupply. Hikers must be prepared to carry food and water for several weeks at a stretch and to fend for themselves in most emergencies.

The Hayduke wanders through the fantastic rock formations of **Arches National Park** before leaping the **Colorado River** on a pedestrian bridge to **Moab.** The outdoor adventure hub is a great place to stock up on whatever you need in the way of food and other supplies for the rest of the hike. From Moab, the trail tags along the river's east side into **Canyonlands National Park** and multihued hoodoos called **the Needles** before slipping into **Glen Canyon National Recreation Area** (NRA).

Jumping the Colorado again on **Hite Crossing Bridge,** the Hayduke runs along the sinuous **Dirty Devil River** and across the supersecluded **Henry Mountains** into the skinny southern extreme of **Capitol Reef National Park.** Crossing back into Glen Canyon NRA, the trail twists its way along the **Escalante River** and then over the top of elongated **Fiftymile Mountain** into sprawling **Grand Staircase-Escalante National Monument.**

After cutting across the southernmost part of **Bryce Canyon National Park,** the trail turns to the south and crosses into Arizona near **the Wave** rock formation in **Vermilion Cliffs National Monument.** There's a temporary respite from the desert in **Kaibab National**

Tall reeds guide a hiker through a canyon in the Escalante River corridor of the Hayduke Trail.

Nearly four million annual visitors frequent Zion National Park, drawn to the ancient—and awe-inspiring—landscape.

Forest before the route uses the **Nankoweap Trail** to dive into the **Grand Canyon.**

During its 80-mile (130-km) passage through the Grand Canyon, the Hayduke follows the **Tonto Trail** to **Phantom Ranch** and then the **North Kaibab Trail** onto the **North Rim.** With the "big ditch" behind, the hike across the **Kaibab Plateau** back into southern Utah seems like a walk in the park. Entering **Zion National Park,** the Hayduke uses the **East Rim Trail** to descend into the main canyon and a grand finale just below **Angels Landing.** ■

LOCAL FLAVOR

• **Milt's Stop n' Eat:** Ask locals about the best burgers in Moab and Milt's is almost always their first suggestion. The vintage diner (founded in 1954) also serves burritos, milk shakes, sandwiches, and six different types of french fries; 356 Millcreek Drive, Moab, UT; miltsstopandeat.com.

• **Needles Outpost:** Serving Section 3 of the Hayduke, this remote campground boasts a general store and showers on the eastern outskirts of Canyonlands; Highway 211, Monticello, UT; needlesoutpost.com.

• **i.d.k. Barbecue:** Brisket, pulled pork, and peach cobbler are the tasty allures of a small-town barbecue joint a little bit off the Hayduke Trail near Bryce Canyon; 161 North Main Street, Tropic, UT; idkbarbecue.com.

• **Jacob Lake Inn:** Before taking on the Grand Canyon, hikers can feast on a cranberry-cream cheese chicken sandwich, mountain trout almondine, blue cheese burger, and other favorites at this roadside eatery in Kaibab National Forest; Highway 89A at Highway 67, Jacob Lake, AZ; jacoblake.com/dining.

A challenging 6.4-mile (10.3-km) route through the wilderness rewards hikers with the astounding ribbons of arching canyon walls that make up the Wave formation (Coyote Buttes North) at Vermilion Cliffs National Monument.

Continental Divide Trail
Montana, Idaho, Wyoming, Colorado & New Mexico

THE BIG PICTURE

Distance: 3,059 miles (4,922 km)

Elevation Gain: approx. 589,980 feet (179,830 m)

Time: 5–7 months

Difficulty: Strenuous

Best Time: Late spring, summer, or early fall

More Info: continentaldividetrail.org

Whether you think of the Continental Divide as a watershed moment for Lewis and Clark or a 1980s John Belushi rom-com, no doubt the geographical landmark occupies a huge space in the American psyche.

Stretching along the crest of the Rocky Mountains from New Mexico to Montana, the divide marks the hydrological boundary among waterways that flow westward into the Pacific and those that flow eastward into the Gulf of Mexico, or in the case of extreme northern Montana, rivers that eventually empty into the chilly Hudson Bay.

Though American maps don't show the demarcation extending beyond the Canada and Mexico borders, the Continental Divide actually runs all the way down the Americas, from the edge of the Bering Sea in Alaska to the outermost tip of Tierra del Fuego in Argentina, a factor that makes hiking the **Continental Divide Trail** (CDT) a journey along one of planet Earth's most significant physical features.

Aside from the physical distance of the CDT, the trail offers a unique opportunity to trek through American history in segments that follow in the footsteps of Lewis and Clark. There are also old mining towns to pass by—or stop at—along the way. Hikers will discover the beauty of the plains and vast swaths of wilderness—along with various ecosystems—that span up and down the Americas.

Part of the "triple crown" of long-distance American trails, with the Appalachian and the Pacific Crest, the CDT has existed in bits and pieces since the 1960s, when backpacking soared in popularity. Although it was declared a national scenic trail in 1978, the route remains unfinished, with around 5 percent of the route (164 miles/264 km) along roadways and sidewalks rather than dedicated footpaths.

The Continental Divide Trail Coalition—an organization that helps maintain the trail with federal,

Founded in 1867 and positioned along the eastern edge of the CDT, South Pass City is a collection of remarkable historic structures preserved amid the wild hills of Wyoming.

A popular biking route, Jones Pass is a seven-mile (11-km) out-and-back trail that races through Arapaho National Forest.

state, and local authorities—says the CDT is the "highest, most challenging, and most remote" of the 11 national scenic trails—in other words, tougher than the Appalachian or Pacific Crest. Emphasizing that point, the AllTrails website recommends that only the most experienced adventurers should attempt the thru-hike.

Although many parts of the CDT are accessible throughout the year, most of those hoping to complete the thru-hike start from the southern end in April or May with a goal of reaching the northern end by September or October. That way, hikers navigate the New Mexico desert before the triple-digit temperatures of summer set in and trek the northern Rockies when the

path carries the least snow and (hopefully) before the first winter storms arrive.

Anyone craving a southbound

hike starting in Glacier National Park should probably wait until June before setting off, and plan on hiking an average of at least 20 miles

OTHER GREAT TRAILS

Great Divide Trail

The Continental Divide doesn't stop at the U.S.-Canada border and neither does the opportunity to hike it. Running roughly 700 miles (1,130 km), Canada's **Great Divide Trail** (GDT) runs across the crest of the Rockies between Waterton Lakes National Park in Alberta and Kakwa Provincial Park in British Columbia.

Along the way are some of the jewels of Canadian nature: Banff, Jasper, and Yoho National Parks, the Willmore and White Goat Wilderness

Areas, and the water- and woods-filled Kananaskis region.

Canadian and American trekkers can argue about which trail is tougher, but there's little doubt that only experienced hikers should attempt the GDT thru-trip. Given its northern exposure, the hiking season is much shorter than the U.S. version, roughly July to mid-September. Among the issues that GDT hikers must overcome are grizzly bears, mosquito swarms, and the possibility of summer snow.

(32 km) a day—through some of the gnarliest terrain in North America—to avoid late autumn or early winter snow in the New Mexico mountains.

The CDT Coalition has established a series of gateway communities, small towns that are especially welcoming to hikers, along the five-state route. There is also a network of "trail angels," local volunteers who can assist trekkers with food and water, as well as transportation between resupply points and trailheads. The coalition and its partners are constantly blazing alternate trails that give hikers a choice of how they traverse certain regions and reduce overuse and stress of the main route.

Northbound hikers take their first steps along the CDT (and undoubtedly snap a selfie) at the **Crazy Cook Monument** next to the international border fence in **New Mexico's** remote Bootheel region. Set along a dirt road around a two-hour drive from **Hachita,** the monument marks the spot where laborer Frank Evans was murdered by the "crazy cook" of his fence-building crew in 1907. A rather strange place to start a cross-country hike. Still, it is what it is.

The opening stretch across the **Chihuahuan Desert** is inevitably hot and dry no matter how early you start in the spring. There's little shade or water, and the town's not especially inspiring until you reach **Silver City,** an old mining burg. Slowly but surely, the route rises into the refreshingly wooded **Gila Wilderness,** established in 1924 as

Discovered in 1870 and named for its reliable eruptions, Old Faithful is an eternally popular draw to Yellowstone National Park.

LOCAL FLAVOR

• **Little Toad Creek Brewery & Distillery:** Celebrate trekking the Chihuahuan Desert with a red chili chocolate martini, green chili cucumber gimlet, or another of the innovative cocktails at this southern New Mexico hangout; 200 North Bullard Street, Silver City, NM; littletoad creek.com.

• **World's End Brewpub:** Prost, Avery, and New Belgium are just a few of the local craft beers that complement the pub grub at a family-owned and -operated public house deep in the Colorado Rockies; 813 Grand Avenue, Grand Lake, CO; worldsendbrewpub.com.

• **Rose's Lariat:** Just steps off the trail, this southern Wyoming eatery has been serving beef flautas, green chiles rellenos, huevos rancheros, and other Mexican dishes since 1954; 410 East Cedar Street, Rawlins, WY; roseslariat.com.

• **Old Faithful Inn Bear Paw Deli:** Grab a quick salad, sandwich, or huckleberry ice cream at this laidback snack counter near Old Faithful geyser; 3200 Old Faithful Inn Road, Yellowstone National Park, WY; yellowstonenationalparklodges.com/ restaurant/old-faithful-inn-bear -paw-deli.

• **Brownies Bakery:** Don't start the final leg of the CDT through Glacier National Park without loading up on carbs at a village eatery that serves wraps, pizza, sandwiches, hot drinks, and ice cream; 1020 Highway 49, East Glacier Park Village, MT; brownieshostel.com.

---

the nation's first federally protected wilderness area.

Pie Town in central New Mexico is a popular stop along the trail because of its namesake pies—with lemon chess, strawberry rhubarb, New Mexico apple, and pecan custard among the local favorites. The CDT skirts the dark black lava fields of **El Malpais National Monument** before leaping over Interstate 40 near **Grants** and scooting into the red-rock country between the towns of **Cuba** and **Chama.**

Crossing into **Colorado,** the trail ascends into the **San Juan Mountains** and what many hikers consider one of the more challenging stretches of the CDT because of the rugged terrain and lofty elevation. Passing through **La Garita Wilderness,** roughly 70 miles (110 km) of the trail hovers at around 11,000 feet (3,350 m). There's a brief respite crossing the **Gunnison River Valley,**

but the route rises once again, to an incredibly scenic passage through the **Collegiate Peaks Wilderness** and its entourage of 14,000-foot (4,270-m) peaks.

Twin Lakes and **Leadville** in central Colorado are great places to chill, resupply, and lick your wounds for a couple of days before resuming the trek. And hikers will definitely want to rest, because up next is **Grays Peak,** highest point along the entire CDT at 14,270 feet (4,350 m). After cutting across the southwest corner of Rocky Mountain National Park, the trail rises into the **Park Range** via **Rabbit Ears Pass** and its namesake rock formation, with Wyoming looming dead ahead.

Hikers who aren't familiar with the Basin and Range geographic of the American West are often shocked that trekking the CDT across **Wyoming** requires a second desert crossing. Descending from

Crossing from New Mexico to Montana and spanning remote, tough conditions, the Continental Divide Trail is a true hiking challenge.

the **Sierra Madre mountains,** the trail crosses the **Red Desert** with its sand dunes, sagebrush flats, and intermittent streams. Within the desert is another natural oddity called the **Great Divide Basin,** a large endorheic drainage area with no outflow. The Continental Divide actually splits in two as it flanks the arid basin.

The shortest path between **Rawlins** and **Bridger-Teton National Forest** is an alternate trail that runs straight across the basin. However, the main CDT makes its way around the basin's eastern edge to historic **South Pass City** ghost town, a onetime way station on the **Oregon Trail.** Climbing into the **Wind River Range,** the route arrives in grizzly country and the potential of encountering bears along the trail. Hikers should pack bear spray and know how to use it.

Farther into the national forest, the **Teton Wilderness** area provides an almost total respite from humanity before hikers almost surely encounter the crowds passing through **Yellowstone.** Sure, the blazers could have curved the trail around the world's oldest national park, but then trekkers would miss the close brush with **Old Faithful** geyser and the **Biscuit Basin** thermal field.

Exiting the park, the CDT traverses the **Bitterroot Range** along the Idaho-Montana border, flitting back and forth between the two states. Along the way is **Lemhi Pass**, where Lewis and Clark crossed the Continental Divide in 1805 on their way to the Pacific. Veering into western **Montana,** the trail offers the possibility of a sojourn in the old copper mining town of **Anaconda** before an amble through **Bob Marshall Wilderness** and its famed **Chinese Wall:** a 1,000-foot (300-m)-high escarpment that towers above the trail for more than 20 miles (32 km).

The northbound CDT ends in dazzling fashion with a trek among the grand lakes, valleys, peaks, and frozen landmarks of **Glacier**

LAY YOUR HEAD

• **Chama River Bend Lodge:** Find comfy motel-style rooms and kitchen-equipped cabins near the CDT in northern New Mexico; from $79; chamariverbendlodge.com.

• **Delaware Hotel:** Butch Cassidy and the "Unsinkable" Molly Brown are a few of the notables who have stayed at this vintage Colorado hotel since it opened in 1886 during the heyday of Leadville's gold and silver rush; from $99; delawarehotel.com.

• **Rivera Lodge:** A definite blast from the past, this 1950s-style cabin resort near Yellowstone and Grand Teton offers cute red cabins with kitchenettes and private bathrooms along Pine Creek; from $69; riveralodge.com.

• **Lincoln Log Hotel:** Established as a halfway house for miners in the 1870s, this historic hotel in Lincoln, Wyoming, really does look as if it were constructed with life-size Lincoln Logs; from $80; facebook.com/LincolnLogHotel1.

National Park. The trail enters the park via Marias Pass in the deep south and then swings around to **East Glacier Park Village** for a last chance to restock before the final push.

On its way to the Canadian frontier, the trail passes two of the park's fjordlike water bodies—**Two Medicine Lake** and **St. Mary Lake.** After climbing over the mountains to **Many Glacier,** hikers have a choice of two routes to the Canadian frontier: a western spur that leads into Alberta's **Waterton Lakes National Park** and an eastern spur that terminates at the **Chief Mountain** port of entry. ■

The American pronghorn *(Antilocapra americana)* is resolutely at home in the wild rabbitbrush of the Great Divide Basin.

Grand Enchantment Trail

Arizona & New Mexico

Venture far off the grid along a trail between Phoenix and Albuquerque that traverses some of the remotest parts of Arizona and New Mexico.

THE BIG PICTURE

Distance: approx. 770 miles (1,240 km)

Elevation Gain: approx. 95,200 feet (29,020 m)

Time: 2 months

Difficulty: Strenuous

Best Time: Winter, spring, or fall

More Info: simblissity.net/get -home.shtml and hikearizona .com/national.php?ID=4

By any stretch of the imagination, the **Grand Enchantment Trail** (GET) is not your average hiking route. Most long-distance paths start and end in secluded wilderness areas. But the GET links two major cities: Phoenix and Albuquerque.

Despite its urban origins, the trail goes out of its way to avoid contact with anything resembling civilization for most of its length. And this is definitely not the express route. Rather than the shortest, most direct walk between **Phoenix** and **Albuquerque,** the GET travels a circuitous path across 14 mountain ranges, 12 federal wilderness areas, 10 peaks rising above 10,000 feet (3,050 m), four national forests, and huge stretches of the Sonoran and Chihuahuan Deserts.

Around two-thirds of the trail runs through cactus- and sagebrush-studded desert terrain, the remainder through the mixed woodland that shades the "sky islands" of the American Southwest. Much of the route is through areas that have yet to be discovered by the vast majority of Arizona and New Mexico residents as well as the tourists that flood other parts of the two states.

It's also a newbie in the annals of long-distance trekking, born after the turn of the 21st century from existing trails and country roads. Topographic maps, a good compass, and a GPS device are a must (although the latter might not function in some of the more remote areas). Here and there, the GET nudges close enough to populated areas for hikers to resupply.

From the Arizona end, the Grand Enchantment kicks off at the **First Water trailhead** in the storied **Superstition Mountains** around 45 miles (72 km) from downtown Phoenix. Thus begins a long transit across **Tonto National Forest** that includes around 70 miles (110 km)

New Mexico thistle *(Cirsium neomexicanum)* grows wild near the First Water trailhead in the Superstition Wilderness Area.

Follow Grand Enchantment Trail to the Gila Cliff Dwellings for a peek at fascinating 13th-century Mogollon structures.

of shared path with the **Arizona Trail.** After conquering 10,724-foot (3,269-m) **Mount Graham** in **Coronado National Forest,** hikers have a chance to rest and resupply in **Safford** before a mountainous trek to the state line via **Gila Box Riparian National Conservation Area** and **Apache-Sitgreaves National Forest.**

Across the border are **Gila National Forest** and tiny **Alma,** an outlaw hideout during Wild West days and now the halfway point of the Grand Enchantment. Dead ahead is one of the most taxing stretches of the entire route, a meandering trek across the **Gila Wilderness** that includes 10,774-foot (3,284-m) **Mogollon Baldy** peak, the highest point in the GET.

Descending from the highlands, the route passes the ancient **Gila Cliff Dwellings** before sharing 45 miles (72 km) of pathway through the rugged **Black Range** with the **Continental Divide Trail.** After crossing the **Rio Grande** near **Polvadera**—a riverside community Spanish settlers founded in the 1620s—the GET climbs into the **Sandia–Manzano Mountains** for a homestretch through **Cibola National Forest** and a terminus at the top of 10,678-foot (3,255-m) **Sandia Peak** overlooking Albuquerque. ∎

OTHER GREAT TRAILS

These sections of the GET are ideal for day hikes:

• **Black Top Mesa:** Starting at First Water, trek the westernmost portion of the GET to Black Top Mesa in the Superstition Wilderness, an 11.4-mile (18-km) round-trip hike.

• **Aravaipa Canyon:** From the end of Aravaipa Road, follow the GET into one of Arizona's most spectacular gorges, a 9.6-mile (15-km) out-and-back hike that includes boulder-strewn and super-narrow Hell's Half Acre.

• **Gila River West Fork:** Sample the GET in western New Mexico along a 2.3-mile (3.7-km) stretch beside the Gila River that kicks off in the Gila Cliff Dwellings Museum parking lot.

• **North Baldy:** Magdalena Ridge Observatory is the jumping-off spot for an 11-mile (18-km) return hike to the summit of 9,853-foot (3,003-km) North Baldy peak in Cibola National Forest.

• **San Lorenzo Canyon:** From the end of the road at San Lorenzo Spring, hike eastward along a two-mile (3.2-km) portion of the GET to a twisted knot of stone hoodoos, arches, and sandstone cliffs.

Idaho Centennial Trail

Idaho

Snaking its way through desert, forest, and mountains, this long-distance route celebrates Idaho's transition from territory to statehood and its incredibly diverse wilderness.

Declared the official state trail in 1990 to mark the 100th anniversary of Idaho statehood, the Centennial was designed to showcase all of the Gem State's natural bounty rather than just the highlights.

The route covers an amazing amount of geography. Idaho measures 479 miles (770 km) from north to south, but the **Idaho Centennial Trail** (ICT) rambles across nearly 900 miles (1,450 km) of terrain between Nevada and British Columbia.

Eclectic aptly describes a trail that meanders amid the state's sagebrush-shrouded high desert, the farm-filled Snake River Valley, the high Rockies, and the lake-spangled Panhandle region.

Thru-hikers most often start at the trail's bottom end to take advantage of the fact that Idaho's high desert is less likely to have snow in the late spring and early summer than the ICT's mountainous sections.

The official start is the Idaho-Nevada state line on Road 288 around four miles (6.4 km) from **Murphy Hot Springs.** Heading across the **Inside Desert,** the route traces the eastern edge of **Bruneau-Jarbidge Rivers Wilderness** into **Morley Nelson Snake River Birds of Prey National Conservation Area.**

Hikers can detour into **Bruneau Dunes State Park** at this point or follow State Route 78 along the small portion of the old **Oregon Trail** and Lewis and Clark's route. Leaping the **Snake River** on a highway bridge, the trail moseys into **Hammett,** one of the few towns along the ICT.

Around 20 miles (32 km) farther north, the trail begins a relentless rise and fall through central Idaho that starts with the **Boise Mountains.** After crossing the **South Fork Boise River,** hikers are presented with a choice of routes around the storied **Sawtooth Range.** The tougher western leg transits the remote **Sawtooth Wilderness** while

Morning fog rises above the Snake River near Hammett, Idaho.

Crest the top of one of the tallest freestanding sand dunes in the interior United States at Bruneau Dunes State Park.

the easier eastern spur traverses the long **Sawtooth Valley.**

The trail becomes one again just north of Stanley for a 10-mile (16-km) stretch beside the **Middle Fork Salmon River.** But the convergence is only temporary. Because at **Dagger Falls,** the trails split again, into east and west legs through the **Salmon River Mountains** and the vast **Frank Church River of No Return Wilderness.**

The separation is much longer this time, more than 250 miles (400 km) before another merger at **Wilderness Gateway Campground** in the **Clearwater Mountains.** But that's the final breakup. The ICT leapfrogs across the **Bitterroot Range** along the Idaho-Montana border into the Panhandle region.

Descending from the **Coeur d'Alene Mountains,** the trail passes through the town of **Clark Fork**

along the eastern shore of **Lake Pend Oreille.** There's one last major climb, this time into the **Cabinet Mountains,** before a passage across the **Purcell Trench** and along **Priest**

Lake. Rounding out the marathon hike is a relatively short trek up the **Priest River Valley** through the **Selkirk Mountains** to the U.S.-Canada frontier near **Snowy Top** peak. ■

DETOURS

Walking on the Moon

In 1969, NASA sent four astronauts to an obscure federal park in southeast Idaho to learn about volcanic landforms and collect rocks on the lunar-like surface.

More than half a century later, earthbound hikers can literally walk in their footsteps along trails in **Craters of the Moon National Monument and Preserve,** which has since expanded to 750,000 acres (305,500 ha) and been nominated for national park status.

The reserve now offers more than a dozen trails. But given the park's

varied terrain, only a few are akin to walking on the moon.

The short hike to the summit of **Inferno Cone,** all of it across dark volcanic debris, offers the closest resemblance. The 3.5-mile (5.6-km) **North Crater Trail** also flows through a twisted landscape scattered with cinders and lava rocks. The **Caves Trail** leads to four large lava tubes.

Hikers can overnight in the volcanic wasteland—and pretend like they're camping on the moon—by backpacking the 10-mile (16-km) **Idaho Wilderness Trail** through the northern part of the preserve.

Snake River Trail

Idaho

Descend into the belly of the deepest canyon in North America along a remote riverside route that was nearly submerged behind hydro dams half a century ago.

THE BIG PICTURE

Distance: 52 miles (83 km) out and back

Elevation Gain: approx. 9,500 feet (2,900 m)

Time: 5–6 days

Difficulty: Strenuous

Best Time: Spring, summer, or fall

More Info: fs.usda.gov/detail/wallowa-whitman/recreation/?cid=stelprdb5238987

Hells Canyon is world renowned for white-water rafting and kayaking along the **Snake River.** But the great divide between Idaho and Oregon is also great hiking country.

Both sides of the canyon boast trails, but the Idaho shore is more user-friendly. In particular, the stretch that harbors the **Snake River National Recreation Trail,** created in 1980, follows earlier paths blazed by the Nez Perce and other Native American groups, as well as 19th-century pioneers and prospectors.

North America's deepest gorge (7,993 feet/2,436 m) was once earmarked for hydroelectric dams. However, the creation of **Hells Canyon National Recreation Area** in 1975 spared its transformation into a second Hetch Hetchy. The lower part of the trail runs through the recreation area; the upper section via the **Hells Canyon Wilderness.** Both areas are administered by **Wallowa–Whitman National Forest.**

Although it's certainly possible to make this a point-to-point hike with a "backdoor" exit through the **Seven Devils Wilderness** east of the canyon, the Snake River Trail is most often done as a multiday out-and-back with backcountry camping along the waterway.

Although the Snake River provides a natural passageway, the trail rarely runs right beside the water. What hikers can expect instead is an up-and-down roller-coaster walk that often runs across slopes high above the river.

Just over 100 miles (160 km) from Lewiston, **Pittsburg Landing** anchors the northern trailhead. It's also the jumping-off point for **jet boat tours** of Hells Canyon between mid-April and mid-September. Thank goodness, the jet boats only run through the middle of the day. Pittsburg's Forest Service campground is an ideal spot to spend a night before hitting the trail.

Kirkwood Ranch is a popular first-night stop or base camp for those who want to explore upstream on day hikes. Part of the **Hells Canyon Archaeological District,** the **historic cabins** and **bunkhouse** offer relics of pioneer days and exhibits on the region's Native Americans.

Reachable by foot or boat, the Kirkwood Historic Ranch is a premier example of early 20th-century pioneer ranching life.

Straddling the border between Idaho and Oregon, Hells Canyon National Recreation Area is home to the deepest river gorge in North America.

Nearby is **Carter Mansion,** a rustic cabin where moonshine was brewed during Prohibition.

Less trodden than the lower section, the route gets rougher as it continues south. One of the biggest challenges is **Suicide Point,** so called because hikers must navigate a narrow ledge high above the river. **Sheep Creek Ranch,** another pioneer-era outpost, is the next major waypoint and another good place to spend a night or two.

Farther upriver are several abandoned pioneer cabins and half a dozen camping spots before the trail reaches **Granite Creek,** seven miles (11 km) downstream from **Hells Canyon Dam.** Those who want to exit via the Seven Devils Wilderness

can peel off onto a side trail that climbs up **Little Granite Creek.** There's also the option of

prearranging a river shuttle back to Pittsburg Landing with **Hells Canyon Adventures.** ■

APRÈS HIKE

• **Nez Perce National Historical Park:** The tribe's epic trek of 1877 is recalled at the visitors center in Lapwai, Idaho, as well as other sites in Idaho and three other states.

• **Lewis and Clark Discovery Center:** On the banks of the Snake River in Hells Gate State Park in Lewiston, the museum screens a half-hour film on the Corps of Discovery journey through Idaho on its way to the Pacific.

• **OARS Salmon River:** Run the white-water "River of No Return"

before its rendezvous with the Snake on a multiday guided raft or dory trip.

• **Artisans at the Dahmen Barn:** Classes, workshops, jam sessions, and art exhibits are all part of the fun at this eastern Washington art collective 20 minutes north of Lewiston.

• **Kenworthy Theatre:** Classic films, stage plays, and MET Live opera performances are on the menu at this restored picture palace in Moscow, Idaho.

With more than a mile of vertical elevation between river floor and the nearby peaks of Seven Devils Mountains, the hike along Hells Canyon gifts trekkers awe-inspiring views.

Grand Canyon Rim to Rim

Arizona

Hiking the Grand Canyon is an epic adventure that tests people's physical limits and opens their mind to what nature is capable of given enough time and rushing water.

THE BIG PICTURE

Distances: Bright Angel, 24 miles (39 km); South Kaibab, 23 miles (37 km), North Kaibab, 36 miles (58 km)

Elevation Changes: Bright Angel, approx. 4,380 feet (1,340 m); South Kaibab, approx. 4,780 feet (1,460 m); North Kaibab, approx. 5,760 feet (1,760 m)

Time: 2–3 days

Difficulty: Strenuous

Best Time: Spring or fall

More Info: nps.gov/grca/ planyourvisit/upload/intro -bc-hike.pdf

Along with the Pacific Crest and Appalachian Trails, a mosey through the Grand Canyon is a goal of nearly every hard-core hiker. Although many are content with a one-way hike down the Bright Angel or South Kaibab Trails to the Colorado River and back, the ultimate challenge is hiking the world's most celebrated gorge on the **Grand Canyon Rim to Rim.**

Given its easy access and myriad support services, the South Rim is the most popular place to kick off the cross-canyon trek. However, starting from the North Rim offers the advantage of around 1,000 feet (300 m) less elevation gain because of its higher altitude (8,000 feet/2,400 m vs. 7,000 feet/2,100 m).

You can tackle the South Rim to Colorado River segment in two ways: via the shorter but more exposed South Kaibab Trail or the slightly longer but often shadier Bright Angel Trail. The following explores both options.

Season is a factor that all cross-canyon hikers must consider. Summer on the rims is warm but not unpleasant. But once you descend into the canyon, triple-digit temperatures and desertlike aridity are the norm. At the opposite end of the Grand Canyon weather spectrum, the rims and higher parts of the canyon trails are often sub-freezing and covered in snow. Without doubt, spring and fall are the best seasons to attempt the hike.

There's also a matter of how long you have. Veteran hikers can polish it off in a single (albeit long) day, an awesome athletic feat that leaves little time for contemplating the canyon's majesty. Two days with an overnight beside the Colorado River is common. However, three days is highly recommended for those hoping to balance fitness and reflection.

BRIGHT ANGEL TRAIL

One of the canyon's oldest known trails, the **Bright Angel Trail** was blazed by Native Americans along a natural fault line in the canyon wall. By the late 1800s, an enterprising miner had transformed the path into a toll road for tourists, a legacy that endures in the mule trains that still clop along the trail today.

Because the Bright Angel is far and

Take the North Kaibab Trail into Roaring Springs Canyon on the north rim for a challenging trek in Grand Canyon National Park.

Packhorses and a hiker cross paths on the South Kaibab Trail in Grand Canyon National Park.

away the most popular way to descend into the canyon, it's also the best maintained and safest route into the gorge, with regular water stations, shade structures, and ranger patrols. The downside for thru-hiking over its first few miles is having to weave your way around countless selfie takers and slow-moving day hikers.

The route drops rapidly via a series of tunnels and switchbacks to **Indian Garden** 3,000 feet (910 m) below the rim, where hikers discover a campground, ranger station, shady cottonwood trees, and potable water. Hikers who aren't in a rush can follow a short spur to **Plateau Point** and a first glimpse of the **Colorado River.**

Beyond Indian Garden, the route continues down **Garden Creek** and

a set of wicked switchbacks called the **Devil's Corkscrew.** Reaching the broad **Tonto Platform** and its Sonoran Desert vegetation, the route finally levels out before an easy

descent to the river. Silver Bridge carries the trail over the river to historic **Phantom Ranch, Bright Angel Campground,** and a rendezvous with the South Kaibab Trail.

OTHER GREAT TRAILS

Hiking Lake Mead

Although it's primarily known for water sports, Lake Mead National Recreation Area also offers plenty of scope for hiking through a Mojave Desert environment that offers a fascinating take on the region's human and natural history.

Just a half-hour drive from the Las Vegas Strip, the **Historic Railroad Trail** is all that remains of a line that enabled the 1930s construction of Hoover Dam. The 3.5-mile (5.6-km)

route features five tunnels and bird's-eye views of Lake Mead.

The **St. Thomas Trail** leads two miles (3.2 km) to the remains of a Mormon pioneer town that disappeared in the 1930s beneath the rising waters of Lake Mead and then reappeared in the early 21st century when the water level fell.

The park's longest hiking trail, the 34-mile (55-km) **River Mountains Loop** circles a desert range between Hoover Dam and Henderson, including a stretch through Boulder City.

SOUTH KAIBAB TRAIL

Perhaps the only reason the **South Kaibab Trail** is a less popular means of getting into the canyon is the fact that hikers have to walk, drive, or hop a shuttle to **Yaki Point**—around five miles (8 km) east of **Grand Canyon Village**—to reach the trailhead.

The South Kaibab is a totally modern creation, blazed by the Park Service shortly after the Grand Canyon became a national park in 1919 as a free-of-charge way for visitors to walk from the South Rim to the river (the Bright Angel wasn't free until 1928). As it descends from the 270-million-year-old **Kaibab limestone** that bolsters the rim to the 1.7-billion-year-old **Vishnu schist,** the route offers an open-air seminar on Grand Canyon geology.

Along the way are **Ooh Aah Point** (named for the astonished response that many early visitors had to its incredible canyon views), **O'Neill Butte** (named for an Arizonan cowboy who rode with Teddy Roosevelt's Rough Riders), and **Skeleton Point** (allegedly named for a ghastly mule accident). The vertiginous **Tipoff** viewpoint offers an aerial perspective of the Colorado River before a final descent into the "basement" of the inner canyon and a saunter across **Black Bridge,** about a mile (1.6 km) upstream from the other suspension span.

NORTH KAIBAB TRAIL

Reaching the canyon bottom, rim-to-rim hikers can sack out at **Bright Angel Campground,** shaded by cottonwoods along a creek of the same name about half a mile

(0.8 km) up from the Colorado River.

Like other in-the-canyon camping spots, a backcountry permit is required to overnight there. Bright Angel offers picnic tables, restrooms, potable water, and a ranger station. Backpackers can cook their own meals or make reservations to chow down in the canteen at nearby Phantom Ranch.

Opened in 1922, **Phantom Ranch** was designed by renowned architect Mary Colter and, like her structures along the South Rim, is considered a masterpiece of rustic American "parkitecture." Backpackers and mule riders are welcome at the stone cabins and dorms, but reservations via a lottery system should be made well in advance.

Although the historic ranch and campground may seem like the halfway point of the cross-canyon trek, it's still 14 miles (22.5 km) to the North Rim. The **North Kaibab Trail** starts with a stroll through a classic slot canyon called **the Box** and then a gradual rise beside **Bright Angel Creek.**

Around six miles (9.6 km) out, a short spur leads to the bottom of 100-foot (30-m) **Ribbon Fall** and its moss-covered rock wall. It's a great place to catch your breath and cool off before the trail gets super steep. From the falls it's a short hike uphill to **Cottonwood Campground,** a convenient lunch place if you're doing the route over two days or a second overnight spot for those extending the hike into a third day. Once again, the camp is equipped with picnic tables, toilets, and potable water (May to October).

The final push to the North Rim entails an elevation gain of 4,200 feet (1,280 m) over the final 6.8 miles (10.9 km). Shade and water are available at **Roaring Springs** and **Manzanita Rest Area**—where there's also a historic artist's cabin—before the final switchbacks.

How do you get back to the South Rim? Super-fit hikers can make it an out-and-back journey. Otherwise, **Trans Canyon Shuttle** offers transport back to Grand Canyon Village; reservations required. ∎

OTHER GREAT TRAILS

• **Grand Canyon Greenway:** Rather than canyon views, this 13-mile (21-km) hiking and biking trail between Tusayan village and the Mather Point visitors center offers a paved, shaded, and easy journey through the woods behind the South Rim.

• **Tonto Trail:** Rambling 70 miles (110 km) between the Little Colorado River and super-remote Granite Canyon, the Tonto is named for the geological bench that provides most of its route across the canyon bottom. It's an even bigger hiking challenge than the Rim to Rim.

• **Havasupai Trail:** Waterfalls and turquoise-colored pools await at

the bottom of a 7.2-mile (11.5-km) hike to Supai village on the Havasupai Reservation west of the national park.

• **Tuckup Trail:** The park's most underused long-distance trail wanders roughly 60 miles (96 km) from Tuweep Campground near the spectacular Toroweap Overlook to 150 Mile Canyon via a sandstone bench called the Esplanade.

• **Widforss Trail:** Named for a 1930s artist who lived at the Grand Canyon, this 10-mile (16-km) out-and-back path along the North Rim offers an artistic blend of serene forest and canyon views.

Hikers encounter snowy conditions on the Grand Canyon's South Kaibab Trail.

Barr Trail
Colorado

Breathtaking views, Rocky Mountain nature, and bragging rights are the allure of an arduous but profoundly rewarding trek to the top of Pikes Peak.

THE BIG PICTURE

Distance: 12.5 miles (20 km)

Elevation Gain: approx. 7,430 feet (2,270 m)

Time: 1 day

Difficulty: Strenuous

Best Time: Spring or fall

More Info: barrcamp.com and pikes-peak.com/hiking-pikes -peak-mountain

If the **Barr Trail** had been blazed 100 years later, they probably would have called it Stairway to Heaven. Because that's basically what it is. An incredibly steep 7,500-foot (2,290-m) ascent to one of the most storied mountains in North America: **Pikes Peak** in the Colorado Front Range.

As it was, the route was named for Fred Barr, who created the vertiginous route between 1917 and 1921, as a way for his guided burro tours to reach the summit. Barr could have never guessed that his narrow mountain track would become one of the nation's most popular high-altitude climbs (150,000 people a year) or the host of grueling long-distance running events like the annual **Pikes Peak Marathon** and **Barr Trail Mountain Race.**

It's not just the length or 11 percent average grade that makes the Barr Trail such a monster. It's also the elevation. Pikes Peak soars to 14,115 feet (4,302 m). But given the fact that the trail begins at 6,700 feet (2,042 m), altitude sickness can occur almost at once and grow progressively worse as the elevation increases.

Hikers have three ways to tackle the route in a single day: a 12.5-mile (20-km) trek straight up the peak from the lower trailhead; a steep but tricky descent from the summit along the same route; or a 25-mile (40-km) out-and-back that only the hardiest hikers should attempt.

With an overnight camp located at around the halfway point—where the Barr Trail intersects with the Elk Park Trail—it's also possible to break the hike into two days.

Barr Trail begins beside the **Cog Railway Depot** on the outskirts of **Manitou Springs.** Right away, hikers are confronted with a major challenge: a series of steep switchbacks called the **W's** that zigzag up the **Manitou Incline.**

The switchbacks peter out around two miles (3.2 km) from the start. Although the trail keeps climbing, the gradient is a lot easier on the lungs and heart, the walk made even more pleasant by the copious spruce, pine, and other trees.

Barr Camp, the nation's highest hiking cabin, sits just below the tree line at 10,200 feet (3,108 m). Built by Fred Barr as an overnight stop on his burro trips, the camp offers a snack bar, picnic area, and

A climber rests at Barr Camp after hiking up Pikes Peak to assist with the AdAmAn Club's annual New Year's fireworks display from the summit.

Old railroad ties line the steep Manitou Incline hike in Manitou Springs, Colorado.

restrooms for day hikers, as well as a bunkhouse, lean-tos, and tent area for those who wish to spend the night.

Beyond Barr Camp is the rocky, treeless alpine tundra zone and another set of steep switchbacks. Here and there, a curious marmot or pika might pop out. Those who rise early have a chance of spotting bighorn sheep or mountain goats grazing the slopes beneath the summit. An A-frame shelter at around 12,000 feet (3,650 m) offers a last chance for shade before a final climb to the summit, where the altitude prohibits plant growth and makes

the mountaintop a virtual desert.

Don't be surprised by the sudden appearance of people at the top; a

popular toll road up the other side of Pikes Peak brings visitors in motor vehicles to the summit ∎

DETOURS

• **Manitou Springs:** With plenty of places to stay and eat at different price ranges, this funky little town below Pikes Peak makes an excellent base for undertaking the Barr Trail.

• **Florissant Fossil Beds National Monument:** Prehistoric Colorado comes to life along the Petrified Forest Loop and Geologic Trail of this federal park northwest of Pikes Peak.

• **Garden of the Gods:** Nature walks, jeep tours, and fun runs make their way around the incredible sandstone formations near Colorado Springs.

• **Mueller State Park:** Hikers, bikers, and equestrians can explore 50 miles (80 km) of trails through forest, grasslands, and rocky outcrops on a one-time cattle ranch that the owners deeded as a wildlife preserve.

The Narrows
Utah

Prepare to get wet on a legendary trail that follows the Virgin River through a deep slot canyon in Zion National Park.

THE BIG PICTURE

Distance: 16 miles (26 km)

Elevation Change: approx. 1,300 feet (400 m)

Time: 1–2 days

Difficulty: Easy to moderate

Best Time: Year-round

More Info: nps.gov/zion

To paraphrase a thousand cop shows, you can hike **the Narrows** the easy way, or you can hike it the hard way.

This iconic route in **Zion National Park** flows through a deep slot canyon the **Virgin River** carved into the red rock of southern Utah over thousands of years. The walls soar as much as 2,000 feet (610 m) and can narrow to between 20 and 30 feet (6 and 9 m) wide in places.

Hikers *always* get wet: More than two-thirds of the route runs through the rock-strewn river, which means walking or wading in water that can range from a few inches to waist level.

Everyone should wear sturdy shoes. Hiking sticks or poles are highly recommended, as is some sort of waterproof covering for your camera or cell phone (if not waterproof). Sure, the water is cold, but it takes the edge off temperatures that can reach triple digits.

No one should attempt to hike the Narrows during flash-flood warnings that can occur at any time of year, but especially during southern Utah's monsoon storm season between July and September.

The "easy way" is hopping the park shuttle along **Zion Canyon Scenic Drive** to stop no. 9 (**Temple of Sinawava**) and trekking the short, paved **Riverside Walk** to the terrace where it ends. From there you simply step into the river and hike upstream for as long as you want in a single day.

Hundreds of people trek this bottom-up route each day during the busy summer season, but most only venture an hour or two into the chasm, which means the farther upstream you journey, the more chance you have of relishing the surroundings in something approaching silence. Ambitious bottom-up hikers can reach **Big Spring** (9.4 miles/15 km) if they set off early enough.

The "hard way" is top down, an intriguing 16-mile (26-km) hike down the entire length of the canyon from **Chamberlain Ranch.** It takes around 12 hours to complete

Canyoneering is one of many outdoor activities families can experience together in the Narrows of Zion National Park.

A photo-worthy mix of vibrant greenery and stark cliffsides unfolds along the Riverside Walk at Temple of Sinawava in Zion Canyon.

the thru-hike from a trailhead on private land on the northeast side of the national park. The Park Service doesn't provide a shuttle to the ranch, so trekkers must arrange their own transport. **Red Rock** and **Zion Shuttles** are two of the companies that provide the service.

Overnight permits are required even for those doing the entire top-down route in one day. Those breaking the trek into two days can overnight at a dozen campsites around halfway down the Narrows. Some are first come, first served; others can be reserved online.

To answer the obvious question, all of the campsites are on dry land above the normal water level. Given the delicate riverine environment, campfires are strictly forbidden and *all* waste must be packed out. Big Springs is the best source of drinking water, but even that should be treated before use. ◼

OTHER GREAT TRAILS

• **Panorama Trail:** The longest route in Kodachrome Basin State Park takes hikers on a six-mile (9.6-km) loop through a fantasyland of ruddy sandstone hoodoos, spires, ravines, and sheer cliffs.

• **Cassidy Arch:** Spanning a hanging canyon high above the Grand Wash, this tribute to famed outlaw Butch Cassidy is accessed via a steep 3.1-mile (5-km) out-and-back trail in Capitol Reef National Park.

• **Frary Peak Trail:** Antelope Island in the Great Salt Lake provides a 6.9-mile (11-km) desert route with views across the water to Salt Lake City and the snowy Wasatch Range.

• **West Rim/Bighorn Overlook:** Late afternoon is the time to walk this five-mile (8-km) route to cliff-top viewpoints in Dead Horse Point State Park with its vertiginous vistas of the Canyonlands country.

Perhaps the best known hike in Zion National Park, the Narrows is home to natural springs, sandstone grottoes, and the spectacular Virgin River.

Delicate Arch Trail
Utah

This short but sometimes strenuous trail leads across a red-rock wilderness to one of America's most admired and photographed rock formations.

THE BIG PICTURE

Distance: 3.2 miles (5.1 km) out and back

Elevation Gain: approx. 630 feet (190 m)

Time: 2–3 hours

Difficulty: Moderate

Best Time: Year-round

More Info: nps.gov/thingstodo/arch-hike-delicate-arch.htm

If **Delicate Arch** looks familiar, it's because the striking landmark has been on Utah's vehicle license plate since 2007 and two U.S. postage stamps. A runner carrying the Olympic flame passed beneath the arch before the 2002 Winter Games in Salt Lake City. It's also a social media star, one of the most sought-after selfie spots in the entire National Park System.

As a result, the short but spectacular hike to Delicate is far and away the most popular trail in **Arches National Park.**

An outstanding example of nature's inadvertent artistry, the arch is composed of Entrada sandstone shaped over 65 million years by the geologic forces of wind, rain, snow, and ice. The setting is also superb: a natural sandstone bowl with panoramic views of the **La Sal Mountains** in the hazy distance.

The trail starts from a parking lot in **Salt Wash,** a creek fed by a natural spring that nurtures greenery amid the red-rock wilderness. The water attracted the **Wolfe Ranch** family to homestead the area in 1898. The remains of their log cabin, root cellar, and corral stand along a short spur off the main trail.

Beyond Wolfe Ranch, the trail is a roller-coaster ride over sandstone ridges, including a steep and slick-rock section about two-thirds of the way along. The final push to the top takes the trail through giant boulders and along a rock ledge with an acrophobia-inducing drop-off. As you round a final corner, Delicate Arch appears in all its majesty.

Take a load off, sit a while, and admire its graceful proportions. Think about all that's transpired since the arch was part of a sedimentary bed uplifted from a shallow prehistoric sea. Watch the parade of humanity waiting in line to snap photos beneath Delicate. Maybe pack breakfast, lunch, or a snack. And be sure to gulp lots of water if you're hiking in the midday summer heat.

The best times to make for Delicate Arch are early morning to catch an almost always awesome sunrise or late afternoon for an equally stunning sunset. Don't be fooled by the short distance: Sections of the trail cut across bare rock that can be surprisingly slippery, especially after a

Petroglyphs in Arches National Park, carved by the Ute tribe sometime between A.D. 1650 and 1850

The Delicate Arch in Arches National Park is composed of Entrada sandstone formed by wind, rain, snow, and ice more than 65 million years ago.

summer rain or winter overnight freeze. If you linger beyond sundown, pack a flashlight or headlamp for the return hike.

On the way back, detour onto the short **Petroglyphs Loop** for a glimpse of a rock-art panel that features bighorn sheep, riders on horseback, and what appear to be dogs. The Ute people, whose descendants still call the region home, carved the images between 1650 and 1850.

For those unable to make the longer trek, the arch can also be admired and photographed from a short, flat, wheelchair-accessible trail at **Lower Delicate Arch Viewpoint.** For those seeking more of a

challenge, the park's other epic hike is the **Devils Garden Trail.** The 7.9-mile (12.7-km) loop runs past dazzling red-rock formations like

the remote **Dark Angel** pinnacle and stupendous **Landscape Arch**— one of the world's five longest natural stone arches. ■

Arizona Trail
Arizona

Stretching from the Mexican border to the Utah state line, the Arizona National Scenic Trail rambles across the cactus-studded Sonoran Desert, up and over the heavily wooded Mogollon Rim, and across the majestic Grand Canyon country.

THE BIG PICTURE

Distance: approx. 800 miles (1,300 km)

Elevation Gain: approx. 103,890 feet (31,670 m)

Time: 6–8 weeks

Difficulty: Strenuous

Best Time: Spring or early fall

More Info: aztrail.org and fs.usda.gov/azt

Anyone who still thinks that Arizona is nothing but unrelenting desert should meet the **Arizona Trail,** an epic 800-mile (1,300-km) walk through a remarkable variety of landscapes, landforms, and human achievements that reflect the state's many moods.

Hikers can undertake the quest in a single shot or knock off the 43 individual passages one at a time. And you don't have to make the whole journey on foot: Much of the Arizona Trail also welcomes mountain bikers, horseback riders, and even Nordic skiers and snowshoers to the parts that get snow each winter.

Although it's tempting to start amid the red-rock wonderland along the Arizona-Utah frontier, starting from the south has distinct advantages. Like the fact that you've already hiked for more than a month before facing the route's biggest challenge: crossing the Grand Canyon. The trail is also numbered from south to north.

The trail's first section—the **Huachuca Mountains Passage**—starts beside a whitewashed international boundary obelisk on a ridge overlooking Mexico in **Coronado National Memorial.** One of the smaller and more obscure units of the National Park System, the memorial marks the arrival of the first Europeans to visit Arizona: a 1540 Spanish expedition led by conquistador Francisco Vázquez de Coronado. Leaving the border behind, the trail climbs into the **Wheeler Peak Wilderness,** the first in a series of "sky islands" (isolated mountain ranges) that offer a tree-covered contrast to the cactus and sagebrush flats and sandy arroyos of the **Sonoran Desert.**

Skirting the eastern edge of **Tucson,** the trail ducks beneath Interstate 10, shoots past **Colossal Cave,** and then slowly rises into the **Rincon Mountains** of **Saguaro National Park.** After a week of solid trekking, you might find the park and its gargantuan cacti to be a great place to linger before pushing on. Because up ahead are the **Santa Catalina Mountains,** one of the toughest, steepest segments of the entire trail. Protected within the

Scarlet hedgehog cactus flowers *(Echinocereus coccineus)* along the Arizona Trail

The Arizona Trail in the Canelo Hills crosses 760 miles (1,220 km), from Mexico to Utah.

confines of **Coronado National Forest,** the highest of all sky islands rises to 9,171 feet (2,795 m) at **Mount Lemmon.** Expect snow and subzero temperatures if you're hiking in winter.

Emerging from woods near **Oracle,** the Arizona Trail enters the so-called "Central Passage" between the Santa Catalinas and the Mogollon Rim. Truth be told, the next 112 miles (180 km) are probably the trail's least inspiring, an undulating walk through the arid **Black Hills, Tortilla Mountains,** and **Gila River Canyons** with little scenic variation. It's not until you reach the storied **Superstition Wilderness** that the landscape gets intriguing again. Forget trying to find the legendary Lost Dutchman Mine—thousands have already tried

and failed. Instead, continue through **Tonto National Forest** and down to the shore of **Roosevelt Lake**

for a quick dip before moving on. Leaving the desert behind, the path leaps across the **Salt River** on a

---

SHORT CIRCUITS

These sections of the Arizona Trail are ideal for day hikes:

• **Passage 7:** Located on the southwest edge of Tucson, this 12.7-mile (20.4-km) hike across the Sonoran Desert is mostly flat but best avoided in summer, when midday temperatures almost always reach triple digits.

• **Passage 13:** The trail's shortest section—8.6 miles/13.8 km between the American Flag Ranch and Tiger Mine trailheads—meanders through the northern foothills of the Santa Catalina Mountains.

• **Passage 29:** Ponderosa pines are your constant companions along a

14.8-mile (23.8-km) stretch that bends around the west side of Mormon Lake in Coconino National Forest.

• **Passage 39:** This relatively easy 12-mile (19-km) jaunt across the Kaibab Plateau starts from the North Rim of the Grand Canyon and ends at the national park entrance gate.

• **Passage 43:** The trail's final segment is also its second shortest (10.6 miles/17 km), a ramble across desert hills between Winter Road and Stateline Campground with the multicolored Vermilion Cliffs stretching off to the east.

handsome steel arch bridge and ascends into the **Four Peaks** and **Mazatzal Wilderness Areas.** With several peaks exceeding 7,000 feet (2,130 m), this is another slice of the Arizona Trail that can get winter snow. Farther along, the aptly named town of **Pine** (yep, there are lots of trees) affords a last chance to take a load off before climbing into the high country via the **Highline National Recreation Trail.**

Established in 1870, the Highline was used by ranchers to move their cattle between summer and winter pastures. The trail was a favorite of Western writer Zane Grey, who had a cabin nearby, and is now part of a grueling ultramarathon called the Mogollon Monster 100.

The Highline climbs up the side of the imposing **Mogollon Rim,** a 200-mile (320-km) escarpment along the southern edge of the

Colorado Plateau. The region beyond the rim is a traditional home of the Apache people. Reaching the crest, the Arizona Trail rambles through the world's largest ponderosa pine forest. The 8,000-foot (2,400-m) altitude takes a little getting used to, but the cooler temperatures are most welcome. There's abundant wildlife too, not just the coyotes, jackrabbits, and rattlesnakes that can appear just about anywhere along the route, but also black bears, mountain lions, and other critters that prefer the high country.

North of **Mormon Lake,** the trail forks and trekkers can choose between an eastern leg that bends around **Walnut Canyon National Monument** and then under Interstate 40, or a western leg that meanders through **Flagstaff.** Although the latter uses parklands as much as possible to cross the city, it also runs beside motels and fast-food outlets for hikers craving at least a temporary break from sleeping bags and campfire meals.

Beyond Flagstaff, the east and west legs merge into a single track amid the lofty pines of **Coconino National Forest** for a scenic end run around **Humphreys Peak** (the state's highest point at 12,637 feet/3,852 m) and the other **San Francisco Peaks.** Given that the trail crosses the **Arizona Snowbowl** winter sports area, hikers can once again expect chilly temperatures and an icy trail if they're making this passage during the colder months.

Dead ahead are the remote ranchlands of the **Coconino Plateau,** relatively flat terrain through grasslands and scattered trees that delivers some of the easiest hiking of the entire route. The horizontal landscape betrays nothing of what's up next: the mighty **Grand**

Cacti tower alongside the Arizona Trail in Saguaro National Park.

Red stones and sweeping views accompany hikers of the South Kaibab Trail as it heads into the Grand Canyon.

Canyon. It's been a long time coming, probably around six weeks since you started the trek. Effort that begs another short break. Treat yourself to a lodge room, a hot shower, and a couple of hearty restaurant meals before dropping into the big ditch.

The Arizona Trail follows the **South Kaibab** (rather than the Bright Angel) route down to the **Colorado River.** After a night at **Phantom Ranch** comes the long uphill march to the **North Rim.** Perched at 8,000 feet (2,440 m), this is another spot where winter hikers are likely to encounter a snow-covered trail. The section on the Rim to Rim hike (see page 88) fills in the details on crossing the chasm.

With the Grand Canyon conquered, it's pretty easy trekking through **Kaibab National Forest** to **Jacob Lake,** a tiny crossroads settlement in the Arizona Strip

and the last vestige of civilization along the Arizona Trail. Only two passages remain: no. 42 **(Kaibab Plateau North)** and no. 43 **(Buckskin Mountain)** before the Utah border. A flight of switchbacks takes the trail down

to **Stateline Campground** and a pillar inscribed with a poem by Arizona Trail founder Dale Shewalter: "In the land of Arizona / through desert heat or snow / winds a trail for folks to follow / from Utah to old Mexico." ■

DETOURS

• **Saguaro National Park:** On the outskirts of Tucson, Tanque Verde Ranch offers workshops in horsemanship and cattle penning, as well as trail rides through the Rincon Mountains of Saguaro National Park.

• **Roosevelt Lake:** Located at the end of Passage 19, Roosevelt Lake Marina rents pontoons, powerboats, and kayaks for a spin or paddle around the big desert reservoir.

• **Verde National Wild and Scenic River:** Mild to Wild guides lead one- and two-day white-water kayak trips along a remote stretch of the Verde

River near Pine and the Mazatzal Wilderness.

• **Walnut Canyon National Monument:** A prehistoric people called the Sinagua built these cliff dwellings nearly 1,000 years ago in a deep gorge not far off the trail's Passage 31.

• **Lowell Observatory:** The heavenly landmark in Flagstaff stages daytime tours, nightly stargazing, family astronomy adventures, and the new Giovale Open Deck Observatory, which opened in 2021.

Fairyland Loop
Utah

The best of Bryce unfolds along a tough canyon and rim trail that meanders through a fantasyland of cliffs, mesas, and towering stone pillars.

According to Paiute legend, the pervasive rock pillars of **Bryce Canyon National Park** were once supernatural beings called the Legend People who were turned to stone by the Coyote god as punishment for squandering the region's water and other resources. The Paiute called them Anga-ku-wass-a-wits (Red Painted Faces) but nowadays they're hoodoos. Bryce Canyon boasts hundreds of them, and although geological forces rather than magic spells may have created them, they're certainly magical.

So is the **Fairyland Loop,** the national park's toughest but most rewarding hike. Tough because it dives deep into the canyon and requires substantial uphill effort to reach the rim again. Extra hard if you're undertaking the walk in the midday heat of summer. Every Bryce trail has some awesome

Bryce Canyon is *the* place to scope out hundreds of rock pillars called hoodoos.

THE BIG PICTURE

Distance: 8 miles (13 km)

Elevation Gain: approx. 1,550 feet (470 m)

Time: 4–5 hours

Difficulty: Strenuous

Best Time: Spring and fall

More Info: nps.gov/brca/planyourvisit/fairylandloop.htm

scenery. But trekking the Fairyland Loop, you're going to have the red-rock wonderland mostly all by your lonesome rather than sharing it with hundreds of others like the popular **Queens Garden Trail.**

Some hikers favor Fairyland Point as the best place to begin. But given its proximity to the campground, lodge, and general store, most people start from the **Sunrise Point** trailhead. The route kicks off with a riveting downhill glide that includes grades as high as 35 percent. Off to the right is **Chinese Wall,** a stupendous stone rampart named after the Great Wall of China.

Chinese Wall offers a case study in hoodoo formation. Portions closer to the canyon rim are rife with joints or cracks caused by water seeping into the rock and freezing during subzero nights, ice that expands and fractures the surrounding stone. As the process continues over millions of years, the joints grow ever wider, to the point where vertical sections or hoodoos become detached from the wall.

The trail continues into **Campbell Canyon,** where older stone pillars have eroded into clay mounds that rangers call a "hoodoo graveyard" because of their tombstone-like appearance. Around 1.5 miles (2.4 km) from Sunrise Point, a

The hoodoos of Fairyland Canyon in Bryce Canyon National Park are particularly stunning at sunset.

short spur trail leads to **Tower Bridge,** a natural arch named after the famous London span. To the left of the bridge is **Keyhole Window,** a large natural hole in the wall with a wannabe hoodoo on its outer edge.

The Fairyland Loop continues around the "prow" of massive **Boat Mesa,** still attached to the rim but destined to one day float on its own like Chinese Wall. There's another maritime metaphor off to the east, a titanic mesa called **Sinking Ship** that seems half-submerged in a red-rock sea.

Around the north side of Boat Mesa is the area that gives the trail its storybook name: **Fairyland.** Trekking through a veritable forest of hoodoos—and with just a smidgen of imagination—it's easy to see

why the Paiute people thought of the pillars as ancient beings turned to stone. The trail returns to the canyon rim at **Fairyland Point.** From there, it's a 2.5-mile

(4.1-km) hike back to Sunrise Point via **Rim Trail,** which undulates along the edge of the **Paunsaugunt Plateau** with its fabulous views of Bryce Canyon. ∎

LAY YOUR HEAD

• **The Lodge at Bryce Canyon:** Unveiled in 1915 and designed by the legendary Gilbert Stanley Underwood, the lodge is a classic example of American national park architecture; from $183; brycecanyonforever.com.

• **North Campground:** Tucked amid towering ponderosa pines between the visitors center and the canyon rim, North Campground is closer to Fairyland Loop than any other overnight digs; from $20; nps.gov/places/000/north-campground.htm.

• **Ruby's Inn:** For more than 100 years, this eclectic motel, campground, and RV park near the park entrance has been hosting Bryce Canyon visitors; from $90; rubysinn.com.

• **Kodachrome Basin:** If the national park campgrounds are full, this chromatic Utah state park offers a juniper-shaded campground and its own spectacular red-rock trails; from $25; stateparks.utah.gov/parks/kodachrome-basin.

The eight-mile (13-km) Fairyland Loop is strenuous, with multiple elevation changes—and some of the most incredible scenery in the park.

East Rosebud Trail
Montana

One of the undiscovered gems of the hiking world ambles up and over the stunning Beartooth Range on some of the oldest rocks on the surface of Earth.

THE BIG PICTURE

Distance: 26 miles (42 km)

Elevation Gain: approx. 3,700 feet (1,130 m)

Time: 2–4 days

Difficulty: Moderate to strenuous

Best Time: Summer or early fall

More Info: fs.usda.gov/recarea/custergallatin/recreation/ohv/recarea/?recid=61377&actid=104

If the East Rosebud traversed a national park or was closer to a major city or was trekked by hundreds of thousands of people each year, it would unquestionably be ranked among the most beautiful trails in North America.

But in the absence of those things, this incredible footpath through the **Beartooth Range** of south-central Montana flies well beneath the radar of most hikers.

And that's what makes it so awesome. Although the **East Rosebud Trail** is also called "The Beaten Path," hikers can relish this woods- and water-laced walk through **Absaroka-Beartooth Wilderness** in almost complete solitude, especially on weekdays.

Although diehard trekkers can complete the thru-hike in a single (albeit long) day, this is the kind of terrain that begs you to hike until

lunch and spend the rest of the afternoon contemplating an alpine landscape blessed with numerous lakes and waterfalls, abundant wildlife, snowy summits, and starry nights.

Along the shore of **East Rosebud Lake** in **Custer Gallatin National Forest,** the tiny town of Alpine marks the northern trailhead. The path follows **East Rosebud Creek** up a mountain valley flanked by towering peaks to **Elk Lake,** the first of 15 named lakes along the route.

With the rocky walls closing in from both sides, the trail slips through a narrow gap carved by the creek to a chain of alpine lakes where many hikers spend their first night. **Lake at Falls** flaunts two cascades, but the camping is better along the shores of **Rainbow Lake** and **Big Park Lake.**

A series of switchbacks takes the trail past **Impasse Falls,** where East Rosebud Creek gushes down a rocky slope into little **Duggan Lake.** A mile and a half (2.4 km) farther along is one of the highlights of the entire hike: **Dewey Lake** set against a backdrop of a snow-filled cirque created by the west walls of **Summit Mountain** and **Mount Dewey.** If you're going to snap one photo along the route, *this* is the spot.

The blue-green waters of East Rosebud Creek in the Beartooth Wilderness meander by a backpacker on the Beaten Path.

A narrow trail leads hikers to the top of Impasse Falls as it plunges into Duggan Lake.

Reaching the crown of the **Beartooth Plateau,** the East Rosebud nearly hits 10,000 feet (3,050 m) above sea level as it weaves around **Fossil Lake,** the largest body of water along the route. Well above the trees, the boulder-strewn shoreline offers plenty of places to camp, admire the views, or consider the fact that the ground beneath is some of the oldest exposed rock on the planet, formed around 3.3 billion years ago when the continents first emerged from the oceans.

From there, it's all downhill, this time following a string of lakes along **Russell Creek.** Surrounded by forest again, the route continues past **Kersey Lake** to the **Clarks Fork Picnic Area.** Then it's about an hour's walk into **Cooke City** along the **Beartooth Highway** (U.S. 212) and a route that John Colter followed in 1807 as the first European to explore the Beartooth and Yellowstone regions. ◼

APRÈS HIKE

- **Montana Candy Emporium:** Fresh fudge, key lime taffy, huckleberry caramels, and a dozen kinds of bubble gum are just a few of the old-fashioned sweets at a Red Lodge store decorated with antique bikes, telephones, old metal signs, and other antiques.

- **Yellowstone Art Museum:** Montana's top contemporary art collection, the "YAM" in downtown Billings specializes in artists of the northern plains and northern Rockies.

- **Fishtail, Montana:** Near the north end of the trail, this tiny town offers the Fishtail General Store (founded 1900), Potter's Rock Shop and Coffee House, and the Cowboy Bar and Supper Club.

- **Paintbrush Adventures:** Saddle up for a guided day ride or a working ranch vacation on a spread beside the Stillwater River in Absarokee, Montana.

- **Cody, Wyoming:** The Night Rodeo, Buffalo Bill Center of the West, and the old-timey Wild West Spectacular at the Cody Theatre are the main events in this northwest Wyoming burg.

Paseo del Bosque

New Mexico

Despite its desert locale, woods and water are the main attractions of this long and variable urban trail through the heart of New Mexico's largest city.

THE BIG PICTURE

Distance: 16 miles (26 km)

Elevation Gain: approx. 70 feet (20 m)

Time: 5–6 hours

Difficulty: Easy

Best Time: Fall, winter, or spring

More Info: cabq.gov/ parksandrecreation/open-space/ lands/paseo-del-bosque-trail

One of America's premier urban trails runs north to south through **Albuquerque** along the eastern edge of the **Rio Grande.** The Spanish word *bosque* (forest) refers to the fact that there's plenty of riverside vegetation, in particular cottonwood trees that provide welcome shade from the often intense New Mexico sun.

The **Paseo del Bosque** is entirely paved and most definitely multiuse; hikers can expect to encounter quite a few bikes and even horseback riders along the way. It links many of the city's best parks, public art, and leading cultural institutions. Locals say trekking the trail is especially awesome during the annual **Albuquerque International Balloon Fiesta** each fall, when hundreds of hot air–filled flying machines hover about the path.

From the north, the trail kicks off from a hiker/biker parking lot beside the **Alameda Boulevard** bridge over the Rio Grande. The first few steps are through the **Bachechi Open Space** preserve, a restored wetlands and woodland area on land where chickens and alfalfa were once raised.

Over its first four miles (6.4 km), the Paseo carves a path between the river and **Los Ranchos de Albuquerque,** an upscale neighborhood where many of the homes have stables. Other than the **Unser Racing Museum,** which features the native New Mexican motor sports family, there's not much to attract hikers off the trail at this point.

But up ahead is **Rio Grande Nature Center State Park,** a unique urban wildlife preserve that features indoor and outdoor viewing areas, as well as a nature shop, native plant garden, and interpretive programs. Just before the **Coronado Freeway** (I-40) underpass, trekkers can hang a right onto a bikeway bridge with great views of the Rio Grande.

South of the interstate is the city's all-time favorite green space—**ABQ BioPark.** In addition to hosting 2.5 miles (4 km) of the Paseo del Bosque, the elongated park harbors a **botanical garden, aquarium, BUGarium live insect**

Cyclists follow the Paseo del Bosque under the Paseo del Norte.

A hot-air balloon ride over the Rio Grande outside Albuquerque, New Mexico, is a memorable way to take in the sights.

habitat, narrow-gauge railroad, and the **ABQ BioPark Zoo.** The **Tingley Beach** section offers **fishing ponds, boat rentals,** and a **small café** easily accessible from the Paseo.

Beyond the zoo, the trail skirts the Barelas district that's even older than Albuquerque, founded in 1662 by Spanish settlers. With a year-round slate of performing arts, exhibitions, and lectures, the National Hispanic Cultural Center has revitalized the old neighborhood over the past two decades.

Many hikers and bikers end their journey along the Paseo del Bosque in Barelas, especially those craving a meal in the local cafés of the Lower 4th Street Historic District. South of Bridge Boulevard, the trail threads an arid route between the river and an industrial zone. It culminates in the fishhook-shaped Chavez Loop through an area of southern Albuquerque that seems far more desert than city. ■

OTHER GREAT TRAILS

• **Wheeler Peak:** Hikers can summit New Mexico's highest point (13,167 feet/4,013 m) via a 4.2-mile (6.7-km) Williams Lake route from Taos Ski Valley.

• **Cloud-Climbing Trestle Trail:** The historic Mexican Canyon railroad trestle (built in 1898) is the main attraction on an eight-mile (13-km) loop through the Sacramento Mountains of southern New Mexico.

• **Zuni-Acoma Trail:** Follow in the footsteps of the ancient Native Americans who blazed this 7.5-mile (12-km) route between the Zuni and Acoma pueblos through the lava fields of El Malpais National Monument.

• **Pueblo Loop Trail:** This 1.4-mile (2.2-km) trail in Bandelier National Monument takes hikers up stairs and wooden ladders to dwellings carved in the canyon walls more than 500 years ago by ancestral Puebloan peoples.

• **Wild Rivers Recreation Area:** More than 20 miles (32 km) of trails lead along the rim and down into the depths of the Red River Canyon and Rio Grande Gorge near Taos.

Colorado Trail

Colorado

Long considered one of the nation's most visually stunning hikes, this long and winding route ventures through a wide variety of Colorado Rockies landscapes and historic sites along pathways blazed by Native Americans, fortune hunters, and narrow-gauge railroads.

THE BIG PICTURE

Distance: 485 miles (780 km)

Elevation Gain: approx. 90,000 feet (27,430 m)

Time: 4–6 weeks

Difficulty: Strenuous

Best Time: Summer into early fall

More Info: coloradotrail.org

There are much easier ways to get from Denver to Durango, but for anyone who wants to understand the Centennial State or escape into the Rocky Mountain wilderness, there's no better way than trekking the **Colorado Trail** (CT).

Stretching nearly 500 miles (800 km) across the central and southwestern parts of the state, the route traverses eight mountain ranges, five major watersheds, six national forests, and six federal wilderness areas during a journey that takes most hikers more than a month to complete.

But that's not all. The CT also passes through historic gold and silver mining towns, a chic winter sports resort, and tiny lakeside towns. Parts of the route are along footpaths blazed hundreds of years ago by Native American hunters and traders, others on tracks pioneered by 19th-century prospectors seeking fame and fortune in "them thar hills."

There's also plenty of elevation. Anyone taking on the challenge—especially users that live at sea level—should be prepared for the fact that the route averages 10,300 feet (3,140 m) and tops out at more than 13,000 feet (3,960 m). Anyone not used to the elevation can expect headaches, nausea, and other symptoms of altitude sickness until they fully acclimatize.

The terrain varies greatly from lush lower-altitude valleys with evergreen and deciduous trees and mountain meadows flush with wildflowers to grassy ridges, rocky summits, and even patches of snow far into summer.

The Colorado Trail Foundation (CTF) maintains the route in partnership with the U.S. Forest Service and a small army of volunteers. Many of those volunteers are also "trail angels" who assist hikers in need of aid or "CT shuttlers" who help get them to/from the trailheads. A list of the latter is available from the CTF.

The **Denver** end of the CT lies on the southern fringe of the metro area near **Chatfield State Park** (which makes an excellent place to camp the night before setting off). The first six miles (9.6 km) follow the onetime path of the **South Platte River** into **Pike National Forest** and up scenic **Waterton**

Backcountry hikers can find maps and other important information about the trails of the San Juan Mountains from the Colorado Trail Foundation.

A hiker makes her way along the Colorado Trail near Molas Pass.

Canyon, a route Native Americans blazed and thousands of prospectors later used to seek their fortunes in the Rockies.

By the 1870s, the narrow-gauge Denver, South Park, and Pacific Railroad was also running up the canyon, a former line that featured in several legs of the Colorado Trail. The trains made a whistle-stop at the top of the canyon, but all that remains from that mining boom settlement is the historic **South Platte Hotel,** where one of Colorado's last Wild West gunfights took place in 1912.

Leaving the river behind, the route ascends above the tree line for

LAY YOUR HEAD

• **Bivvi Hostel:** Open throughout the year, this Breckenridge lodge caters to winter ski bums and summer hikers or bikers with a range of digs from hot-tub suites to six-person dorms; from $45; thebivvi.com/home.

• **Delaware Hotel:** Opened in 1886 at the height of Leadville's gold and silver boom, this historic redbrick abode offers Victorian-style rooms with antiques and modern baths; from $70; delawarehotel.com.

• **Twin Lakes Roadhouse:** Located right beside the saloon and general store in the town's tiny historic district, the roadhouse has a Hiker's Room with queen bed and claw-foot tub as well as a separate Carriage House; from $130; twinlakes colorado.com.

• **Kendall Mountain Lodge:** Recently upgraded from backpacker hostel to boutique hotel, the lodge offers queen or twin rooms along Silverton's historic Blair Street near numerous eating and drinking establishments; from $85; kendallmountainlodge .com.

• **Siesta Motel:** A towering neon cactus sign announces this classic 1950s motel along Durango's main drag; the modern Western-style decor comes with kitchenettes and an outdoor barbecue area; from $85 (summer), $58 (winter); durango siestamotel.com.

the first time as it scoots around the north side of **Raleigh Peak** in the **Kenosha Range.** A long traverse of the **Lost Creek Wilderness** takes the trail to **Kenosha Pass.** Perched at exactly 10,000 feet (3,050 m), Kenosha is one of the state's most celebrated passes because of its gold- and silver-era history, views of the snowcapped **Front Range,** and appearance in several episodes of the *South Park* animated TV series.

The actual **South Park**—a high-altitude grassland where bison once roamed—is just south of Kenosha Pass and viewable from the CT as it continues west toward a rendezvous with the **Continental Divide Trail** (and 235 miles/ 378 km of shared path). Up ahead

is **Breckenridge,** hometown of many world-class skiers and snowboarders. The **Swans Nest trailhead** is just four miles (6.4 km) from downtown Breckenridge for hikers who feel the need for an urban break.

Beyond the **Copper Mountain ski area,** the route dips down into a valley that once harbored **Camp Hale,** where the U.S. Army trained thousands of Mountain Division and winter-weather troops during World War II.

After entering **San Isabel National Forest,** the trail reaches **Turquoise Lake,** which offers nine campgrounds and access to **Leadville,** Colorado's most colorful and notorious boomtown. Such was Leadville's repute during Wild West

days that it attracted many distinguished (and unsavory) characters, ranging from Doc Holliday and Oscar Wilde to the Unsinkable Molly Brown of *Titanic* fame.

Tacking to the south, the trail passes through the **Mount Massive Wilderness** and along the eastern base of **Mount Elbert** (at 14,440 feet/4,401 m, the highest peak in the Rocky Mountains and second highest in the lower 48 states after Mount Whitney).

Arriving at **Twin Lakes,** hikers have a choice of following the CT east or west around the **Collegiate Peaks,** named by a group of Harvard students during an 1869 expedition led by Yale graduate Josiah Whitney. **Collegiate East** is shorter,

A view of Mount Elbert, the highest peak in Colorado and second highest in the lower 48 after Mount Whitney

Fall color brings a splash of splendor to the Colorado Trail near Kenosha Pass.

easier, and comes close to **Buena Vista** with its white-water rafting on the **Upper Arkansas River. Collegiate West**—only completed in 2012—offers a truer wilderness experience and more dramatic landscapes but adds 82 miles (132 km) to the length of the CT thru-hike.

The two routes merge again near **Monarch Pass** at the northern end of the **San Juan Mountains.** After skirting the west side of **Mount Ouray**—named for a 19th-century Ute chief who met three American presidents—the path goes up and over **Marshall Pass,** where the Denver and Rio Grande Western Railroad became the first train line to cross the Continental Divide in Colorado in 1881.

Swinging to the southwest, the route wanders into the **San Juan volcanic field.** Formed 30 to 40 million years ago during the tail end of the mountain building that

formed the Rockies, the region still boasts landmarks like the immense **Cochetopa Dome** near the CT's **Lujan Pass trailhead.** Then it's into

Gunnison National Forest and **La Garita Wilderness.**

The CT finally parts ways with the Continental Divide Trail near the remnants of **Beartown,** an 1890s gold mining outpost, before crossing the **Durango and Silverton railroad** tracks and the **Animas River** on a footbridge. Dead ahead is **Molas Pass** and the **Million Dollar Highway** (U.S. 550), which afford hikers a fast downhill walk into **Silverton** with its many hotels, restaurants, and historic sites.

Straying far away from civilization again, the last stretch of the Colorado Trail meanders through **San Juan National Forest** and along the western edge of **Hermosa Creek Wilderness** before a series of switchbacks takes it down to **Junction Creek** and the end of the long walk from Denver. Junction Creek sports a large campground, but it's just a 3.5-mile (5.6-km) walk into downtown **Durango** from there and a celebratory drink at one of the many craft breweries. ■

APRÈS HIKE

• **Mesa Verde National Park:** The nation's largest archaeological preserve and one of its oldest national parks safeguards more than 600 cliff dwellings built by ancestral Puebloans between A.D. 750 and 1300 on the side of a huge mesa in southwest Colorado.

• **Pagosa Springs:** The planet's deepest geothermal hot spring bubbles to the surface at several spots along the San Juan River in and around the town of Pagosa Springs. Hikers can soothe their weary bones (and feet) post-trek in steamy pools at the Healing Waters, the Springs, and Overlook resorts.

• **Durango Drinks Scene:** Like the rest of Colorado, Durango is heavy

into designer libations produced at eight brewpubs/craft breweries and two craft distilleries; most of them also serve food.

• **Animas River Rafting:** Take your choice of an easy float trip down the Lower Animas or a roller-coaster ride through the Class IV to V rapids of the Upper Animas on a guided white-water rafting or inflatable kayaking trip upstream from Durango.

• **Basecamp Pack Trips:** Durango-based Over the Hill Outfitters offers three- to five-day horseback camping forays into the remote Weminuche Wilderness in the San Juan Mountains.

Lamar River Trail

Wyoming

Hike where wolves howl, buffalo roam, and wildlife rather than hot water is the main attraction on a trail through a remote corner of Yellowstone National Park.

THE BIG PICTURE

Distance: 32 miles (51 km)

Elevation Gain: approx. 2,170 feet (660 m)

Time: 2 days

Difficulty: Easy to moderate

Best Time: Summer and fall

More Info: nps.gov/yell/planyourvisit/backcountryhiking.htm

There are no lakes, geysers, or awesome waterfalls, but the **Lamar River Valley** in the northeast corner of **Yellowstone** is without doubt the best place for wildlife viewing in America's oldest national park.

Lush grasslands and sagebrush attract bison, pronghorn, and mule deer, sometimes in sizable herds. Grizzly bears also frequent the area, as do Yellowstone's two wolf packs. Bighorn sheep inhabit the heights around the valley, while the watercourse provides a perfect habitat for river otters. Look to the sky for bald eagles and other raptors.

Meanwhile, the wide-open terrain makes the valley an ideal place to view and photograph wildlife, especially for those willing to venture away from the park's notoriously traffic-plagued roadways. And like the valley itself, the best route for wildlife viewing is the **Lamar River Trail.**

Given the prevalence of wild things, hikers should always carry bear spray and know how to aim the nozzle at the approaching bruin rather than at themselves. Likewise, they should never approach wild animals, in particular bison, bears, and wolves.

The full trail is 32 miles (51 km) out and back, an easy two-day trip with several places to bed down for a night. But the trail also offers the possibility of day or even half-day walks into the wilderness. It really depends on how far you want to hike.

The trailhead is a parking lot on the park's **Northeast Entrance Road** (U.S. 212) around 15 miles (24 km) from **Tower Junction.** A narrow wooden bridge takes hikers across **Soda Butte Creek** and an eventual rendezvous with the **Lamar River** as it meanders down the valley from the **Absaroka Range,** which forms the park's eastern boundary.

Around four miles (6.4 km) from the trailhead is Cache Creek, which marks a sharp divide between the valley's grassland and forest. Many

Sometimes called "America's Serengeti," the Lamar Valley is home to numerous large animals, including bison.

Soda Butte Creek, a major tributary of the Lamar River in Yellowstone National Park

day hikers about-face at this point and head back to the trailhead. Those with a backcountry permit can camp beside the creek.

From there, it's a fairly steady uphill hike along the eastern edge of the river to the **Lower Lamar** backcountry campsite and **Calfee Creek Patrol Cabin.** Built in 1915 by the U.S. Army when the military was still in charge of safeguarding Yellowstone, the log structure is one of only a few remaining in the park.

Past **Miller Creek,** the route joins the historic **Nez Perce National Historic Trail,** which Chief Joseph and 800 members of his tribe trekked with more than 2,000 horses in the summer of 1877 while fleeing the U.S. Army, which was trying to force them onto a reservation.

Warm Spring Meadow provides a temporary respite from the trees before the trail reaches **Cold Creek Junction,** where out-and-back hikers doing the whole route normally camp. However, there's also an option of progressing into a point-to-point hike that follows the **Mist Creek Trail** and **Pelican Valley Trail** another 17 miles (27 km) to the north shore of **Yellowstone Lake.** ■

OTHER GREAT TRAILS

• **Observation Point:** Starting from Old Faithful, this 1.6-mile (2.5-km) lollipop trail makes a steep ascent to a spectacular viewpoint overlooking the steamy Upper Geyser Basin.

• **Mount Washburn:** Reach the fire lookout tower on the summit (10,219 feet/3,115 m) via trails from Dunraven Pass or Chittenden Road.

• **South Rim:** Walk along the Grand Canyon of the Yellowstone to Artist Point, with an option to descend the super-steep Uncle Tom's Trail to an even more jaw-dropping view of Lower Yellowstone Falls.

• **West Thumb Geyser Basin:** Short but action-packed, this one-mile (1.6-km) route meanders through a very active thermal field beside Yellowstone Lake.

• **Mammoth Hot Springs:** Starting from Mammoth village, a double loop trail with boardwalks and stairs wraps around the volcanic hot spots of the Lower Terraces.

Jenny Lake Loop
Wyoming

Gorgeous lake and mountain views and wildlife sightings reward those who follow this lakeshore trail in Grand Teton National Park.

One of the easier hikes in **Grand Teton National Park** wraps around picture-perfect **Jenny Lake,** with the park's celebrated sawtooth peaks rising above the western shore. Although a short section of the trail along the eastern shore is paved, most of the route rambles unpaved through trees, around boulders, and across several wooden bridges.

Given its quick and effortless access from some of the park's major visitor nodes, the Jenny Lake Trail can get a little crowded at times. But those seeking more solace (or exercise) can duck down side trails leading into wilderness canyons and mountain passes.

Who was Jenny? A Shoshone woman who married Richard "Beaver Dick" Leigh, an English fur trapper and mountain man who spent much of the year in the Jackson Hole Valley with Jenny and their six kids. Leigh also guided the landmark 1872 survey of the Teton Range.

THE BIG PICTURE

Distance: 7.6 miles (12.2 km)

Elevation Change: approx. 600 feet (180 m)

Time: 3–5 hours

Difficulty: Easy

Best Time: Late spring to early fall

More Info: nps.gov/grte

Hikers can start the loop from several points along the eastern shore, including the **Jenny Lake Visitor Center** and **Jenny Lake Lodge.** There's also the option of hopping the **Jenny Lake Boating** shuttle service to the **West Shore Boat Dock** and kicking off from there.

Starting out from the visitors center, the trail leaps **Cottonwood Creek** and the boat dock on a sturdy log bridge before swinging around the lake's south shore and probably the best chance to spot a moose along the route. Tacking north, the trail makes for the **Cascade Creek** area. Hikers can ride the water taxi back to the eastern shore or clamber up spur trails to 100-foot (30-m) **Hidden Falls** or **Inspiration Point** with its stunning views of the lake and **Gros Ventre Mountains** in the distance.

A long but incredibly scenic side trail climbs 4.4 miles (7 km) through **Cascade Canyon,** jagged **Teewinot Mountain** and the brawny **Rock of Ages** rising on either side. Reaching a fork at the top of the canyon, trekkers can hang a left onto the **Teton Crest Trail,** a rugged 45-mile (72-km) route through the heart of the range to **Teton Village.**

Continuing along the west shore, Jenny Lake Trail intersects the **Lake**

Jenny Lake Loop is a perfect trail for those seeking an easy jaunt through nature.

The still waters of Jenny Lake in Grand Teton National Park reflect the impressive scope of the Teton Range.

of the Crags Trail—a short but difficult route that ascends to three remote alpine tarns—and passes through an area still recovering from the 1999 Alder fire. Ash-colored logs testify to lush woods before the blaze, but the undergrowth has bounced back nicely.

Another wooden bridge takes the trail across the **String Lake Outlet,** a shallow waterway that connects **String Lake** and Jenny Lake. Up ahead are the historic **Jenny Lake Lodge** and the start of a paved portion that runs down the eastern shore from **Jenny Lake Overlook** to the campground and visitors center. ∎

LAY YOUR HEAD

• **Jenny Lake Lodge:** Opened in the 1920s as a rustic dude ranch, the lodge is often mentioned among the best wilderness digs in North America. The decor is log cabin chic, the cuisine is Grand Teton's best, and there's a nightly Wine and Wickets social hour; cabins from $636; gtlc.com/lodges/jenny-lake-lodge.

• **Jenny Lake Campground:** Drop-dead lake and mountains views are the lure of a summer-only national park campground with 61 no-hookup sites, 10 of them reserved for walk-in or boat-in campers; $6.50–$36; nps.gov/grte/planyourvisit/jennylakecg.htm.

• **Lost Creek Ranch & Spa:** Luxury dude ranch digs and top-notch cuisine are complemented by float trips or fly-fishing on the Snake River, yoga and Pilates, heated pool and hot tub, and a range of horseback activities; from $6,450 a week, all inclusive; lostcreek.com.

• **Grand Teton Climbers' Ranch:** The American Alpine Club offers climbers and trekkers rustic bunkhouse accommodations with communal cooking and shower facilities around four miles (6.4 km) south of Jenny Lake; $22–$33; americanalpineclub.org/grand-teton-climbers-ranch.

Midwest

The Garden of the Gods sandstone formations overlook Shawnee National Forest.

Buckeye Trail
Ohio

Walk all the way around Ohio on an epic route through small towns and big cities, along historic towpaths, over the Appalachian Plateau, and across the Great Lakes Plains.

THE BIG PICTURE

Distance: 1,444 miles (2,324 km)

Elevation Change: Unknown

Time: 2.5–4 months

Difficulty: Strenuous

Best Time: Spring, summer, or fall

More Info: buckeyetrail.org

One of the nation's most audacious state trails, the **Buckeye Trail** (BT) makes a huge loop around Ohio, a bucolic trek along country roads and wilderness paths through a mix of farmland and forest.

Given its tremendous length (1,444 miles/2,324 km), a continuous thru-hike is rare. More likely is knocking off the 26 sections one by one over months or even years.

Opened in 1960 and one of the country's oldest state trails, the BT can be divided into four main sections that exemplify different aspects of the Ohio hiking experience. Starting from the trail's southernmost point near Cincinnati, our description runs counterclockwise.

Overlooking the **Ohio River** on the east side of **Cincinnati, Eden Park** marks the start of a southern leg that rambles across the gentle hills of Ohio's **Bluegrass Region** before rising into the **Appalachian Plateau.**

Easily the state's most rugged and remote corner, the highlands' undulating topography conveys the trail over numerous ridges and through myriad river valleys. It's tough going at times, but the reward includes long walks through the wilds of **Wayne National Forest,** several state forests, and half a dozen state parks.

Among the highlands of this southern swing are the caves, waterfalls, and incredible fall colors of **Hocking Hills State Park,** the ancient American Indian Hopewell mounds of the **Fort Hill Earthworks,** and a chance to dip your toes in the Ohio River at the **Edge of Appalachia Preserve.**

The BT's eastern leg offers a journey through the industrial revolution that starts with the 1842 **Stockport Mill** (now a hotel and restaurant) on the **Muskingum River.** The route follows the **Ohio and Erie Canal Towpath** into **Akron's** vintage **Canal District** and the possibility of watching the minor-league **RubberDucks** at Canal Park stadium or an outdoor concert at **Lock 3.**

Continuing along the canal, the trail traverses **Cuyahoga Valley National Park** before a wide swing around **Cleveland** suburbia takes

The Buckeye Trail snakes south of Cleveland through Cuyahoga Valley National Park.

Tucked in a remote corner of Hocking Hills, Cedar Falls is a hidden gem amid Blackhand sandstone and lush woodlands.

hikers to **Headlands Beach State Park.** Having crossed the entire state, many people end their BT trek with a dip in **Lake Erie.** Those who want to keep truckin' need to backtrack 65 miles (105 km) to the **Brecksville Reservation** in Cuyahoga Valley and the start of the Buckeye's northern leg.

Rather than run along the heavily developed lakeshore, the trail dips below Cleveland and ambles across the flat and farm-filled **Great Lakes Plains** to **Fremont** (hometown of President Rutherford B. Hayes) and the **Maumee River Valley** near **Toledo.**

The **Miami and Erie Canal Towpath** provides much of the BT's path through the rolling hills of the **corn belt** along the state's western

edge. The route follows the **Great Miami River** through **Dayton** and its various **Wright brothers** sites

before a final push along the **Little Miami Scenic Trail** back to Cincinnati. ■

OTHER GREAT TRAILS

• **Olentangy Trail:** Trek across Columbus on a 13.6-mile (22-km) riverside route through woodland, wetlands, and the Ohio State University campus.

• **Cincinnati Riverwalk:** Stretching two miles (3.2 km) along the downtown waterfront, this easy stroll includes a chance to leap across the Ohio River into Kentucky on the Purple People Bridge.

• **Ohio and Erie Canal Towpath (Cleveland):** The Towpath Mounds landscape art installation, the house from *A Christmas Story,* and the

ArcelorMittal Steel Heritage Center are some of the offbeat sights along this 25-mile (40-km) urban trail through Cleveland.

• **Holmes County Trail:** This 22-mile (35-km) paved path through Ohio's Amish country features a lane for hiking, biking, and in-line skating, and a second lane for horseback riders and Amish buggies.

• **Western Reserve Greenway:** Ohio's premier rail trail spans 43 miles (69 km) of scenic countryside between inland Warren and lakeside Ashtabula.

George S. Mickelson Trail

South Dakota

Highland meadows, ponderosa pines, and an overwhelming sense of history embellish this rousing rail trail through the heart of the Black Hills.

Gold miners, gunslingers, and the Lakota Sioux. Wyatt Earp, Calamity Jane, Wild Bill Hickok, George Armstrong Custer, and Tȟašúŋke Witkó (Crazy Horse). All of them traveled the north-south passage through the Black Hills that conveyed the trains of yesteryear and the hikers, bikers, and horseback riders of today.

Constructed in the early 1890s to serve the region's wild and woolly mining towns, the railroad line chugged along for nearly a century before Burlington Northern terminated service and donated the right-of-way to South Dakota State Parks.

Stretching 109 miles (175 km) between **Deadwood** and **Edgemont,** the **George S. Mickelson Trail** features four stone tunnels and more than 100 bridges. Sixteen trailheads

THE BIG PICTURE

Distance: 109 miles (175 km)

Elevation Change: approx. 5,400 feet (1,650 m)

Time: 4–6 days

Difficulty: Easy to moderate

Best Time: Late spring, summer, or early fall

More Info: gfp.sd.gov/parks/detail/george-s--mickelson-trail

offer parking, picnic tables, restrooms, and stations for the daily use fee that all users must pay. Camping isn't allowed along the trail; however, campgrounds and indoor accommodations are available in towns along the route.

Starting beside **Powerhouse Park** in Deadwood, the trail snakes its way up **Whitewood Creek** into the densely wooded highlands above the town. Only a few stone foundations are left at **Flat Iron City,** a trailside ghost town devastated by a 1927 flood. Reaching **Englewood,** the route starts its long run across **Black Hills National Forest.**

Along the way, the Mickelson passes through several long-forgotten settlements. **Dumont** and **Nahant** started life as frontier lumber mills. One of the oldest towns in the Black Hills, **Rochford,** with its little log chapel, was founded in 1877 by gold seekers. Farther south, the trail passes through three of its vintage railroad tunnels.

Hill City offers a range of eateries and overnight digs, as well as **South Dakota State Railroad Museum** and the dinosaur fossils of the **Black Hills Institute. Mount Rushmore** is just 10 miles (16 km) east of Hill City. For the time being, the only way to hike or bike between the two is along fairly busy

With a history steeped in railway lore, the Mickelson Trail reaches for 109 miles (175 km) across South Dakota.

Morning sunlight catches in the granite crevices of the Needles spires in the Black Hills.

roadways. However, the state has applied for permission to build a **Rushmore Connector Trail** across national forest land to the presidential memorial.

The next stretch of the Mickelson offers views of the colossal **Crazy Horse Memorial,** sculpted into a granite hillside beside the trail. The town of **Custer** is another chance for hikers and bikers to overnight or resupply, as well as a 3.2-mile (5.1-km) spur leading to **Stockade Lake** on the western edge of **Custer State Park** (with its wildlife and numerous hiking trails).

Pringle features an oddball **Bicycle Sculpture** and another possible detour off the Mickelson— a 6.2-mile (10-km) hike or bike along Highway 385 to **Wind Cave National Park.**

Beyond Pringle, the Mickelson exits Black Hills National Forest and begins a homestretch across grassy ranchland to Edgemont. The trail finally peters out in **Edgemont City Park** beside the **Trails, Trains &** **Pioneers Museum** and a nicely restored **covered wooden bridge** dating from the 1890s, when Edgemont was a busy rail junction. ■

LAY YOUR HEAD

• **Whistler Gulch Campground:** With cabins, RV hookups, and tent sites along Whitewood Creek in Deadwood, this is the most convenient place to overnight at the start or end of the Mickelson; from $27; whistlergulch.com.

• **Oreville Campground:** Aspens and ponderosa pines shade the 26 vehicle and tent sites at a Black Hills National Forest campground with picnic tables, fire rings, drinking water, and vault toilets; from $20; recreation.gov/camping/camp grounds/231841.

• **Heritage Village Campground:** Located near the Crazy Horse Memorial about halfway along the Mickelson Trail, the village offers showers, laundry, internet, and the Prairie Dog Café; from $22.

• **Buffalo Ridge Camp Resort:** Splurge for a cozy glamping tent at a campground on the outskirts of Custer that also offers cabins, tree houses, teepees, RV hookups, and a swimming pool; from $39; custerhospitality.com/buffalo-ridge -camp-resort.

• **Edgemont Campground:** Modest but friendly digs for tents and RVs near the southern end of the Mickelson Trail; from $15; edgemont -campground.business.site.

Chicago Lakefront Trail
Illinois

Trek the "toddlin' town" via an eclectic shoreline trail that offers everything from beaches and water sports to world-class museums, breezy waterfront cafés, iconic public art, and incredible views of the Windy City skyline.

A s early as the 1830s, the city of Chicago reserved a section of the Lake Michigan shoreline as public space where ordinary citizens could stroll, sit, and take in the air. The ever expanding route now measures 18 miles (29 km) from top to bottom.

In addition to a dozen beaches, the **Chicago Lakefront Trail** offers access to the city's three largest parks, legendary sports venues, and celebrated

THE BIG PICTURE

Distance: 18 miles (29 km)

Elevation Gain: Negligible

Time: 3 days

Difficulty: Easy

Best Time: Late spring to early fall

More Info: chicagoparkdistrict.com/parks-facilities/lakefront-trail

cultural institutions. There's also the aesthetic value: Lake Michigan set against the Chicago skyline.

NORTH SHORE

R ide the **Red Line** subway to **Bryn Mawr** or **Thorndale** to start walking south from **Kathy Osterman Beach.** You know you're headed in the right direction when you pass the **Large Walking Figure** statue along the shore.

Up ahead is **Montrose Point,** a human-made cape fashioned with sand trucked from Indiana that features Chicago's largest beach, a **sanctuary for migratory birds, fishing charters,** and **canoe/kayak rentals.** Even if you didn't bring your pooch, watch the happy hounds frolic in the water at **Montrose Dog Beach.** The entrance to **Montrose Harbor** is flanked by two **moonrise observation points** that are also great for sunrise if you happen to be an early riser.

Just past the **Waveland** waterfront golf course and sports fields, walkers can detour down Addison Street to **Wrigley Field,** home of the **Chicago Cubs,** the second oldest major league baseball diamond after Boston's Fenway Park.

Back along the shore, the Lakefront Trail soon slips into **Lincoln Park,** which started life as a public burial ground before its 1860 transformation into a recreational

Chicago's Lakefront Trail leads tourists and locals alike to nearby Navy Pier and along almost the entire length of the city.

The Chicago skyline rises in the distance in front of the Shedd Aquarium and the Lakefront Trail.

green space. The city's largest park offers a broad range of activities from the **Lincoln Park Zoo** and **Peggy Notebaert Nature Museum** to sailboat charters in **Belmont Harbor** and **Theater on the Lake** (home of the **Chicago Summer Theater Festival**).

The lakeshore sports scene reaches fever pitch at **North Avenue Beach** with its **beach volleyball courts,** and **paddleboard** and **Jet Ski** rentals. The "shipwreck" near the jetty is actually the ocean liner–inspired **North Avenue Beach House,** which features

portholes, faux funnels, and a top-deck cocktail bar.

DOWNTOWN

The Lakefront Trail segues into its middle section at **Slab Cove,** which is also one of the best spots to snap a picture of the skyline with the

---

LAY YOUR HEAD

• **Majestic Hotel:** Half a block from Lincoln Park and an easy walk to Wrigley Field, this North Shore hotel in a vintage 1921 building doubles as a shrine to the Chicago Cubs; from $89; majestic-chicago.com.

• **The Drake:** Four American presidents, British royalty, the Rat Pack, and Marilyn Monroe are among the many notables who have stayed at this classic lakeshore hotel. Overlooking Oak Street Beach, it opened in 1920; from $163; thedrakehotel.com.

• **Sable at Navy Pier:** Launched in 2021, this upscale boutique abode—with its panoramic lake and skyline views—feels more like a luxury cruise ship than a land-based hotel; from $129; sablehotel.com.

• **Chicago Lake Shore Hotel:** Located in the Kenwood neighborhood near Promontory Point, this revamped two-story motor lodge is perfect for exploring the southern section of the Lakefront Trail; from $109; chicagolakeshorehotel.com.

LOCAL FLAVOR

- **Waterfront Café:** A 10-minute walk north of Osterman Beach, this super laid-back eatery offers live tunes, a large lakefront patio, and reasonably priced lunch and dinner dishes; 6219 North Sheridan Road; waterfrontcafechicago.com.

- **Clock Tower Café:** Tucked inside a 1931 Gothic Revival structure in Waveland Park that resembles an English church, the café complements its salads, burgers, and Chicago dogs with craft beers and signature cocktails; 3701 North Recreation Drive; clocktower cafechicago.com.

- **Shore Club:** Salmon ceviche, lobster tacos, and tuna poke are among the seafood delights at a

popular North Avenue Beach hangout that also flaunts an alfresco cocktail lounge; 1603 North Lake Shore Drive; shoreclubchi.com.

- **Caffé Oliva:** A Mediterranean menu and strategic location between Ohio Street Beach and Navy Pier make this outdoor eatery the perfect place to chill along the downtown waterfront; 550 East Grand Avenue; caffeoliva.com.

- **Reggies on the Beach:** The Jackson Park waterfront provides a sandy venue for a bar and restaurant that sports a big wooden deck, live music, and beach cabanas; 6259 South Lake Shore Drive; facebook.com/reggiesonthebeach.

100-story **John Hancock Center** rising higher than anything else.

Oak Street and **Ohio Street Beaches** offer small sandy strands in the shadow of all that high-rise luxury. Yet not even the skyline can overshadow the massive **Navy Pier.**

The 3,300-foot (1,010-m)-long behemoth has morphed from its role as a Great Lakes naval training center into an eclectic over-the-water attraction with **carnival rides, lake cruises,** multiple bars and restaurants, the **Chicago Children's**

Museum, and the **Chicago Shakespeare Theater.**

Just south of the pier, the **Chicago River** emerges from a skyscraper canyon as it flows into Lake Michigan. **Grant Park** soon appears on the left. Its landmarks range from the globally significant **Art Institute of Chicago** to the gleaming **Cloud Gate** and the **Maggie Daley Ice Skating Ribbon** (which also offers rock climbing).

The park's **Queen's Landing** is where Elizabeth II and Prince Philip stepped ashore from their royal yacht during the first ever visit by a British monarch to Chicago in 1959. Inspired by the rococo fountains of Versailles, nearby **Buckingham Fountain** is especially attractive during its evening illumination. Reaching the bottom end of Grant Park, the trail offers another stunning skyline view, one that includes the 108-story **Willis (nee Sears) Tower,** tallest building on the planet from 1974 to 1998.

Bringing up the bottom end of the downtown waterfront is the **Museum Campus** and an unrivaled assemblage of science and nature that includes **Shedd Aquarium, Adler Planetarium,** and the **Field Museum of Natural History.** Adjacent **Northerly Island** continues to morph from its past as a small airfield that closed in 2003 into a city park with a **beach, sailing programs,** and an **outdoor concert venue.**

SOUTH SHORE

Although **Soldier Field** of the Chicago Bears is considered part of the Museum Campus, it also marks a transition into the southern section of the Lakefront Trail. Opened in 1924 and easily the oldest NFL stadium, the giant arena has hosted many nonsporting

With its roots dating back to the 1830s, Chicago's Lakefront Trail now connects some of the city's main attractions to the beauty of Lake Michigan.

Lake Michigan's sandy shoreline grants sunbathers a warm retreat from the nearby hustle of the city.

events, including appearances by Amelia Earhart, President Franklin D. Roosevelt, and Rev. Martin Luther King, Jr.

The trail passes **Burnham Harbor** along a stretch of shoreline with its yachts, stadium, and memorials to Chicago police and firemen who fell in the line of duty, and colossal **McCormick Place,** the largest convention center in North America. Spreading out from the building's south side, **McCormick Bird Sanctuary** features an elevated nature trail and viewing platforms in six acres (2.5 ha) of native prairie and woodland vegetation.

Farther along, **31st Street Harbor** is another haven for water sports, ranging from **kayak, paddleboard,** and **Jet Ski** rentals to **guided fishing trips** and a private luxury **yacht charter.** Perched at the south end of **Oakwood Beach** is **"The Secret Mermaid,"** an unauthorized sculpture created by four "guerrilla artists" in 1986 and hidden for 14 years before the Chicago Park District adopted her as official public art.

Looming off **49th Street Beach** is the rusting hulk of the ***Silver Spray,*** a steamboat that ran aground on the offshore **Morgan Shoal** in 1914. An artificial peninsula extending into the lake, **Promontory Point** features a historic 1937 field house with a castle turret, lake-view seating, and wonderful fall foliage.

Anchoring the southern end of the Lakefront Trail is storied **Jackson Park,** longtime location of the **Museum of Science and Industry,** and future home of the **Barack Obama Presidential Library.** Designed by Frederick Law Olmsted and Calvert Vaux—the same pair that planned New York City's Central Park—the green space opened in 1871 and later hosted the World's Columbian Exposition of 1893. All that remains of the fabled "White City" are the artificial waterways and museum building.

The Lakefront Trail officially ends at the spot where 67th Street hits Lake Michigan. However, nothing is preventing you from strolling the sidewalk past the golf course to the **South Shore Park,** with its **sandy beach, nature sanctuary,** and historic **South Shore Cultural Center.** ∎

The Adler Planetarium's sundial sculpture, "Man Enters the Cosmos," looks out over the twinkling expanse of downtown Chicago.

Flint Hills Nature Trail
Kansas

The tallgrass prairie offers a unique setting for a rail trail along a route originally blazed by wagon trains, oxcarts, and stagecoaches rumbling down the Santa Fe Trail.

THE BIG PICTURE

Distance: 117 miles (188 km)

Elevation Gain: approx. 1,800 feet (550 m)

Time: 5–8 days

Difficulty: Easy to moderate

Best Time: Spring, summer, or fall

More Info: kanzatrails.org/flint-hills -nature-trail

As the name suggests, this multiuse trail across eastern Kansas revolves around nature, in particular a region that harbors the largest tract of tallgrass prairie left in North America.

The wild bison and elk that once grazed on the bluestem and switch-grass are long gone. But the Flint Hills eco-region continues to support many other native species, from white-tailed deer, coyotes, and prairie chickens that cross the trail to hawks, kestrels, falcons, and other feathered friends that hover above the rolling grassland.

But it's not all Mother Nature. The modern pathway traces the route of the old **Santa Fe National Historic Trail,** which trappers, traders, settlers, and soldiers followed to the Southwest starting in the 1820s. In the decade before the Civil War, the region was on the front line of Bleeding Kansas, the deadly violence between pro-slavery and antislavery groups.

The Council Grove, Osage City and Ottawa Railway arrived in the 1880s to support the region's booming cattle industry. A century later, the line was obsolete. However, a group of Kansas hikers and bikers formed a grassroots nonprofit conservancy to transform 117 miles (188 km) into the **Flint Hills Nature Trail.**

Hikers, horse riders, and cyclists are welcome on the Sunflower State's longest trail of any kind and the nation's seventh longest rail trail. Camping is not allowed along the route, which means users must plan on spending nights in towns or parks with accommodations.

Located about an hour's drive south of downtown **Kansas City,** the town of **Osawatomie** anchors the trail's eastern end. Before hitting the road, trekkers should visit the town's **John Brown Museum** for an overview of Bleeding Kansas in an old stone structure that was once a stop on the Underground Railroad and headquarters of the famous abolitionist.

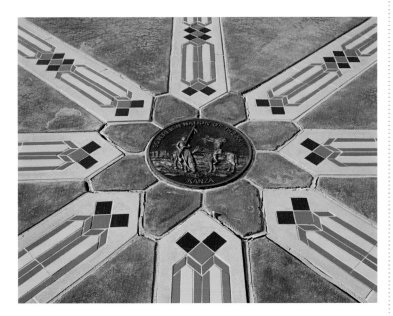

This emblem of the Kaw Nation is located in Allegawaho Memorial Heritage Park, which is being developed by the Kaw (Kanza) tribe as they reestablish their Kansas heritage after being forcibly relocated.

Called mile zero of the Flint Hills Nature Trail, Osawatomie, Kansas, marks the starting or stopping point of the trail.

The trail follows the **Marais des Cygnes River** upstream to **Ottawa,** where the **Old Depot** (opened in 1888) and **Dietrich Cabin** (built in 1859) reflect 19th-century frontier life in the Flint Hills region. Farther along, **Pomona State Park** offers shady lakeside camping, fishing, and boat rentals.

Basecamp Flint Hills in little **Allen** offers another chance to camp beside the trail before a long stretch of open prairie that includes **Allegawaho Heritage Memorial Park.** Created by the modern descendants of the Native Americans who once called this region home, the park safeguards the remains of three Kaw villages.

Up ahead are **Council Grove** and the **Kaw Mission State Historic Site,** as well as the aptly named **Last Chance Store,** where thousands of Santa Fe Trail travelers restocked before heading into the wilds of western Kansas. The Flint Hills route reaches its western end in **Herington,** not far from where President Dwight D. Eisenhower was raised. ∎

LOCAL FLAVOR

• **Chris' Café:** Meatloaf, mashed potatoes, chicken-fried steak, and barbecued beef are some of the traditional Great Plains comfort food at this low-key eatery near the start of the trail; 537 Main Street, Osawatomie, KS; facebook.com/OsawatomieCafe.

• **Smoked Creations:** Cuban sandwiches, barbecued burritos, and St. Louis–style spareribs complement the brisket and pulled pork at this Ottawa eating institution; 222 East Logan Street, Ottawa, KS; smokedcreationsbbq.com.

• **Marilynn's Place:** A cinnamon roll with chili is one of the local favorites on a menu that also features gumbo, shepherd's pie, and other dishes from way beyond Kansas; 1216 Laing Street, Osage City, KS; facebook.com/marilynnsplaceks.

• **Trail Days Café & Museum:** The historic Rawlinson-Terwilliger Home beside the old Santa Fe Trail provides an atmospheric setting for arguably the best cooking along the entire trail; 803 West Main Street, Council Grove, KS; traildayscafeandmuseum.org.

Knobstone Trail
Indiana

Indiana's longest hiking trail wanders through the rugged woods, ridges, and valleys of the Knobstone Escarpment between Indianapolis and Louisville, Kentucky.

THE BIG PICTURE

Distance: 45 miles (72 km)

Elevation Change: approx. 7,300 feet (2,230 m)

Time: 3–4 days

Difficulty: Strenuous

Best Time: Spring, summer, or fall

More Info: knobstonehikingtrail.org

Rambling across the top of its namesake escarpment, the **Knobstone Trail** (KT) is strewn with deep ravines and steep hills, topography that makes a relatively short walk through the woods more strenuous than expected.

The escarpment is named for its underlying Knobstone shale, formed more than 300 million years ago when most of the American Midwest was submerged beneath a vast inland sea. Uneven erosion and weathering over the intervening years created the extreme terrain of the state's most rugged and remote region.

Pioneers tried to farm the area but found the steep slopes nearly impossible to cultivate. Unlike the rest of Indiana, the Knobstone region remained largely untamed and underpopulated until the 1930s, when the state annexed much of the land. As a result, today's hikers can easily imagine how the mixed hardwood forest of southern Indiana looked and felt to young Abe Lincoln, who lived nearby between the ages of seven and 21.

Nearly all of the KT runs through state forests, multiuse reserves that facilitate hunting and timber extraction as well as recreation. Hikers should take note of hunting seasons (fall and winter) and wear bright colors.

The only organized campgrounds along the route are located at Delaney Park and Deam Lake at either end. Primitive dispersed camping is allowed along most of the trail. However, hikers must pitch their tents at least 100 feet (30 m) from the trail and at least a quarter mile (0.4 km) from trailheads, roads, and designated recreation areas.

Starting from the south, hikers take their first few steps along the KT at **Deam Lake State Recreation Area.** Named for the forester who wrote *Trees of Indiana,* the park offers campsites and cabins, as well as rowboat and kayak rentals, and a nature center with programs and exhibits on the Knobstone region. Slipping around the lake's eastern shore, the trail dives into **Clark State Forest.**

Around 5.5 miles (8.8 km) from

A butterfly alights on greenery along the ruggedly beautiful backcountry Knobstone Trail.

The untamed nature of the Knobstone area means hikers gain a glimpse into the past while traversing the steep terrain.

the start, the KT crosses a wide area ravaged by a monster EF4 tornado that ripped through southern Indiana in March 2012. The forest is still recovering. However, the lack of mature trees means the rebuilt trail across the destruction zone offers the best views along the entire route.

Farther along, the **Virginia Pine-Chestnut Oak Nature Preserve** safeguards a small but exquisite tract of pristine forest. Reaching **New Chapel trailhead** beside the slow-flowing **South Branch of Big Ox Creek,** hikers can take a detour to **Dr. John Richey Cemetery,** which preserves the moss- and lichen-covered headstones of early 19th-century settlers.

The KT tiptoes along cornfields near the **Leota trailhead** before veering west into the **Elk Creek Fish and Wildlife Area.** The last

11 miles (18 km) of the Knobstone pass through **Jackson-Washington State Forest.** Hikers have a choice of finishing at the **Spurgeon**

Hollow trailhead or trekking another two miles (3.2 km) to **Delaney Park** with its campground, cabins, and showers. ■

APRÈS HIKE

• **Columbus:** Eero Saarinen, Robert Venturi, I. M. Pei, and César Pelli are among the celebrated architects who designed structures in an Indiana city that boasts seven national historic landmark buildings.

• **Fort Vallonia:** This reconstruction of an early 19th-century frontier outpost offers a museum, guided tours, and a living history fest with music, food, crafts, and reenactors every October.

• **Muscatatuck National Wildlife Refuge:** More than 280 avian species call on this "continentally important" birding area during

their annual migration across the Midwest.

• **French Lick West Baden Museum:** The world's largest circus diorama and Larry Bird memorabilia are the top attractions of an awesome small-town collection that began as a pop-up museum in 2007.

• **Louisville, Kentucky:** Churchill Downs and the Kentucky Derby Museum, the Muhammad Ali Center, and Louisville Slugger Museum & Factory are the triple crown of sights in the big Kentucky city less than 20 miles (32 km) from Deam Lake.

Cowboy Trail
Nebraska

A Wild West railroad line across northern Nebraska has found new life as a hiking, biking, and horseback trail across some of the Cornhusker State's most distinctive landscapes.

THE BIG PICTURE

Distance: 321 miles (516 km)

Elevation Gain: approx. 1,790 feet (550 m) Norfolk to Valentine

Time: 10–14 days

Difficulty: Easy to moderate

Best Time: Spring, summer, or fall

More Info: outdoornebraska.gov/cowboytrail and bikecowboytrail.com

In the 1870s, the Fremont, Elkhorn and Missouri Valley Railroad began laying tracks across the Great Plains of northern Nebraska, a route that would soon be called the Cowboy Line because it served the region's booming cattle industry. After the line was abandoned and the tracks ripped up in the 1980s, the route morphed into the state's first long-distance recreational trail and the nation's most ambitious rails-to-trails conversion.

Although it's tempting to think the **Cowboy Trail** traverses nothing more than flat open range, that couldn't be further from the truth. From the Niobrara River Valley and other major watersheds to the inimitable Sandhills region and wooded Pine Ridge, the multiuse hiking, biking, and horseback route flaunts a surprising variety of Nebraska landscapes.

Far off the interstate and largely forgotten, lots of small towns have shady city parks with campgrounds and other amenities for those making their way across the plains. Around two-thirds of the trail is surfaced in gravel-like crushed limestone and the route rambles across hundreds of bridges left over from railroad days, including the monster span across the Niobrara River.

A two-hour drive northwest of **Omaha,** the city of **Norfolk** anchors the route's eastern end. Trekkers can duck into the **Elkhorn Valley Museum** for a quick overview of regional history (and hometown hero Johnny Carson) before setting off. Beyond Norfolk, the first leg of the Cowboy Trail runs through seemingly endless farms and ranches on a 100-mile (160-km) dash through the **Elkhorn Valley.** Here and there are curiosities, like the historic gristmill and retro drive-in movie in **Neligh,** or the old brick train depot in **O'Neill.**

Reaching little **Stuart,** the trail finally breaks away from the Elkhorn Valley and heads west into the heart of the **Sandhills.** Considered a separate eco-island from the surrounding Great Plains, the region features prairie grass–covered rolling dunes that can reach as high as 330 feet (100 m). Thanks to a railroad right-of-way that never exceeds a 2 percent grade, hikers and bikers don't have to deal with the undulating elevation.

Newport's claim to fame is one

Young students plant milkweed seedlings near the Cowboy Trail.

A sweeping view of a section of the multiuse Cowboy Trail over Long Pine Creek

of the world's smallest pool halls, a former hay-weighing station converted into a billiards room beside the trail. Around 70 miles (110 km) farther west, the trail leaps across the Niobrara River on the stupendous **Valentine Bridge.** The town of **Valentine** is home base for outfitters like **Brewers Canoers** and **Little Outlaw** that offer paddling and tubing on the **Niobrara National Scenic River.**

The 140 miles (225 km) of trail between Valentine and Chadron are the least developed, the old railroad tracks only recently removed and much of the route across dirt and grass rather than nicely crushed limestone. But it's also one of the more scenic, a homestretch through the **Pine Ridge** region and landscapes

more reminiscent of the nearby Black Hills than the rest of Nebraska. Shaded by ponderosa pines, the ridge was once a homeland of Crazy Horse and the Lakota Sioux.

Chadron marks the end of the line with three museums that celebrate the Pine Ridge region's human and natural history, and the mighty fine **Chadron State Park,** where hikers and bikers can camp amid the towering ponderosa. ■

LAY YOUR HEAD

• **Ta-Ha-Zouka Park:** Camp beside the Elkhorn River in Norfolk; $12–$18; norfolkne.gov.

• **Riverside Park:** Neligh's municipal campground offers Wi-Fi, showers, and a swimming pool; $5–$15; neligh.org.

• **The Pines:** Enjoy rustic cabins near the trail in Long Pine; from $85; thepineslongpine.com.

• **Cottonwood Lake:** This state recreation area near Merriman has shoreline camping amid the Sandhills; $10–$35; outdoornebraska .gov/cottonwood.

• **Chadron State Park:** Nebraska's oldest state park offers cabins, campsites, trail rides, and a trading post; $15–$90; outdoornebraska .gov/chadron.

Originally laid in the 1870s, the tracks for the modern Cowboy Trail
spanned a route across the Great Plains of northern Nebraska.

Ice Age National Scenic Trail

Wisconsin

Plunge into North America's frozen past along an epic trail that wanders the edge of the huge Pleistocene ice field that formed the geography of modern Wisconsin.

THE BIG PICTURE

Distance: approx. 1,200 miles (1,930 km)

Elevation Gain: approx. 130 feet (40 m)

Time: 48–60 days

Difficulty: Strenuous

Best Time: Late spring, summer, or early fall

More Info: iceagetrail.org and nps.gov/iatr

Wisconsin's **Ice Age Trail** is all about the geological forces that shaped the Upper Great Lakes region.

Drumlins, kames, eskers, and erratics may sound like the names of tribes in *Game of Thrones,* but they're actually some of the glacial features that trekkers encounter along the Ice Age Trail. They were created by the massive Laurentide Ice Sheet that covered half of Wisconsin and much of North America until around 12,000 years ago. The trail traces the terminal moraine that marked the farthest advance of that frozen giant.

Running through 30 of the state's 72 counties, the route spans roughly 1,200 miles (1,930 km) between **Lake Michigan** and the **St. Croix River** just above its confluence with the Mississippi. The Ice Age Trail remains a work in progress: Around two-thirds of the footpath is finished, the segments linked by walks along roads and sidewalks.

Hiking the trail, it's natural to imagine what the flora and fauna were like during Pleistocene days. Woolly mammoths, caribou, and musk ox grazed on the stunted tundra vegetation along the immediate edge of the great ice sheet. As the ice retreated, spruce forest inhabited by mastodons, saber-toothed cats, giant beavers, and giant bears slowly replaced the tundra. The first humans, ancient ancestors of the Native Americans who would later inhabit the region, arrived around 10,000 years ago.

Ten millennia later, Wisconsin conservationists decided the state's glacial landmarks needed to be safeguarded from future development. One of those geological movers and shakers was Ray Zillmer, who in the 1950s proposed a 500-mile (800-km)-long national park in Wisconsin that would showcase the impact of continental glaciation. His proposal was turned down, but it spurred the Park Service to create the **Ice Age National Scientific Reserve,** with most of its nine units located in state parks or forests along the terminal moraine.

Devil's Lake State Park boasts steep quartzite cliffs along a 1,000-mile (1,600-km) footpath that dates to the Ice Age.

Summer evenings make for magical hiking on the South Shore Beach of Devil's Lake State Park during sunset.

Trekking from east to west, the trail starts at **Potawatomi State Park** on the **Door Peninsula.** An elongated landform that juts into Lake Michigan, the peninsula is often lauded as one of the most beautiful places in the Midwest. And the trail takes full advantage of the scenery during an opening 25-mile (40-km) leg through the pastoral countryside between **Sturgeon Bay** and **Algoma.**

The route finally hits hard-core glacial terrain between **Glenbeulah** and **Rice Lake** on segments that ramble across the top of **Kettle Moraine.** Around 100 miles (160 km) long, the moraine is so large it was called the Kettle Range during pioneer days. It takes its name from the many "kettles," depressions caused by melting ice that

eventually filled with water to become small lakes and ponds. The region harbors two units of the national scientific reserve: **Kettle Moraine State Forest** and the **Campbellsport Drumlins.**

The big bend at the southern end of the Ice Age Trail is mostly

OTHER GREAT TRAILS

- **Hank Aaron State Trail:** Named for the Milwaukee Braves baseball legend, this 14-mile (22.5-km) paved urban trail links Milwaukee's lakefront with the Harley Davidson Museum, the Mitchell Park horticultural domes, and American Family Field stadium.

- **Glacial Drumlin State Trail:** Stretching 52 miles (83 km) between Waukesha and Cottage Grove—with connectors to Milwaukee and Madison—this crushed limestone trail is popular with bikers traveling between the state's biggest cities.

- **Timms Hill Trail:** Summit Wisconsin's highest point (1,951 feet/595 m) on a 10-mile (16-km) spur off the Ice Age Trail near Ogema.

- **Military Ridge State Trail:** Shooting due west from Madison, this 40-mile (64-km) route traces the path of a wilderness road blazed by the U.S. Army in the 1830s.

- **Gandy Dancer Trail:** Named for the men who laid the tracks, this rail-to-trail conversion travels 47 miles (76 km) along the Wisconsin-Minnesota border between Danbury and St. Croix Falls.

roadway rather than dedicated hiking trail, although the **Janesville** greenbelt does provide at least temporary relief from traffic and a chance for hikers to pamper themselves with an urban overnight.

Beyond Janesville, the trail enters the **Driftless Area,** another geological oddity. Because it was never covered by an ice cap, even during the maximum extent of North American glaciation, the terrain was never smoothed or flattened and never covered by glacial deposits or "drift." Reaching **Monticello,** the trail skirts around the western edge of Madison before arriving at **Cross Plains** village, where the **Ice Age Trail Alliance** headquarters welcomes visitors.

Along with vehicles and pedestrians, the trail crosses **Lake Wisconsin** on the vintage **Merrimac Ferry** (founded in 1844). Before boarding, pick up a cone at the **Merrimac Scoop,** an old-timey ice-cream stand beside the ferry landing. Reaching the north shore, the trail climbs to **Devil's Lake,** one of Wisconsin's most scenic state parks. Although it boasts a glacial interpretive center, the park is actually an outstanding example of Driftless terrain—a deep valley flanked by steep quartzite cliffs with dramatic outcrops like **Cleopatra's Needle** and **Elephant Rock.**

Hikers can crash at the park's **Ice Age Trail Campground** while they decide on their next move. Beyond Devil's Lake, the trail temporarily splits into two different routes: a 92-mile (148-km) western bifurcation via the boisterous **Wisconsin Dells** summer resort area and the 75-mile (120-km) eastern branch via **Portage** and **Montello.**

Those following the western route

Catch beautiful fall colors while hiking the Ice Age Trail near Gibraltar Rock.

should linger a few hours in **Baraboo,** an official Ice Age town and a bustling little place with several claims to fame. It's the hometown of **Bradbury Robinson,** who in 1906 threw the first legal forward pass in American football history during a college game in Waukesha, Wisconsin. It's also the place where five local siblings founded the **Ringling Brothers Circus** in 1884. As such, Baraboo is home to both the **International Clown Hall of Fame** and the **Circus World Museum** with its live performances.

Once the branches form a single trail again near **Coloma,** the route continues through **Hartman Creek State Park,** the **Dells of the Eau Claire County Park,** and **Kettlebowl Ski Hill.** Slipping into the vast **North Woods,** the Ice Age Trail finally comes into its own as a dedicated hiking trail, a sinuous westward run that includes the **Harrison Hills,** the upper **Wisconsin River Valley,** and **Chequamegon-Nicolet National Forest.** The route is

sprinkled with moraines, kettle ponds, and other glacial features, as well as remote campsites where the outside world seems far away.

Another unit of the national scientific reserve, **Obey Ice Age Interpretive Center** in **Chippewa Moraine State Recreation Area** is one of the best places along the trail to learn more about glaciation, as well as the region's human and natural history. Nature films and ranger-led wildlife encounters complement the interactive exhibits.

Sticking to the woods as much as possible, the trail makes a big loop around the north end of the farm-filled **Red Cedar Valley** (celebrated for its strawberries) and passes through **McKenzie Creek State Wildlife Area** and **Straight Lake State Park** on a final lunge toward the St. Croix River. The Ice Age Trail reaches a stunning conclusion on a cliff top overlooking the **Dalles of the St. Croix River** on the Wisconsin side of **Interstate State Park.** ∎

LOCAL FLAVOR

• **Greystone Castle:** Despite its grandiose name, this Sturgeon Bay eating and drinking institution is really a vintage American diner tucked inside a sturdy stone stagecoach station erected in 1898; 8 North Madison Avenue, Sturgeon Bay, WI; greystonecastlebar.com.

• **The Braising Pan:** West Bend's German heritage inspires a menu featuring schnitzel, sauerkraut, braunschweiger sausages, Bavarian pretzels in a beer cheese sauce, and nachos made with bratwurst, onions, and Swiss cheese; 1100 N. Main Street, West Bend, WI; thebraising pan.com.

• **Lark:** The adventurous menu at this edgy eatery in downtown Janesville

ranges from kimchi mac and cheese and sushi pizza to more traditional fare like tenderloin and pork belly; 60 S. Main Street, Janesville, WI; www.larkjanesville.com.

• **Driftless Glen:** Burgers slathered in bourbon barbecue sauce and brandy-glazed salmon complement the locally made spirits and cocktails at this Baraboo distillery restaurant; 300 Water Street, Baraboo, WI; driftlessglen.com.

• **Moonridge Brewing Company:** This North Woods brewery right off the trail in Cornell offers a thirst-quenching selection of stout, hefeweizen, amber, IPA, blonde ale, and other beers; 501 Bridge Street, Cornell, WI; moonridgebrewery.com.

Katy Trail
Missouri

America's longest rail trail flows up the Missouri River Valley from St. Louis to Jefferson City and Clinton on the edge of the Ozarks.

THE BIG PICTURE

Distance: 240 miles (386 km)

Elevation Gain: approx. 6,800 feet (2,070 m)

Time: 8–12 days

Difficulty: Moderate

Best Time: Spring, summer, or fall

More Info: katytrailmo.com

Traveling the **Katy Trail** along the **Missouri River,** one sometimes wonders if Lewis and Clark would have preferred a smooth, level waterside path to fighting against a robust current, dodging half-submerged trees, and battling wicked whirlpools in a keelboat and dugout canoes.

Cutting across Missouri's midsection, the trail takes its name not from the wife, daughter, sister, or mother of a local luminary but rather the nickname of the train company—the Missouri-Kansas-Texas (MKT) Railroad—which locals dubbed the "KT" during frontier days.

A 1986 flood that washed out a significant section of track near St. Louis sparked development of the foot and cycle path when the KT railroad decided to forgo repairs and sell the right-of-way to the state. Around two-thirds of the trail (165 miles/265 km) runs beside the Missouri River on a route that Lewis and Clark and many other 19th-century travelers followed to the American West.

Much of the Katy Trail is through typical Midwest farmland, but it also takes hikers and bikers through a region rich in German American history and past Jefferson City and its imposing State Capitol Building. The route features 24 trailheads, 18 campgrounds, and numerous towns where travelers can stock up on food and drink, sleep with a roof over their heads, or get their bike repaired.

Although the newest, easternmost portion of the trail flirts with the **Mississippi River** north of **St. Louis,** many folks commence their journey at **DuSable Park** along the historic

The Katy Trail spans 237 miles (381 km), covering much of the state of Missouri via an old rail line.

Sunflowers turn their heads to the sky along the Katy Trail near Weldon Spring, Missouri.

riverfront in **St. Charles.** Right off the bat there's a worthwhile stop: the **Lewis and Clark Boat House and Museum,** which houses full-scale reproductions of various Corps of Discovery vessels.

Heading upriver, the Katy Trail threads the Missouri wine country between **Augusta** and **McKittrick.** Near **Lake Creek Winery** is the grave of frontiersman **Daniel Boone,** who hunted and trapped the region until his 1820 death. Across the river from McKittrick, the town of **Hermann** celebrates its German heritage with beer steins, bisque dolls, and a **Wurst Haus** restaurant that serves 47 varieties of bratwurst sausage.

Next up along the river, the massive **State Capitol** dominates **Jefferson City's** skyline. But the coolest things in town are a cliff-top **Lewis and Clark monument** and creepy **Missouri State Penitentiary Museum.**

Tacking to the northwest, the trail climbs to **Eagles Bluff Overlook** with its panoramic views of the Missouri Valley. The old railroad station at **Hindman Junction** marks the Katy's confluence with the **MKT Trail,** an 8.9-mile (14.3-km) spur that leads into downtown **Columbia** and the **University of Missouri** campus.

Boonville marks the route's departure from the Missouri River and a 72-mile (116-km) trek through farmland and small towns. The Katy ends in **Clinton,** a market town near **Truman Lake** on the northwest edge of the **Ozarks** region. Backtracking to **Windsor,** hikers and bikers can travel all the way to **Kansas City** on the 47-mile (76-km) **Rock Island Spur.** ■

APRÈS HIKE

• **Truman Lake:** Rent a pontoon, powerboat, or paddleboard for a spin on Missouri's largest human-made water body.

• **St. Louis:** Glide to the top of the Gateway Arch, take a riverfront cruise on the Mississippi, attend a Cardinals game at Busch Stadium, and savor a St. Louis–style thin-crust pizza with Provel cheese.

• **Kansas City:** Marvel at wonderfully renovated Union Station, snap selfies in front of the lawn art at Nelson-Atkins Museum of Art, and munch burnt ends at Arthur Bryant's BBQ joint.

• **Columbia:** Tailgate with Tiger fans at Faurot Field, party with students along 9th Street or Broadway, and buy something you really don't need at Midway Antique Mall and Flea Market.

Maah Daah Hey Trail
North Dakota

Channel the frontier spirit of young Teddy Roosevelt on a trail along the Little Missouri River Valley through the badlands and grasslands of western North Dakota.

The name **Maah Daah Hey** (MDH) has two meanings in the language of the Mandan and Hidatsa people who have called this region home for hundreds of years. It translates into both "grandfather" and "something that's been around for a long time." Either one befits a path steeped in both natural and human history.

The route passes through all three units of **Theodore Roosevelt**

National Park, which safeguards 70,446 acres (28,508 ha) of pristine prairie and badlands, as well as the legacy of the 26th president. Two decades before he moved into the White House, Roosevelt ventured to the Dakota Territory on a buffalo hunt. After the death of his mother and first wife on the same day in 1884, he was back in the badlands, hoping the cowboy life would eventually vanquish his grief.

More than half a million bison live in North America today, many in the wilds of Theodore Roosevelt National Park.

THE BIG PICTURE

Distance: 144 miles (232 km)

Elevation Gain: approx. 15,140 feet (4,620 m)

Time: 6–8 days

Difficulty: Moderate

Best Time: Late spring, summer, or early fall

More Info: mdhta.com

Maah Daah Hey boasts eight segments and 14 trailheads, the middle ones for those who aren't traveling the entire trail. Along the way are 10 campsites and eight water boxes where trekkers can refill their canteens or hydration packs.

Crossing the **Little Missouri River** is the biggest challenge along the route. Hikers, bikers, and horseback riders must ford the waterway at two places. Given the swift current, underwater sinkholes, and shifting water level, this can be very tricky. Trekkers should consult the USGS North Dakota flow data chart available through the trail website.

Starting from the south, the MDH kicks off from the **Juniper trailhead** beside the **Burning Coal Vein Campground** about an hour's drive south of **Medora.** The trail bends around the Medora Oil Field before reaching the Little Missouri at **Sully Creek State Park.**

After crossing the Little Missouri at Sully, the trail skirts around Medora, ducks underneath Interstate 94 and slips into Teddy Roosevelt National Park. This stretch through the park's **Cottonwood** area is the best chance to spot bison and wild horses grazing the riverside grass. Trekkers willing to wade the river again can overnight at the park's shady Cottonwood Campground

Plan time to visit Maltese Cross Cabin, the rustic home where Teddy Roosevelt lived for a time, now preserved at the Cottonwood Campground.

and explore a visitors center that preserves the rustic **Maltese Cross Cabin** where Roosevelt lived before building his ranch house.

Beyond Cottonwood, the trail rambles across the **Theodore Roosevelt Wilderness** area with prairie dog towns and a spur leading off to a petrified forest. The remains of Teddy's treasured **Elkhorn Ranch** and a nearby campground are a two-day hike to the north. Fording the Little Missouri again at **Elkhorn Crossing,** the MDH dives into the badlands via **Devil's Pass,** the trail balanced on a narrow, heavily eroded ridge with 150-foot (45-m) drops on both sides.

The Maah Daah Hey continues into **Little Missouri National Grassland** and geological oddities like the **Ice Caves** and **China Wall.** It runs down **Corral Creek** in the northern unit of Theodore Roosevelt National Park before a fork at Milepost 142 offers trekkers a choice of ending at the **Summit** or **CCC campgrounds.** ■

OTHER GREAT TRAILS

- **White Butte Trail:** An hour's drive south of Medora, this 3.4-mile (5.5-km) return hike climbs to North Dakota's highest point—3,506-foot (1,069-m) White Butte.

- **Little Soldier Loop:** Across the river from Bismarck, this easy 2.1-mile (3.3-km) trail in Fort Abraham Lincoln State Park marches across the army post where George Armstrong Custer lived prior to Little Bighorn.

- **Greater Grand Forks Greenway:** Although the Greenway spans both sides of the Red River, the longest hiking/biking route is a 6.5-mile (10.5-km) stretch along the North Dakota side between the North Pedestrian Bridge and 47th Avenue South.

- **Pipestem Creek Trail:** This adventurous eight-mile (13-km) route near Jamestown is a favorite with local bikers but also attracts hikers and trail runners.

Golden light and a view of the Little Missouri River accompany cyclists on the Maah Daah Hey Trail.

Great Lake-to-Lake Trail No. 1
Michigan

Explore the rail trails, footpaths, and country roads of Michigan's Lower Peninsula along the first of five long-distance routes that will eventually crisscross the Great Lakes State.

It should come as no surprise that Michigan has a long coast, encompassing two peninsulas and scores of islands surrounded by four of the five Great Lakes. At 3,288 miles (5,291 km), the "Water Wonderland" of the Midwest has more shoreline than any other state except Alaska.

It also flaunts a cool way to hike or bike between two of its largest water bodies. **Great Lake-to-Lake**

Trail No. 1—the first of five proposed routes across the Upper and Lower Peninsulas—rambles across farmland, forest, townships, and suburbs between **Lake Michigan** and **Lake Huron.**

Given southern Michigan's topography, the 275-mile (442-km) route is relatively flat. And although undertaking a thru-hike may take some effort, many sections

THE BIG PICTURE

Distance: 275 miles (442 km)

Elevation Gain: Unknown

Time: 2–3 weeks

Difficulty: Easy to strenuous

Best Time: Year-round

More Info: greatlaketolaketrails.org

of the route expedite short, easy treks for walkers of just about any skill level.

Season is another consideration. Summer in the lower Great Lakes region tends to be hot and steamy. But it's also the festival season along the Great Lake-to-Lake Trail, with summer events like the **Leilapalooza festival** in Battle Creek, the **Pontiac Music Festival,** and **Kalamazoo Ribfest** (where music meets grilled meat).

During fall—if incredible fall colors don't float your boat—hikers can catch a college football game (or at least the tailgating and after-parties) in **Ann Arbor.** Michigan winters are notoriously brutal, but the silver lining is enough snowpack along the trail for awesome snowshoeing and Nordic skiing.

Kicking things off from Lake Michigan, the trail starts near the red lighthouse on **South Beach** in **South Haven.** A short walk along city streets eventually fades into a multiuse trail that passes across the **Black River covered bridge** on its way out of town. The trail covers the 30-odd miles (48 km) to **Kalamazoo** via an arrow-straight rail trail along the former route of the Kalamazoo and South Haven Railroad.

The Lake-to-Lake traces the **Kalamazoo River** upstream to **Battle Creek** before a road-sharing portion along rural Michigan

Follow the Great Lake-to-Lake Trail into Marshall for a stop at the American Museum of Magic and a peek at the largest collection of magic artifacts on permanent display in the United States.

Linked to the shore by a trail of glimmering lights, the Muskegon South Pierhead Light was built in 1903.

Avenue carries the route into **Marshall.** Besides a lively weekend **farmers market** where hikers can stock up on local tasty treats, Marshall also harbors the **American Museum of Magic.**

An old right-of-way of the Michigan Central Railroad complements rural roads as the trail crosses the middle of the peninsula between **Albion** and **Jackson.** The trail meanders along the **Mike Levine Lakelands Trail** and a woodsy passage through **Island Lake Recreation Area** northwest of Ann Arbor before the route slides into the big city.

A sequence of suburban footpaths—the Hudson Valley, West Bloomfield, Clinton River, and Macomb Orchard Trails—carries the Lake-to-Lake around the northwest edge of the **Detroit Metro Area.** Another road walk takes hikers from **Richmond** to the **St. Clair River** and a walk along the **Bridge to Bay Trail** to the grand finale of the trans-state route in **Lighthouse Park** on **Lake Huron.** ∎

DETOURS

• **Kalamazoo Growlers:** Minor-league baseball at its best, the Growlers play collegiate summer ball against Northwoods League opponents at cozy Homer Stryker Field beside the Kalamazoo River; northwoodsleague.com/kalamazoo-growlers.

• **Leila Arboretum:** The Kingman Museum of natural history, the whimsical wooden sculptures of the Fantasy Forest, and expansive gardens color this sprawling park on the outskirts of Battle Creek; lasgarden.org.

• **Bohm Theatre:** This restored 1929 movie house in Albion presents new and classic films, regular live blues, and other music events; bohmtheatre.org.

• **Hell:** The central Michigan town takes full advantage of its name with devilish attractions like Screams From Hell souvenirs and Hell Hole Diner, as well as non-satanic canoe and kayak rentals; gotohellmi.com.

• **Pine River Stables:** Get off your feet and onto a horse during guided rides around this 100-acre (40-ha) spread near St. Clair; pineriverstables.net.

North Country Trail

Multiple States

Far and away the nation's longest national scenic trail, this epic trek between North Dakota and Vermont rambles across an array of American landscapes, from the tallgrass prairies and majestic North Woods to the Great Lakes, Adirondacks, and Green Mountains.

THE BIG PICTURE

Distance: 4,760 miles (7,660 km)

Elevation Gain: Unknown

Time: 8–10 months

Difficulty: Strenuous

Best Time: Spring, summer, or fall

More Info: northcountrytrail.org

If America's long-distance hiking community ever decides to expand its celebrated "triple crown" of epic trails into a grand slam, a shoo-in should be the **North Country Trail** (NCT).

Stretching across eight states and spanning more than 4,760 miles (7,660 km), the NCT is nearly twice as long as the Appalachian Trail, and more than a third longer than the Pacific Crest and Continental Divide routes.

Unlike the trails that grew organically over many years along the nation's three great mountain chains, the North Country was established by visionary hikers and outdoor enthusiasts. The idea was hatched in the early 1960s, but it wasn't until 1980 that the NCT was substantial enough to become a national scenic trail.

Rather than blaze it from scratch, the route was cobbled together from a number of existing state trails starting with the Buckeye Trail in Ohio, the Baker Trail in Pennsylvania, and the Finger Lakes Trail in New York. Over the years, the Wabash Cannonball Trail, Superior Hiking Trail, Kekekabic Trail, Border Route Trail, Iron Belle Trail, and Mesabi Trail were also invited to the party.

Like other national scenic trails, the North Country is administered by the National Park Service. However, the North Country Trail Association (NCTA) handles much of its continued development and maintenance through 29 regional chapters and thousands of volunteers who help clear the path, paint the blue blazes that mark the route, organize guided hikes, and stage special events to celebrate the trail and lure newbies into the wilderness.

There's still significant trailblazing to undertake. As of 2020, around 1,600 miles (2,575 km) of the total route were along highways, roads, and sidewalks that served as connectors between completed segments. But the amount of nonmotorized miles continues to creep upward, with Vermont, Pennsylvania, and

A barred owl peeks out from a Michigan stretch of the North Country Trail.

The vast expanse of the Boundary Waters Canoe Area Wilderness in northern Minnesota offers ample opportunity to paddle, hike, and camp.

Wisconsin the closest to achieving 100 percent footpath status.

The NCTA also offers an excellent website for volunteering with one of the chapters, learning more about the trail, or planning your hike (emphasis on the latter). Though the North Country doesn't ramble across potentially treacherous mountain terrain like a couple of its long-distance cousins, the extreme length presents a major planning challenge.

Assuming you can average 20 miles (32 km) a day, you would need roughly 238 days to walk the entire route. That's more or less eight months. March is about as late as you can start if you hope to complete the NCT in a single shot.

DETOURS

• **North Dakota Badlands:** Before or after the NCT, visit the land where buffalo still roam. The tortured landscapes out West are home to Theodore Roosevelt National Park, Little Missouri National Grassland, and Sully Creek State Park; beautiful badlandsnd.com.

• **Boundary Waters Canoe Area Wilderness:** Get off your feet and into a boat for a float across one of the nation's premier paddling places. A number of outfitters can help plan your route and provide everything you need (including food) for a float through the Minnesota wilderness; friends-bwca.org.

• **Isle Royale National Park:** From Grand Portage, Minnesota, NCT hikers can hop a ferry over to the big wilderness island in the middle of Lake Superior to chill at one of the waterfront campgrounds or tramp one of the cross-island trails to Rock Harbor; nps.gov/isro.

• **Watkins Glen Raceway:** While crossing the Finger Lakes region, make a pit stop at "The Glen" for the almost weekly car-racing events, the self-drive experience, or special events like the annual beer festival; theglen.com.

• **Hudson River Gorge:** Take a wild and crazy raft trip down the headwaters of the Hudson River in the Adirondacks, a one-day ride down Class III and IV rapids near Indian Lake, New York; wildwaters.net.

Whether you start from east or west, you're going to be hiking in winter weather with the probability of rain, sleet, and snow.

Starting from the Vermont end gives hikers more options for shelter and creature comforts if the weather gets ornery. However, on average, North Dakota offers sunnier skies and less precipitation in the later winter and early spring—which is why our description starts out west.

Located about halfway between Bismarck and Minot, **Lake Saka-kawea State Park** anchors the western end of the North Country Trail with big skies, endless prairie, and one of the largest reservoirs along the entire length of the **Missouri River.**

On its march across North Dakota, the route passes through **Audubon National Wildlife Refuge** (246 bird species!) and **Sheyenne National Grassland.** Reaching **Fort Abercrombie State Historic Site**—the reconstruction of the 1860s frontier stronghold—hikers cross the **Red River** into Minnesota.

Contradicting the state's image as a woodsy wilderness, west-central Minnesota is prairie and farmland with streams and creeks rather than 10,000 lakes. Low population and lack of towns make this stretch of trail one of the most reclusive along the entire route. But that's not to say there's nothing to see but the horizon. Hikers should definitely take a selfie with the **World's Largest Prairie Chicken** statue in Rothsay.

The woods and water start to kick in as the trail traverses **Maplewood State Park** on its way to the source of the **Mississippi River** in **Itasca**

The multitiered falls of Upper Falls at Old Man's Cave in Hocking Hills State Park

The NCT crosses into Michigan, where colder weather months offer explorations to icicle-laden caves.

State Park. By the time the trail reaches northeastern Minnesota, it's deep into the North Woods and a remote leg through the **Boundary Waters Canoe Area Wilderness** along the U.S.-Canada border.

Emerging from the woods near **Grand Portage,** the NCT hangs a sharp right and follows the 310-mile (500-km) **Superior Hiking Trail** along the big lake they once called Gitche Gumee. **Duluth** provides an opportunity for urban adventures, especially the bars, restaurants, and museums of the waterfront **Canal Park District.**

SHORT CIRCUITS

These sections of the NCT are ideal for shorter hikes:

• **McClusky Canal:** The NCT crosses the Continental Divide during its 70-mile (110-km) transit along this irrigation canal in central North Dakota.

• **Itasca State Park:** More than 10 miles (16 km) of the NCT meander beside lakes and through thick woods along the southern edge of this Minnesota park.

• **Pictured Rocks:** Hikers can follow up to 42 miles (67 km) of the NCT by trekking the old Lakeshore Trail along the Lake Superior coast of Pictured Rocks National Lakeshore on Michigan's Upper Peninsula.

• **Cook Forest State Park:** The NCT shares the path with six trails in this western Pennsylvania preserve, including a segment of the Hemlock Trail that runs through the Forest Cathedral old-growth trees.

It's back into the wilderness after that, a meander through the backwoods of northern Wisconsin and Michigan's **Upper Peninsula** that includes segments through **Porcupine Mountains Wilderness State Park, Hiawatha National Forest,** and super-scenic **Pictured Rocks National Lakeshore** on the south side of **Lake Superior.**

After crossing the colossal **Mackinac Bridge,** the NCT flirts briefly with **Lake Michigan** before veering inland at **Petoskey** on a route it shares with the older **Iron Belle Trail** down the middle of the **Lower Peninsula.** It makes a lengthy wander through plenty of farmland and **Manistee National Forest.** And although the trail comes close to **Grand Rapids** and **Kalamazoo,** other than a riverside trek through **Battle Creek,** the route remains refreshingly bucolic all the way down to the Michigan-Ohio state line.

Slipping into Ohio west of **Toledo,** the North Country hooks up with the **Buckeye Trail** in the **Maumee River Valley** on a run that nearly reaches the **Ohio River.** Much of the route in western Ohio

The North Country Trail has grown organically into the longest U.S. national scenic trail.

is along a towpath beside the **Miami and Erie Canal,** which facilitated shipping between the Great Lakes and the Ohio River prior to the Civil War.

Once again, the trail manages to avoid major population centers. The one big exception is a segment through the middle of **Dayton** that runs close to the **National Museum of the U.S. Air Force** and **Huffman Prairie,** where the Wright brothers experimented with their homemade flying machines. After a brief flirtation with **Cincinnati's** outer burbs, the trails peel off to the northeast and a rendezvous with the cave- and waterfall-suffused **Hocking Hills.**

After 900 miles (1,450 km) of shared path, the Buckeye and North Country finally part ways in **Zoar,** the former heading for **Canton,** the latter making a beeline

LOCAL FLAVOR

• **Outstate Brewing:** Spray Tan Sour, Blue Northern Light Lager, and Star Island IPA are but a few of the drafts available at a microbrewery beside the Otter Tail River (and just off the NCT) in west-central Minnesota; 309 South Vine Street, Fergus Falls, MN; outstatebrewing.com.

• **Hog Wild BBQ:** Tucked into the woods just west of Upper St. Croix Lake, this local smokehouse offers pulled pork, brisket platters, and barbecued sandwiches prepared with the

chef's own homemade dry rub seasoning; 10688 Highway 53, Solon Springs, WI; hogwildbbqwi.com.

• **Petoskey Brewing:** Take a load off near Lake Michigan at a taproom located in a redbrick 1890s brewery that also serves burgers, wings, and Smokin' Betty sandwiches; 1844 Harbor-Petoskey Road, Petoskey, MI; petoskeybrewing.com.

• **Donnie's Tavern:** Right beside the NCT/Buckeye Trail in north-central

Ohio, this family-run restaurant creates fresh takes on regional favorites like walleye, meatloaf, strip steak, fried chicken, and pasta; 162 Main Street, Zoar, OH; donniestavern.com.

• **ZEMS Ice Cream and Mini Golf:** Break your trek across the Mohawk Valley with a frosty and a round of 19 at this old-timey ice-cream stand in upstate New York; 124 West Hickory Street, Canastota, NY; zemsicecream.com.

across the state line into the coal country of northwest Pennsylvania. The **Allegheny River** provides a natural pathway into **Allegheny National Forest** along the eastern edge of the Pennsylvania Wilds followed by a seamless crossing via the **Baker Trail** into upstate New York's rugged **Allegheny State Park.**

For much of its trek across western New York, the NCT shares sod with the **Finger Lakes Trail,** a path that takes hikers along the southern edge of the elongated glacial lakes through a region renowned for its food and wine. **Watkins Glen Beach** on **Seneca Lake** provides the best chance to take a dip and soak

feet that are surely weary by now. But you're nearing the homestretch.

The North Country crosses the old and venerable **Erie Canal** in **Canastota,** where hikers with an interest in pugilism can visit the **International Boxing Hall of Fame.** More than 20 miles (32 km) of towpaths carry the trail through the **Mohawk Valley** to **Rome,** where it turns to the north and rises into **Adirondack Park.**

Much of the proposed NCT route across the Adirondacks is yet to be blazed, with hikers taking to highway shoulders and country roads to complete the transit. However, stretches of nonmotorized trail

through the **Little Moose** and **Siamese Ponds Wilderness Areas** provide plenty of peace and quiet.

The trail reaches **Lake Champlain** at **Crown Point,** where the ruins of a Revolutionary War stone fort stand guard beside a modern steel arch bridge that carries vehicles and hikers across the water into Vermont.

The Green Mountain State joined the North Country Trail in 2019. The extra 45 miles (72 km) includes a wrap around the college town of **Middlebury,** an easy ascent into **Green Mountains National Forest,** and an eastern end to the epic trek at **Maine Junction.** ■

Snaking from the west side of the Lower Peninsula around to the Upper Peninsula, the 1,273-mile (2,048-km) Iron Belle Trail carries hikers right to the water's edge.

River to River Trail

Illinois

Stretching from the Mississippi to the Ohio, this long-distance route in southern Illinois meanders through a thickly forested wilderness that seems little changed since the days when Abe Lincoln wandered the region.

THE BIG PICTURE

Distance: 160 miles (257 km)

Elevation Gain: approx. 15,290 feet (4,660 m)

Time: 1–2 weeks

Difficulty: Moderate

Best Time: Spring or fall

More Info: rivertorivertrail.net

Most visitors know Illinois for its seemingly endless farmland and "stormy, husky, brawling" Chicago (to quote Carl Sandburg). But the state boasts a third mood that remains largely undiscovered by those outside of the region: the densely wooded Shawnee National Forest region down south.

The **River to River Trail** flows through the latter, an unexpectedly wild side of a state where you don't expect to come across much wilderness. As much as skyscrapers reflect the Windy City, regenerated forest and oddball rock formations define this region and its namesake **Shawnee National Forest.**

Like the rest of the state, this area has plenty of history, too. Hikers are following in the footsteps of those who crossed these woods long ago: Cherokee along the Trail of Tears; African Americans on the Underground Railroad; and George Rogers Clark and his men during a surprise attack on the British during the American Revolution.

Rather than a single eastern terminus, the River to River offers dual starting spots. The more secluded is **Battery Rock,** which featured in several minor Civil War skirmishes, while the more popular is a gazebo overlooking the **Ohio River** in **Elizabethtown.**

After meandering around a dozen miles (19 km) on their own, the trails converge near the rocky **Garden of the Gods.** In addition to fantastically carved sandstone formations—like **Camel Rock,** which featured on the state's 2016 "America the Beautiful" quarter—Garden of the Gods offers a campground and cabins in which hikers can overnight.

Continuing west, the route passes ruins and remnants of the 19th-century pioneer days when the Shawnee region was far more populated than now. Early settlers named many of the geological features along the trail, landmarks like narrow **One Horse Pass** and even skinnier **No Horse Pass.** But not everything is vintage. Among the late-model landmarks along the trail are **Petticoat Junction,** which past hikers have decorated with undergarments, and the creepy **Max**

Bring your furry friends along to catch the sunset atop the awe-inspiring rock formations of the Garden of the Gods.

Known as Giant City Streets, these sandstone bluffs were shaped by geologic forces 12,000 years ago.

Creek Vortex, allegedly haunted by floating "earth light" balls.

Goddard Crossing on State Highway 45 is considered the trail's halfway point, but a much more formidable barrier is Interstate 24, which hikers cross via two underpasses. After skimming the south shore of **Dutchman Lake,** the route rises into lovely **Ferne Clyffe State Park.** It's thought that both George Rogers Clark and Cherokee on the Trail of Tears passed this way. Modern trekkers can sack out at several campgrounds and explore the park's waterfalls and rock formations.

Giant City State Park affords another chance to overnight (and yet more rocky marvels) before the trail crosses the rock spillway between the twin **Cedar Lakes** and descends onto the **Mississippi River** floodplain beneath **Inspiration Point.** Once the haunt of river pirates but now about as mild-mannered as a town can be, **Grand Tower** ends the hike with waterfront camping at **Devil's Backbone Park.** ∎

LOCAL FLAVOR

• **E-Town River Restaurant:** It's all about catfish at a floating eatery on the Ohio River that serves it by the pound, in a sandwich, with shrimp, or on a platter; 100 Front Street, Elizabethtown, IL; facebook.com/etownriverrestaurant.

• **Whiffle Boy's Pizza & More:** The "more" at this modest but tasty eatery near Ferne Clyffe State Park includes salads, sub sandwiches, chicken wings, and cheesecake; 221 South Broadway, Goreville, IL; whiffleboyspizza.com.

• **Peachbarn Winery & Café:** Located right beside the trail on the outskirts of Alto Pass, the winery complements its whites, rosés, and sangrias with artisan cheese and sausage boards, salads, and a "very berry" sundae; 560 Chestnut Street, Alto Pass, IL; peachbarn.com.

• **Giant City Lodge:** Load up on protein and carbs in a state park restaurant that offers fried chicken dinners with mashed potatoes in country milk gravy, buttered corn, creamy coleslaw, and biscuits with apple butter; 460 Giant City Lodge Road, Makanda, IL; giantcitylodge.com

Ancient rock formations bask in the sunshine amid fall foliage in the Garden of the Gods in Shawnee National Forest.

Paul Bunyan Trail

Minnesota

The nation's longest paved rail trail, the Paul Bunyan meanders 120 miles (193 km) through the woods and watery wonderland of north-central Minnesota.

THE BIG PICTURE

Distance: 120 miles (193 km)

Elevation Change: approx. 2,300 feet (700 m)

Time: 5–6 days

Difficulty: Easy to moderate

Best Time: Year-round

More Info: paulbunyantrail.com

The folks who manage and maintain the **Paul Bunyan Trail** like to emphasize that it's multiuse: not just a hiking or biking route, but also a recreational path perfect for other outdoor enthusiasts including in-line skaters, as well as snowshoers, cross-country skiers, and snowmobile riders during the region's eternally snowy winters. Manual and electric wheelchairs can also travel the nation's longest accessible trail.

Running north to south between Brainerd and Bemidji, the trail meanders through a gorgeous region that personifies Minnesota's "Land of 10,000 Lakes" nickname. It's also a nexus for venturing onto other great hiking and biking routes like the Heartland Trail, Mississippi River Trail, North Country Trail, and Blue Ox Trail to the U.S.-Canada border.

Like most rail trails, the route owes its life to the death of a railroad line. In this case, the state Department of Natural Resources took over a Burlington Northern line that was abandoned in 1983 to transform into a linear state park.

Crow Wing State Park marks the southern end of the Paul Bunyan with relics of a historic 19th-century trading post and a campground beside the **Mississippi River.** The route uses surface streets through the twin towns of **Baxter** and **Brainerd** before the start of the actual rail trail near **Westgate Mall.** Snaking its way through the **Brainerd lakes,** the trail passes through tiny Nisswa, where a craft brewery, ice-cream parlor, and gourmet coffee shop flavor the trek and offer welcome spots to rest your feet.

Passing through **Pequot Lakes,** trekkers can climb the 100-foot (30-m) **Paul M. Thiede Fire Tower** for a one-of-a-kind bird's-eye view of Minnesota's North Woods. Those walking the route in August can attend (and camp at) the **Lakes Bluegrass Festival,** right beside the trail in **Pine River.**

Farther north, the route runs beside a giant statue of **Lucette Diana Kensack** (Paul Bunyan's sweetheart) in **Hackensack.** Located at around the halfway point of the trail, the lakeside town celebrates **Sweetheart Days** in July with an old-timey main street parade,

The Paul Bunyan Trail is a multiuse recreational path that connects to a variety of other popular trails.

The historic Paul Bunyan and Babe the Blue Ox statues reside on the shore of Lake Bemidji, where Paul Bunyan was born.

horseshoe tournament, arts and crafts fair, and dachshund derby.

Reaching the town of **Walker,** Paul Bunyan users can segue onto the epic **North Country Trail**—a hiking route that runs all the way from North Dakota to Vermont—or the much shorter and multiuse **Heartland Trail** that runs 49 miles (79 km) between **Cass Lake** and **Park Rapids.**

Traversing an area of mixed forest and farmland, the stretch between **Laporte** and **Bemidji** is probably the most tranquil section of the entire route, straying away from the towns and lake resorts that flank the trail farther south. Users can end their trek in downtown Bemidji with a selfie beside the famous lakefront statues of **Paul Bunyan** and **Babe the Blue Ox.** Or they can trek up the east shore of **Lake Bemidji**—with a chance to swim at **Nymore Beach** and camp (tent sites and on-site cabins available) and fish at **Lake Bemidji State Park.** ■

DETOURS

• **Paul Bunyan Land:** Kids love this vintage amusement park with its carnival rides, miniature train, pioneer village, and two-story talking lumberjack.

• **Brainerd International Raceway:** Hot rod drag races, muscle car shoot-outs, the Trans Am series, and snowmobile watercross are just a few of the events held from April to October at this prestigious motorsport facility.

• **Leech Lake Band of Ojibwe:** The public is welcome at any of the eight traditional powwows the nation stages between May and September on tribal lands near Walker.

• **Fishing Charters:** Professional guides offer half- and full-day boat trips to angle for bass, walleye, and huge muskie on Leech Lake.

• **Crow Wing River State Water Trail:** Local outfitters rent canoes, kayaks, tents, and other equipment for wilderness float trips along 90 miles (145 km) of the Crow Wing upstream from its confluence with the Mississippi.

Iowa Great Lakes Trail

Iowa

A cluster of glacial lakes in northwest Iowa provides an eclectic farmland, small-town, and shoreline setting for a paved multiuse trail.

They may not be large compared to Superior, Huron, and those other Great Lakes, but to the Native Dakota people, the deep-blue lakes in what is now northwest Iowa were grand indeed. They called one of the larger lakes Minnetonka, or "great waters," an appellation that 19th-century pioneers and holiday cabin hucksters Anglicized into their own name for the region.

An ever expanding project, the **Iowa Great Lakes Trail** has grown from an original 14-mile (22.5-km) "spine" linking the largest lakes into a 60-mile (96-km) network of routes that forms a loose figure eight around the three big water bodies.

Sixty miles (96 km) now connect a figure eight of trails that meander around three waterways and an eclectic mix of settings on the Iowa Great Lakes multiuse trail.

THE BIG PICTURE

Distance: 14 miles (22.5 km)

Elevation Change: approx. 360 feet (110 m)

Time: 1 day

Difficulty: Easy

Best Time: Year-round

More Info: vacationokoboji.com/bike-okoboji

The spine takes its name from its appearance on a map: a sturdy central trail with numerous spurs that shoot off like ribs from a spinal cord. It runs north to south from **Big Spirit Lake** across the narrow isthmus that separates the twin **Okoboji Lakes** to the town of Milford. Paved the entire way, the path is open to hikers, bikers, dog walkers, in-line skaters, cross-country skiers, and snowshoers.

Its northern terminus is near **Maple Oaks Beach** along the eastern shore of Big Spirit Lake. The first stretch runs between lakeside homes and farm fields and past the cute little redbrick city hall in **Orleans.** Beyond the **Spirit Lake Fish Hatchery**—where more than 95 million walleye, northern pike, and muskellunge are reared each year—the route rendezvouses with **East Okoboji Lake.**

The town of **Spirit Lake** offers low-key eateries where thru-hikers can grab a snack or drink. Or continue into **Okoboji** town, where shoreline restaurants like **Tweeter's** and the **Outrigger** offer lake views and more substantial meals.

A pedestrian bridge takes the trail across the narrow passage between the twin lakes to **Arnolds Park** and the hub of the lake region's historic summer vacation district. Trail users can rent a boat

The mirrored surface of Okoboji Lake

or take a dip at **Arnolds Park Public Beach** before strolling down the busy Hiawatha Pioneer Trail (U.S. 71) through downtown Arnolds Lake.

Hanging a left onto Bascom Street, the route snakes its way between **Lake Minnewashta** and **Lower Gar Lake** before a home-stretch past farms and budding sub-divisions to **Milford,** one of the older towns in the lakes region.

Among the spurs are a route around **West Lake Okoboji** that includes the **Barney Peterson Memorial Nature Trail** and **Gull Point State Park** along the lake's western shore. From Orleans, a route that curves around the west and north shores of Spirit Lake fea-tures a trumpeter swan observation area, **Kettleson Hogsback Nature Trail,** and a walk along **700th Street** (aka the Iowa-Minnesota state line).

Rent or bring your own bike to explore the 31-mile (50-km) **Terril Loop** or the 29-mile (46-km) **Superior/Swan Lake Loop** through the surrounding countryside. ∎

DETOURS

• **Indian Motorcycle Factory:** Book reservations for a tour of the Spirit Lake assembly line and showroom of a legendary motorcycle company founded in 1901.

• **Higgens Museum of National Bank Notes:** "Money, money, money" is the theme of an Okoboji collection that safeguards the nation's largest collection of Ameri-can paper money.

• **Arnolds Park Amusement Park:** One of the world's oldest amuse-ment parks (founded 1889) features dozens of old-timey rides, including the 1930 wooden Legend roller coaster.

• *Queen II:* Take a spin around West Lake Okoboji on the latest iteration of a pleasure boat that's been cruis-ing the Iowa Great Lakes region since the late 19th century.

• **Iowa Rock 'n Roll Music Associ-ation Hall of Fame & Museum:** Superstars like Buddy Holly and the Everly Brothers as well as long-lost acts like the Trashmen, the Fabulous Morticians, and Koats of Male are among the inductees.

South

Known for its oceanside sand dune, Jockey's Ridge State Park offers a myriad of outdoor experiences, from paddling to nature hikes.

Greenbrier River Trail
West Virginia

The Greenbrier River Valley provides a verdant setting for a rail trail that chugs through wilderness tracts and remote waterfront towns in southeast West Virginia.

THE BIG PICTURE

Distance: 78 miles (125 km)

Elevation Change: approx. 3,000 feet (910 m)

Time: 4–5 days

Difficulty: Moderate

Best Time: Spring, summer, or fall

More Info: greenbrierrivertrail.com

This country road may not take you home, but it certainly runs through one of the most scenic parts of West Virginia, a journey along the **Greenbrier River** through the Alleghany Highlands.

Like many of the nation's newer multiuse routes, the **Greenbrier River Trail** is a rail-to-trail conversion, in this case the transformation of a Chesapeake and Ohio Railway (C&O) line that serviced the region's

sawmills and timber operations until the 1930s, when the forests were largely depleted.

Almost a century later, the valley's woods have mostly recovered and provide a shady canopy over much of the route. What makes the Greenbrier different from other rail trails is its extraordinarily sinuous nature. Rather than straight lines—which would have required far more bridges, trestles, and tunnels—the

original C&O roadbed hugs the banks of a river with abundant twists and turns.

Although the trail is numbered from south to north, a 732-foot (223-m) elevation drop between Cass and Caldwell makes hiking or biking the opposite direction a much easier proposition. That also follows the natural flow of the Greenbrier on its way to a confluence with the New River and an eventual rendezvous with the Gulf of Mexico.

More than a dozen campsites and camping shelters along the route give backpackers and bikepackers a place to overnight between segments. Users can also bed down at state parks and forests, and small riverside towns along the route.

A walk down Main Street in **Cass**—flanked by identical whitewashed houses erected when it was a pulp-and-paper company town—brings hikers to the north end of the Greenbrier River Trail. Starting along the west bank, the route weaves through **Seneca State Forest.** The vintage railroad tunnel-and-bridge combination (built in 1900) conveys the trail to the east bank and a long segment through Monongahela National Forest.

Founded in 1749 by the early Europeans settlers, Marlinton is the

This rails-to-trails conversion follows the flow of the original rail line, crossing winding Greenbrier River before dipping back into the canopy of the forest.

The bike-friendly 78-mile (125-km) Greenbrier River Trail was once a part of the Chesapeake and Ohio Railway system.

first town heading south along the trail. Among its many historic buildings are the old C&O depot and the tiny Pocahontas County Opera House, which offers a year-round slate of live mountain music.

Switching back to the right bank near **Watoga State Park,** the trail slips through Seebert village, where an old Methodist church provides a photo op, and Jack Horner's Corner store an opportunity for hot food, cold beverages, and resupply.

Up ahead is the 402-foot (122-m) Droop Mountain Tunnel, named for a nearby Civil War battlefield that was the last major skirmish fought in West Virginia. Just past the tunnel, a side trek down Julia Road from Horrock trailhead leads to pick-your-own blueberries

on Friendly Goat Fruit Farm.

The trail ends in Caldwell, a small riverside settlement on the outskirts of Lewisburg, where myriad bars, restaurants, and accommodations offer hikers and bikers a quick post-journey recharge. ■

APRÈS HIKE

• **Cass Scenic Railroad:** Relive the days when the Greenbrier River Trail was a railroad line at a state park with vintage locomotives that pull passenger cars around an 11-mile (18-km) circuit.

• **Green Bank Telescope:** Take a walking, biking, or bus tour of the world's largest single-dish fully steerable radio telescope and its science center museum.

• **New River Gorge National Park:** White-water rafting and kayaking are the main attractions at the nation's newest national park, an 80-minute drive west of Caldwell.

• **The Greenbrier:** See how the other half lives at a historic resort opened in 1778 and rebuilt by the Chesapeake and Ohio Railway in 1913.

• **West Virginia Renaissance Festival:** Jousting, jesters, and jugglers are all part of the fun as a merry band of reenactors takes over a big field near Lewisburg over four weekends in June.

Pinhoti National Recreation Trail

Alabama & Georgia

Explore the national forests and remote wilderness areas along a national recreational trail that rambles across the southernmost peaks and valleys of the Appalachian Range.

Envisioned by its creators as a southern extension of the Appalachian Trail, the **Pinhoti National Recreation Trail** rambles from the wild mountains of northwest **Georgia** to the slash pine and loblolly forests of central **Alabama.**

The trail's advocates continue to lobby the National Park Service for the Appalachian Trail honor. Meanwhile, the Pinhoti has gained its own renown, evolving from a relatively obscure route several decades ago into an increasingly popular long-

THE BIG PICTURE

Distance: 337 miles (540 km)

Elevation Gain: approx. 45,000 feet (13,700 m)

Time: 3–5 weeks

Difficulty: Moderate to strenuous

Best Time: Year-round

More Info: www.greenbelly.co/pages/pinhoti-trail-map and pinhoti.info/joomla

distance route with its own merits.

Pinhoti means "place where turkeys live" in the language of the Creek people, and the trail's diamond-shaped blaze features a black turkey foot. Spanish explorer Hernando de Soto encountered the Creek on his epic trek across Georgia and Alabama in 1540. It's no coincidence that the Pinhoti parallels the route that de Soto and his men likely followed through the same region.

The route is numbered south to north, with segment one commencing from the top of **Flagg Mountain** in **Weogufka State Forest.** In the 1930s, the Civilian Conservation Corps built the vintage stone tower at the summit, which was recently restored.

Coming down from Flagg, the trail crosses a short stretch of Alabama farm country before rising into the wilds of **Talladega National Forest** and a 126-mile (202-km) hike to the Georgia state line. Along the way are waterfalls, remote mountain hollows, and pockets of old-growth forest—like **Cheaha Wilderness** and **Dugger Mountain Wilderness**—that safeguard rare and endangered plant species. The 2,413-foot (735-m) **Cheaha Mountain** is the highest point in Alabama.

Crossing from northwest Georgia into central Alabama, the Pinhoti National Recreation Trail is a perfect choice for those looking to hike year-round.

Established in 1933, Cheaha State Park is the oldest park in Alabama, with 2,799 acres (1,133 ha) of granite boulders and woodlands.

Just past the Georgia state line, the Pinhoti transitions onto country roads for a stretch that includes the historic town of **Cave Spring** and its refreshing waters. After leaping the **Coosa River,** the route rises into the highlands again on a run that includes a 20-mile (32-km) walk across the crest of **Taylor Ridge** in **Chattahoochee National Forest.** Landmarks along the ridge include **James H. "Sloppy" Floyd State Park** and the ruins of creepy **Corpsewood Manor,** where one of Georgia's most notorious homicides took place.

The trail crosses the broad **Conasauga Valley**—and the largely urbanized corridor between **Atlanta** and **Chattanooga**—with another road shoulder and sidewalk section that includes a trek past big-box stores, car dealerships, and fast-food restaurants. However, the sideshow is fleeting and the Pinhoti soon escapes into the forest again.

Climbing into the rugged mountains of **north Georgia** and the main part of Chattahoochee National Forest, the trail peters out beside the **South Fork of the Jacks River**—around 45 miles (72 km) from the southern terminus of the Appalachian Trail for those who want to keep on walking. ∎

DETOURS

• **Alabama Theatre:** Opened in 1927 as a picture palace, this downtown Birmingham cultural institution now stages live music, dramas, comedies, and classic movies.

• **Tuskegee National Historic Sites:** Black history comes into focus at national park units that showcase the prestigious Tuskegee Institute and Tuskegee Airmen of World War II fame.

• **Talladega Superspeedway:** A longtime mecca of American motor sport and one of the world's fastest car-racing tracks, the "Dega" hosts a variety of NASCAR events.

• **Coosa River Adventures:** This Alabama outfitter rents kayaks and canoes for day trips on the gentle Coosa River and multiday camping along the Tallapoosa River.

• **Fort Mountain State Park:** The "fort" at this north Georgia park is a mysterious stone wall built by ancient Native Americans or (according to another theory) a medieval Welsh explorer who beat Columbus to the Americas.

Outer Mountain Loop
Texas

Blending parts of six other trails, this trek around the Chisos Mountains of Big Bend National Park underscores the region's radically different desert and forest landscapes.

Big Bend might be best known for its desert wilderness and that huge curve in the **Rio Grande.** But the sprawling national park also boasts substantial highlands.

Formed by volcanoes that erupted 40 to 60 million years ago, the **Chisos Mountains** offer a whole different take on West Texas nature: a richly wooded and relatively well-watered ecosystem with a range of flora and fauna more at home in the Rockies than the **Chihuahuan Desert.**

A great horned owl perches above Cottonwood Campground in Big Bend National Park.

THE BIG PICTURE

Distance: 33 miles (53 km)

Elevation Gain: approx. 6,000 feet (1,830 m)

Time: 3 days

Difficulty: Strenuous

Best Time: Late fall, winter, or early spring

More Info: nps.gov/ bibe/planyourvisit/bc_ outermountainloop.htm

Rising to almost 8,000 feet (2,438 m), the Chisos normally run 20°F (11°C) cooler than the surrounding desert no matter what time of year, which makes them ideal for hiking, especially during the warmer months. Although it should be noted that higher elevations get a sprinkling of snow nearly every winter.

The **Outer Mountain Loop** is the area's most challenging trail, a rugged 33-mile (53-km) hike that borrows segments of six other trails along a route that includes desert, forest, and rocky outlooks with views across West Texas and northern Mexico.

Hikers can strike off from two vastly different trailheads. One lies beside the **Homer Wilson Ranch** pull-off at mile 8.1 (13 km) along **Ross Maxwell Scenic Drive.** Other than a water cache storage box— which hikers must stock themselves—there are no amenities.

The alternative is starting from the **Chisos Basin,** a huge volcanic bowl that dominates the middle of the range. Besides a park visitors center, the basin offers a general store, restaurant, campground, cabins, and motel rooms for crashing before and after the hike. Given those creature comforts,

A cluster of opuntia cacti (*Opuntia* sp.) in the Chisos Mountains of Big Bend National Park

many loop hikers choose the basin as their basecamp.

Starting from the visitors center parking lot, the route follows the **Pinnacles Trail** up switchbacks that climb to 7,000-foot (2,130-m) **Toll Mountain Pass.** Catch your breath, take in the view, follow the route downhill along the **Boot Canyon** and **Juniper Canyon Trails** as the forest gradually fades away into desert, and settle in for the night amid sagebrush and cactus.

Day two starts with a long, hot trek along the 11-mile (18-km) **Dodson Trail** that skirts the southern edge of the Chisos Range. This stretch features a couple of desert ridges but is reasonably horizontal compared to the previous day. The challenge is a glaring lack of shade and the relentless Big Bend sun; packing enough water for this leg is crucial.

The trail eventually reaches historic Homer Wilson Ranch house, a solid stone structure built in 1929. Just beyond is liquid refill in the water cache that hikers will hopefully have stashed ahead of time. Turning back toward the mountains, **Blue Creek Canyon Trail** offers plenty of places to bed down.

Day three is another doozy, a 2,500-foot (760-m) climb back into the Chisos Basin. Thank goodness, the woods resume as hikers near the rim. From there, it's an easy downhill glide along the **Laguna Meadows Trail** to the visitors center and surrounding amenities.

Those who want to linger longer at the summit can camp at one of the dozen or so **High Chisos backpacking sites.** After, it's possible to undertake side trips to the **South Rim** and **Emory Peak** (at 7,825 feet [2,385 m], the highest point in both the Chisos Mountains and Big Bend National Park). ■

OTHER GREAT TRAILS

- **Skyline Drive Trail:** This 4.5-mile (7.2-km) route in Davis Mountains State Park climbs from the campground and lodge to viewpoints above Fort Davis National Historic Site and its namesake town.

- **Guadalupe Peak Trail:** Summit the highest point in Texas (8,751 feet/2,667 m) on a steep out-and-back route from Pine Springs Visitor Center in Guadalupe Mountains National Park.

- **Cinco Tinajas Trail:** An easy hike among the many gnarly routes in Big Bend Ranch State Park, this 3.4-mile (5.5-km) loop winds through slot canyons to five remote desert pools.

Follow the Pinnacles Trail through Boulder Meadow for views of Casa Grande in the distance.

Black Creek Hiking Trail
Mississippi

Step back in time to the Gulf of Mexico coastal plain of pre-European times on a De Soto National Forest trail along one of the South's most remote wild and scenic rivers.

Rather than black water, this wild and scenic waterway is actually caramel or copper colored, an eye-catching hue caused by the tannic acid in decaying vegetation that drops into the river from the surrounding forest.

And what a forest it is: a largely unfettered blend of bald cypress, sweet gum, red maple, and other floodplain hardwoods with higher elevation trees like the loblolly pine.

Canoeing Black Creek gives visitors a waterside view of this wilderness area.

THE BIG PICTURE

Distance: 41 miles (66 km)

Elevation Gain: approx. 1,750 feet (530 m)

Time: 2–3 days

Difficulty: Moderate

Best Time: Year-round

More Info: hikinginmississippi .com/?page_id=583

Although **De Soto National Forest** is named for the first European to explore the region (Spaniard Hernando de Soto), the reserve and its pristine Black Creek Wilderness are a throwback to precontact days, when the Choctaw and earlier Native American peoples inhabited the region.

Meandering along the south side of its namesake waterway, **Black Creek Trail** is easily accessible from **Gulfport** and **Biloxi** on the Mississippi coast or **Hattiesburg** and **Jackson** in the middle of the state. The whole trail is within the national forest, with around 10 miles (16 km) through the wilderness area. Hikers cross over smaller streams along the route on more than 100 bridges and boardwalks.

Primitive camping is allowed along the entire route, but hikers must bivouac at least 100 feet (30 m) off the trail. Camping is free and no permit is required.

Starting from the southeast end, the trail kicks off from **Fairley Bridge Landing,** named for one of the early Euro-American families that settled the area. Before reaching the creek, the route runs through the densely forested **Red Hills** and a few high spots where hikers can snatch views of the surrounding countryside. A spur leads off to a tiny **pioneer cemetery** largely lost

Fallen needles from the surrounding pine trees in De Soto National Forest create the ideal acidic pH for carnivorous pitcher plants *(Sarracenia)* to thrive.

and forgotten among the woods.

Roughly seven miles (11 km) from the start, the trail slides into **Black Creek Wilderness** and its unique coastal plain environment. In addition to the old-growth trees, the area is also a refuge for a rich variety of animals. Hikers should keep an eye out for threatened species like the yellow-blotched map turtle *(Graptemys flavimaculata)* and pearl darter *(Percina aurora)* in streams and ponds. Immersed in the primal forest, many hikers spend their first night in the wilderness area.

Exiting the wilderness area, the route skirts a primitive Forest Service camping area at **Janice Landing** before diving back into the forest. Much of this middle section runs right beside Black Creek. Reaching **Old Highway 49,** hikers can detour into the town of

Brooklyn for a cold drink at the gas station or **Dollar General** before the final push through the piney woods to **Big Creek Landing** and the trail's western terminus.

In addition to canoes and kayaks for running the wild and scenic river, **Black Creek Canoe Rental** in Brooklyn offers a hiker shuttle service to Fairley Bridge Landing and other spots along the Black Creek Trail. ■

OTHER GREAT TRAILS

• **Tuxachanie Trail:** Just a half-hour drive from Mississippi's Gulf Coast, this 11.9-mile (19.1-km) route through De Soto National Forest features old railroad trestles, African American historic sites, and an abandoned World War II German POW camp.

• **Fontainebleau Nature Trail:** Bird-watchers twitch at the prospect of sighting a wide variety of feathered friends along a 1.7-mile (2.7-km) route through Sandhill Crane National Wildlife Refuge that includes forest and bayou.

• **Al Scheller Hiking Trail:** This rugged 12-mile (19-km) route through the backwoods of Vicksburg National Military Park was originally built for Boy Scouts to practice orienteering and compass use.

• **Clark Creek Primitive Trail:** Many of the Clark Creek Nature Area's 50-plus waterfalls—and the world's largest bigleaf snowbell and Mexican plum trees—are viewable along a 4.3-mile (6.9-km) loop in the state's southwest corner.

Wilderness Road Trail

Virginia

Trek the legendary Cumberland Gap along a path inspired by the trailblazing efforts of Daniel Boone and thousands of others who migrated west via southwest Virginia.

O n the cusp of the American Revolution, the Transylvania Company (nothing to do with vampires) commissioned frontiersman Daniel Boone to blaze a path through the Appalachians into the little-known Kentucky country on the other side.

Largely using footpaths that Native Americans trekked for

centuries, Boone pushed his trail through the Cumberland Gap, a journey into terra incognita that came to be called the Wilderness Road. Although a fraction of the original length, the 10.7-mile (17-km) **Wilderness Road Trail** makes for a great day hike through the natural and human history of southwest Virginia.

Pass by McHargue's Mill as the trail winds through Wilderness Road State Park.

THE BIG PICTURE

Distance: 10.7 miles (17 km)

Elevation Change: approx. 2,000 feet (610 m)

Time: 1 day

Difficulty: Easy

Best Time: Year-round

More Info: nps.gov/cuga and dcr.virginia.gov/state-parks/wilderness-road

Starting from a park-and-ride lot beside the **Wilderness Road Highway** (U.S. 58) near **Caylor**—near the spot where Boone's oldest son and five other frontiersmen were killed in a 1773 ambush by Native Americans—the route follows the path of the old Louisville and Nashville Railroad line through the bucolic Virginia countryside.

Just two miles (3.2 km) into the journey, the trail slips into **Wilderness Road State Park.** Hikers should definitely duck into the visitors center for the frontier museum, gift shop with trail swag, and the short film, *The Wilderness Road: Spirit of a Nation.* Elsewhere in the park are the stately 1870 **Karlan Mansion** and a reconstruction of **Martin's Station,** a frontier-era fort and trading post that served travelers on Wilderness Road.

The trail continues along the former train line past several flooded quarries and a timber mill to **Gibson Station,** founded in 1775 by an Irishman who later fought for the Continental Army. Veering away from the railroad right-of-way, the footpath tags along beside Highway 58 to **Cumberland Gap National Historical Park.**

After skirting the park campground on the short **Colson Trail,** hikers segue onto the **Boone Trail**

A scenic view of the Tennessee River Gorge

and a 1.6-mile (2.5-km) walk to the park's **Daniel Boone Visitor Information Center.** The outdoor pavilion offers exhibits on early travelers along the Wilderness Road, while the info desk can tell you all about overnight hiking along trails in the park's surprisingly large backcountry.

The Wilderness Road Trail picks up again beyond the visitors center on an uphill leg that features side trails to an 1819 stone **Iron Furnace** and **Gap Cave** with its stalagmites and flowstone cascades (two-hour guided tours).

At the top of the climb is **Cumberland Gap,** where hikers can look across the blue ridges of Virginia and down at Kentucky's **Middlesboro Basin,** gouged by a long-ago meteor impact. Spur trails flare off across the mountaintops to **Pinnacle Overlook** and **Tri-State Peak,** where Virginia, Kentucky, and Tennessee rendezvous at a USGS triangulation cap.

Slipping into Kentucky, the Wilderness Road descends to the park's **Cumberland Gap Visitor Center,** where a bookshop and films about Daniel Boone and the park's human and natural history complement hands-on exhibits. For those who want to keep walking, **Middlesboro's** main drag (**Cumberland Avenue**) is just half a mile (1 km) past the visitors center. ∎

OTHER GREAT TRAILS

The Cumberland Trail

A work in progress, the Cumberland Trail is a new long-distance route across the Cumberland Plateau of eastern Tennessee. When completed, it will stretch roughly 300 miles (480 km) between Cumberland Gap National Historical Park and Chickamauga and Chattanooga National Military Park.

Running parallel to the Appalachian Trail (AT)—and designed by hikers who envision the Cumberland as less crowded and more off the beaten path than the uber-popular AT—the trail starts its southward journey at Tri-State Peak in Cumberland Gap.

By 2022, around 215 miles (346 km) of the route had been completed. Among the longer sections already open to hikers are a 35-mile (56-km) leg between Cove Lake and Frozen Head State Parks, a 30-mile (48-km) segment linking Nemo Bridge and Daddy's Creek, and a 29-mile (46-km) section between Upper Leggett Road and Mowbray Pike.

Appalachian Trail
Multiple States

The gold standard by which all other long-distance walks are judged, the Appalachian Trail stretches just over 2,190 miles (3,500 km) between Georgia and Maine across one of the planet's oldest mountain ranges.

THE BIG PICTURE

Distance: 2,190 miles (3,500 km)

Elevation Gain: approx. 464,000 feet (141,430 m)

Time: 5–7 months

Difficulty: Strenuous

Best Time: Spring, summer, or fall

More Info: appalachiantrail.org

The **Appalachian Trail** (AT) isn't anywhere near the longest American hiking trail—the North Country Trail is nearly twice its mileage. It isn't the most scenic—treading through the likes of Yosemite, Tahoe Basin, Crater Lake, and the North Cascades, the Pacific Crest Trail is an easy winner of the eye candy category. Neither is it the oldest U.S. long-distance hiking route. That honor belongs to the Long Trail, a Vermont path blazed a decade earlier that inspired creation of the AT.

But the Appalachian is the toughest. Its peaks and knobs may not reach as high as the Sierras or Rockies, but conquering them requires an excruciating amount of up and down. Total elevation gain for those who hike the entire 2,190-mile (3,500-km) route is around 464,000 feet (141,430 m). As many sources point out, that's the equivalent of scaling Mount Everest.

Going beyond geography into the realm of human perception, the AT is far and away the most famous of America's many footpaths. Millions of people who have never been near the wilderness or set foot on a hiking route have heard of the Appalachian Trail. And you must be doing something right when Robert Redford stars in a feature film about walking the route (his 2015 film, *A Walk in the Woods*).

The Appalachian Trail is also the most popular ultra-long-distance trail. Around three million people hike at least a portion of the AT each year. Of course, the number of "2,000-milers" who have trekked the entire trail is much smaller: only around 1,000 per annum. But that

The Appalachian Trail intersects New York's Long Path in Harriman State Park.

The AT spends more time in Virginia than any other state, with more than 100 miles (160 km) of the famous trail rolling through Shenandoah National Park.

number has grown steadily since the trail was completed in the 1930s, when only around one hiker a year made it all the way through.

Many of the early "2,000-milers" are the stuff of hiking legend. World War II veteran Earl V. Shaffer—aka "The Crazy One"—was the first person to thru-hike the Appalachian Trail in a single season, a feat he first accomplished in 1948 as a way to "walk the Army" out of his system. Shaffer was also the first person to thru-hike the AT in both directions (1965), and just two weeks short of his 80th birthday, he became the oldest person to hike the entire trail (1998).

LAY YOUR HEAD

- **Mountain Crossings:** This historic 1930s stone structure just 31 miles (50 km) from the southern terminus includes a rustic hostel, hiking clothing and equipment, and an AT swag shop; $20; mountaincrossings.com.

- **Laughing Heart Lodge:** The hostel portion of this Hot Springs, North Carolina, hangout features bunks, private rooms, and tent sites, plus showers, laundry, kitchen area, and Wi-Fi; from $15; laughingheartlodge.com/hostel.

- **Bear Garden Hiker Hostel:** Just steps from the AT in southern Virginia, the hostel offers bunkhouse rooms, breakfast, hot showers, and washer/dryer; $20; facebook.com/beargardenhikerhostel.

- **The Doyle Hotel:** Welcoming AT hikers since the 1930s, the historic Doyle offers hot food, cold beer, and comfy beds before crossing the Susquehanna River in east-central Pennsylvania; from $49; facebook.com/doylehotel.

- **Appalachian Mountain Club:** Founded in 1876 as the nation's oldest outdoor group, the AMC offers lodges, cabins, huts, and campsites in five northeastern states between Maine and New Jersey; rates vary; outdoors.org/destinations.

Even more renowned is Emma "Grandma" (and mother of 11 children) Gatewood, who completed the first solo female thru-hike in 1955 at the age of 67 with her trademark headscarf, duffel bag, walking stick, and Keds tennis shoes. She would trek the AT twice more.

From *Grandma Gatewood's Walk* by Ben Montgomery to Bill Bryson's best-selling *A Walk in the Woods* (the inspiration for Redford's film), there are plenty of accounts about trekking the AT. Ditto when it comes to guides. Among the most popular are the official *Appalachian Trail Thru-Hikers' Companion* by the Appalachian Long Distance Hikers Association and *How to Hike the Appalachian Trail* by Chris Cage.

With more than 260 shelters, around 125 designated campsites, and indoor digs at 50 AT communities along the route, hikers have plenty of overnight options. Dispersed or stealth camping is allowed along portions of the trail that pass through national forests, primarily in the four southern states. However, camping is forbidden in national and state parks, and along much of the middle Atlantic and New England portions.

Whether you're thru-hiking, segment hiking, or sampling just a small portion of the AT, **Georgia** offers the best weather and trail conditions earlier than any other state. By March and early April, the 77 miles (124 km) of trail that flow over the **Blue Ridge Mountains** in north Georgia are usually ready for walking.

Around a 90-minute drive north

You'll find designated campsites and dispersed camping along the length of the Appalachian Trail.

LOCAL FLAVOR

- **Smoky Mountain Diner:** Salmon patties, roast beef, chicken and dumplings, and peach cobbler comfort hikers at this Hot Springs hot spot; 70 Lance Avenue, Hot Springs, NC; facebook.com/Smoky -Mountain-Diner-153411231377293.

- **Three Li'l Pigs:** Jerk, teriyaki, tomato, and vinegar sauces flavor the pork, chicken, and beef at this trailside barbecue joint; 120 Kingston Drive, Daleville, VA; threelilpigs bbq.com.

- **Port Clinton Peanut Shop:** Passing through Pennsylvania, restock your snack cache with gummy bears, licorice, chocolates, trail mix, and fresh roasted peanuts; 97 Center Street,

Port Clinton, PA; portclintonpeanut shop.com.

- **King Arthur Baking Company:** The menu of this combo café, bakery, and culinary school runs a broad gamut from pastries and breakfast sandwiches to salads, artisan breads, and pizza; 135 U.S. 5 South, Norwich, VT; kingarthur baking.com.

- **Monson General Store:** Hikers in a hurry can snatch a grab-and-go special at an old-timey store in the Maine woods just steps from the AT Visitor Center; 12 Greenville Road, Monson, ME; facebook.com/ monsongeneral.

of **Atlanta, Springer Mountain** is the trail's southern terminus, but to reach the 3,782-foot (1,153-m) peak, hikers need to walk a mile (1.6 km) or more from the nearest trailhead parking areas. With fresh legs, it feels like a sprint (rather than a slog) through **Chattahoochee National Forest** to **Bly Gap** on the Georgia–North Carolina border.

Nantahala National Forest carries the trail across western **North Carolina,** through a remote region known for deep valleys, thick forest, and more annual rainfall than anywhere in the continental U.S. other than the Pacific Northwest. On the other side of colossal **Fontana Dam**—at 480 feet (150 m), the highest dam east of the Mississippi—the AT slips in the back door of **Great Smoky Mountains National Park.**

Making its way across the park's **Twentymile Ridge,** the AT passes near **Shuckstack Fire Tower** and its incredible views of the Smoky Range. Reaching **Buck Gap,** the

route starts a 218-mile (350-km) mountaintop run along the North Carolina-**Tennessee** border that includes **Clingmans Dome,** highest point along the entire AT at 6,643 feet (2,025 m).

Exiting the nation's most visited national park, the trail continues across ridges and summits that mark the boundary between **Pisgah National Forest** (North Carolina) and **Cherokee National Forest** (Tennessee), with the towns of **Hot Springs, Erwin,** and **Roan Mountain** offering the possibility of rest and restock along the way.

Descending from **Holston Mountain,** the route moves into **Virginia,** which boasts more of the AT (531 miles/854 km) than any other state. The passage across Old Dominion includes lengthy treks through **George Washington and Jefferson National Forests** and **Shenandoah National Park.** In addition to trail towns like **Damascus, Waynesboro,** and **Front Royal,** the trail passes through nine

Fingerboard Shelter in Harriman State Park is one of the oldest remaining shelters along the Appalachian Trail.

federal wilderness areas with old-growth forest.

The AT's short but fascinating stretch through **West Virginia** includes **Harpers Ferry** with its Civil War sites and headquarters of the **Appalachian Trail Conservancy** (ATC). Leaping the **Potomac River** on a railroad bridge, the route rambles across the top of 80-mile (128-km)-long **South Mountain** on its way across **Maryland.**

The 229 miles (368 km) of the AT in **Pennsylvania** start with an easy walk across bucolic **Cumberland Valley** and a bridge across the **Susquehanna River** at **Duncannon.** Then comes a deep dive into a **Valley and Ridge province** with steep up and down climbs. **Pine Grove Furnace State Park** (near **Gettysburg Battlefield**) harbors the **Appalachian Trail Museum.**

On the far side of the **Delaware Water Gap,** the AT uses **Kittatinny Mountain** to cut across **New Jersey'**s heavily wooded northwest corner via lofty **High Point State Park.** Crossing into **New York** near the outer edge of the **New York City** metro area, the route glides into **Harriman State Park,** where the first section of the Appalachian Trail opened in October 1923. Majestic **Bear Mountain Bridge**—at 124 feet (38 km) above sea level, the lowest elevation on the AT—takes the trail across the **Hudson River.**

Tacking up the west side of the Hudson Valley, the trail runs through **Hudson Highlands** and **Clarence Fahnestock State Parks** in the **Taconic Mountains** before reaching the New York-**Connecticut** state line. A walk through the **Housatonic River Valley** spirits the path into the scenic **Berkshires** region of western **Massachusetts,** past towns like **Stockbridge, Pittsfield,** and **North Adams** that blend early American history and iconic cultural institutions.

Green Mountain National Forest—and 100 miles (160 km) of dirt the AT shares with the **Long Trail**—takes the route much of the way across **Vermont.** After hopping the **Connecticut River** into **New Hampshire,** the trail navigates the **Dartmouth College** campus and soon rises into the **White**

SHORT CIRCUITS

These sections of the AT are ideal for day hikes:

• **Crawford Notch:** From the Ripley Falls/Webster Cliff turnoff on Highway 302, it's a six-mile (9.6-km) return to Ethan Pond in one direction and a 5.6-mile (9-km) out-and-back to the summit of Mount Webster the other way in New Hampshire's White Mountains.

• **Harriman State Park:** The first completed section of the AT meanders 19.2 miles (30.9 km) between Elk Pen and Bear Mountain Bridge, an hour's drive north of the Big Apple.

• **Shenandoah National Park:** Stretching just over seven miles

(11 km), a portion of the AT between Big Meadows and Skyland rambles through woods along the crest of the Blue Ridge.

• **Harpers Ferry:** Cross from West Virginia to Maryland on the railroad bridge and walk a section along the Potomac River that the AT shares with the C&O Canal Towpath.

• **Newfound Gap:** From the parking area on Highway 441, day hikers can trek out and back to Clingmans Dome (14 miles/22.5 km) or Icewater Spring Shelter (6 miles/9.6 km) in Great Smoky Mountains National Park.

Mountains. One of the most scenic stretches of the entire trail includes **Franconia Notch, Crawford Notch,** and **Mount Washington** before a long-awaited rendezvous with **Maine.**

Although it doesn't present the extreme topography of the Smoky Mountains or Blue Ridge, the 281 miles (452 km) of the route across western Maine are more remote than anything farther south along the AT. Carved by long-ago glaciers, the landscape features deep forest, bald-topped mountains, numerous lakes, and the possibility of close encounters of the critter kind with moose and black bear.

Maine kicks off in gnarly fashion at **Mahoosuc Notch,** a boulder-strewn gap that many consider the AT's single toughest mile. Making their way across the rugged **Height of Land** region, hikers ford the **Kennebec River** at **Caratunk** on a canoe ferry (May to September).

The **AT Visitor Center** in **Monson** offers the lowdown on the impending trek through the **100 Mile Wilderness** and big **Baxter State Park,** where the final section of the trail was completed in 1937. The final steps take hikers to the summit of **Mount Katahdin,** tallest point in Maine at 5,269 feet (1,606 m) and the northern terminus of the Appalachian Trail. Summit the peak from the **Hunt Trail,** which is anything but an easy end to the trek. The 10.9-mile (17.5-km) out-and-back route climbs more than 4,000 feet (1,219 m), but the scenic overlooks are worth the effort—and the perfect finale to the AT. ∎

Nestled in the Roanoke Valley, McAfee Knob is one of the most iconic—and photographed—spots on the AT.

Sheltowee Trace National Recreation Trail
Kentucky & Tennessee

Follow the white turtle blazes on a route across the Cumberland Plateau through a region that Daniel Boone tramped when Kentucky was still America's western frontier.

THE BIG PICTURE

Distance: 333 miles (535 km)

Elevation Gain: approx. 60,000 feet (18,300 m)

Time: 3–5 weeks

Difficulty: Strenuous

Best Time: Spring, summer, or fall

More Info: sheltoweetrace.org and sheltoweetrace.com

The Shawnee people whom Daniel Boone encountered during his explorations of the Kentucky wilderness thought the broad-shouldered frontiersman resembled a huge turtle. And when he was adopted into the tribe in 1778, Chief Blackfish dubbed him Sheltowee, or "Big Turtle."

So when a long-distance trail was established in the state's Daniel Boone National Forest almost exactly two centuries after that event, it was christened the **Sheltowee Trace** and was marked with blazes featuring a white turtle.

The current route stretches for more than 300 miles (480 km) from north to south across the **Cumberland Plateau** of eastern Kentucky, an area also called the Eastern Kentucky Coal Field or Kentucky Appalachia.

Although the trace is primarily for hikers, some sections are open to bikers and horseback riders. And one section between **Turkeyfoot** and **S-Tree** allows dirt bikes and ATVs. With only a handful of organized campgrounds, camping is allowed as long as you bivouac at least 300 feet (90 m) from the trail. Users can also overnight (and restock provisions) in five trail towns.

The trail starts its long journey through the backwoods at the northern tip of **Daniel Boone National Forest.** Crossing over Interstate 64, the route makes its way through

Sheltowee Trace stretches across two states for 319 miles (513 km), through Daniel Boone National Forest and Big South Fork National River and Recreation Area.

It's worth the early wake-up to catch the sunrise over the expansive Red River Gorge.

Morehead State University and into downtown Morehead. Catch an exhibition at the Kentucky Folk Art Center before hitting the trail again.

Cave Run Lake Dam provides a perch for hikers to gaze down the Licking River Valley before a meander along the lake's western shore. Up ahead are Red River Gorge and Natural Bridge State Park. Crossing the Kentucky River, the route slips into McKee, where Prohibition famously endured until 2019.

A road-walk section takes the trail past the Camp Wildcat Battlefield, where Kentucky's first Civil War clash unfolded in 1861. Laurel River Lake enables another waterfront sojourn before tagging along the Cumberland River for 11 miles (18 km) to Cumberland Falls State Park and its namesake cascade.

West of U.S. 27, the trace runs beside the Big South Fork of the Cumberland River. Along the way is Yahoo Falls.

Crossing the border into Tennessee, the trail finishes with a 49-mile (79-km) wander through Big South Fork National River and Recreation Area. Hikers can bed down at rustic Charit Creek Lodge or Bandy Creek Campground before tramping the John Muir Trail (Tennessee version) to Honey Creek and the last few steps at Burnt Mill Bridge. ■

DETOURS

- **Rockcastle Outdoor Company:** Take guided motorcycle tours through Daniel Boone country and unguided paddleboard floats down the Rockcastle River from Livingston, Kentucky.

- **Sheltowee Trace Adventure Resort:** Paddle to the spray-drenched base of Cumberland Falls on guided kayak and rafting trips or hop aboard the *Cumberland Star* for a scenic voyage along the river.

- **Holly Bay Marina:** Rent a pontoon boat for the day or a motorboat for half a day to cruise on Laurel River Lake; check out three-, four-, or seven-night houseboat rentals, too.

- **Red River Gorge Zipline:** Soar 300 feet (90 m) above the chasm on five lines ranging up to 1,900 feet (580 m) in length.

- **Big South Fork Scenic Railway:** This seven-mile (11-km) journey through the history and culture of Kentucky Appalachia includes a layover and lunch at historic Barthell Coal Camp (established in 1902).

The Sheltowee Trace trail will lead you to Van Hook Falls, surrounded by a sandstone cathedral and picturesque Cane Creek.

Wild Azalea Trail
Louisiana

Louisiana's longest hiking trail offers a burst of pink-and-white flowers each spring and a journey through the region's piney hills, hardwood bottoms, and boggy seeps throughout the year.

THE BIG PICTURE

Distance: 27 miles (43 km)

Elevation Gain: approx. 1,800 feet (550 m)

Time: 1–2 days

Difficulty: Moderate

Best Time: Spring

More Info: townofwoodworth
.com/wild-azalea-trail

Not a lot of trails beg to be trekked during a very specific time of year. But those who want to see, smell, and photograph the namesake blooms along the **Wild Azalea Trail** better have hiking boots on the ground between March and May.

Louisiana's longest wilderness trail snakes through the Evangeline District of Kisatchie National Forest. Depending on your walking speed—and how often you stop to admire the pinkish white flowers—the hike takes one or two days between terminal trailheads at **Valentine Lake** and Woodworth village.

Trekking the route in summer means hot, humid weather not especially conducive to hiking. Winter brings chilly mornings and more sparse vegetation. So weatherwise, spring really is the best time to tramp the Wild Azalea. Or fall, for those who aren't inspired by brilliant floral displays.

Around 20 minutes south of Alexandria, **Woodworth** marks the trail's eastern end with several cafés and convenience stores where you can grab a last bite or extra supplies before striking out. Starting from the **Woodworth Town Hall** parking lot, the Wild Azalea follows **Castor Plunge Road** for almost two miles (3.2 km) before veering off onto its own woodland track past **Little Bayou Clear.**

Tacking northwest into **Kisatchie National Forest,** the trail crosses several creek beds and hilly watershed divides. Some of the hike's best wild azaleas flank the stretch along **Loving Creek.** Around a dozen miles (19 km) from the start, the path crosses **Hamp Smith Road** and descends into **Castor Creek Scenic Area,** a 90-acre (36-ha) wilderness tract shaded by a blend of beech, ash, magnolia, and bald cypress trees, as well as tall loblolly pines.

More or less the halfway point, the forest on either side of the scenic area makes a good place to break for

A wooden bridge along the Wild Azalea Trail

An eastern tiger swallowtail butterfly alights on an azalea bush in the Calcasieu Ranger District of Kisatchie National Forest.

the night. Hikers can camp anywhere along the Wild Azalea as long as their site is at least 30 feet (9 m) from the trail centerline.

Day two starts with a turn to the north and a leap across State Highway 488 to **Evangeline Primitive Camp** on Messina Road, another favorite overnight spot for those who have spread the trek over two days. Just west of the camp is the **Wild Azalea Seep,** an area of rich saturated soil that supports orchids and other floral species as well as the only bog moss colony west of the Mississippi River. This unusual ecosystem is an official Louisiana Natural Area.

Swinging around to the west, the trail crosses marshy **Lamotte Creek** on a narrow wooden bridge. Off to the right, hikers can see where the

creek flows into one of the many arms of **Kincaid Lake.** From there, it's around eight miles (13 km) to the trail's western end at **Valentine Lake,** a Forest Service recreation

area with a waterfront campground, two fishing piers, and nonmotorized boating. The lake's north shore is another place where wild azaleas flourish in the spring. ■

OTHER GREAT TRAILS

Urban Azalea Trail

An hour's drive south of Woodworth, the city of **Lafayette** offers an urban version of the azalea journey with parks, gardens, and front yards that flash their own flamboyant colors each spring.

Launched in the 1930s, the **Lafayette Historic Azalea Trail** can be hiked, biked, or driven. Rather than a linear start-to-finish route, the trail fans out like a spider's web through downtown, residential neighborhoods, and the

University of Louisiana at Lafayette campus.

Along its 25 miles (40 km), the trail passes many of the city's landmarks and attractions, including the **Cathedral of St. John the Evangelist, Alexandre Mouton House** (built ca 1800), **Acadiana Center for the Arts,** and **Sterling Grove Historic District.**

Neighborhoods like the **Arbolada Addition, Bendel Gardens,** and **Mouton Gardens** are the stuff of azalea legend. And anyone trekking the university campus should keep an eye out for gators in **Cypress Lake.**

Palmetto Trail
South Carolina

Still a work in progress, this ever expanding route from mountain to sea reveals the incredible cultural and natural variety of the smallest state in the American South.

THE BIG PICTURE

Distance: 380 miles (610 km)

Elevation Gain: approx. 2,600 feet (800 m)

Time: 1 month

Difficulty: Easy to strenuous

Best Time: Year-round

More Info: palmettoconservation.org/palmetto-trail

From the Blue Ridge Mountains and the Piedmont region to the sand hills that run across the middle of the state and wetlands along the subtropical shoreline, the **Palmetto Trail** does a remarkable job of including all of South Carolina's major geographic regions.

Around 380 miles (610 km) of the nonmotorized route is finished, with another 150 miles (240 km) still to be blazed, mostly in the state's midsection and up-country. The route encompasses a variety of surfaces, including rail trails, bikeways, city sidewalks, forest paths, country roads, and even the steps of the State Capitol.

With 30 segments that range from short, flat, and easy to long, steep, and tough, the Palmetto is a trail that just about anyone can walk, bike, or horseback ride. Although starting from the Atlantic coast may seem appealing—after all, the South Carolina shore is enticing—it makes a lot more sense to start in the **Blue Ridge** and work your way downhill rather than up.

The first three segments are in and around **Oconee State Park** in the state's far western corner. Hikers and bikers can fish for bass and catfish, paddle across **Lake Oconee,** or even play 18 holes of miniature golf in the park before hitting the trail. Although much of the up-country route is still in development, hikers can trek foot-only portions of the Palmetto at **Eastatoe Creek, Table Rock State Park,** the **Jocassee Gorges,** and **Roundtop Mountain.**

The **Foothills Trail** provides a temporary link to the **Mountain Bridge Wilderness Area** and a long stretch of the Palmetto that includes **Jones Gap State Park,** the **Saluda Mountains,** and the Nature Conservancy's **Blue Wall Preserve,** which harbors a variety of native plant communities and more than 100 bird species.

Landrum and its assorted antique shops mark the transition from the Blue Ridge to the **Piedmont** region of the Palmetto Trail. After traipsing through **Spartanburg** on nine miles (14.5 km) of urban greenways and city sidewalks, the route slips back into the woods for a passage across **Croft State Park** and **Blackstock Battlefield,** where colonial militia bested British

Once completed, the Palmetto Trail will link the state's varied geographies, from the shores of Charleston to the Blue Ridge Mountains.

The Palmetto Trail runs the gamut, from leisurely to challenging terrain, crossing forests, cities, rail trails, and rural countryside.

regulars in November 1780. Up next is the route's second longest wilderness section, a 36-mile (58-km) leg across **Sumter National Forest.**

Rambling down the **Broad River,** the trail marches through the middle of **Columbia,** past the **State House** (built in 1855), the **University of South Carolina** campus, and the backwoods of **Fort Jackson** army base. Snaking its way through **Wateree Swamp,** over the sandy **High Hills,** and along the shore of **Lake Marion,** the trail segues into subtropical wetlands inhabited by alligators, waterfowl, flooded cypress groves, and its namesake palmetto tree.

The grand finale is 47 miles (76 km) of backwoods hiking and biking through **Francis Marion National Forest,** a hideout for the forest's namesake, South Carolina–born militia leader "Swamp Fox," during the American Revolution.

Awendaw Creek takes the trail down to the **Intracoastal Waterway,** about a 40-minute drive up the coast from Charleston. ■

LOCAL FLAVOR

• **Stone Soup Market & Cafe:** Restock your grub with local cheese and meat, cookies and brownies, deli salads, and casseroles or soups you can heat over your campfire; 1522 East Rutherford Street, Landrum, SC; stonesoupoflandrum.com.

• **FR8yard:** This lively beer garden has pub grub, live music, and a large outdoor seating area just off the Palmetto Trail in downtown Spartanburg; 125 E. Main Street, Spartanburg, SC; fr8yard.com.

• **The Devine Cinnamon Roll Deli:** Tasty rolls might be their specialty, but this eclectic eatery in Columbia's Shandon neighborhood also offers breakfast, lunch, and southern sides like Carolina chili and shrimp and grits; 2617 Devine Street, Columbia, SC; thecinnamonrolldeli.com.

• **Figaro Market:** Grab an Italian sub, chicken Alfredo, or fruit bowl at this gourmet deli in downtown Newberry; 1202 Caldwell Street, Newberry, SC; facebook.com/FigaroMarket.

Ouachita National Recreation Trail

Oklahoma & Arkansas

These backwoods provide a surprisingly pristine setting for a long-distance trail that wanders the highest mountains between the Rockies and Appalachians.

A few highways weave their way through this remote region of eastern Oklahoma and southwest Arkansas, but the best way to explore the heights is along hiking/mountain biking routes like the **Ouachita National Recreation Trail** (OT).

Stretching 223 miles (360 km) from east to west, the trail rambles through pine and oak forest across mountaintops and through secluded valleys watered by pristine streams. Ouachita National Forest hosts roughly 90 percent of the route (192 miles/308 km), including

The majority of the Ouachita National Recreation Trail passes through national forest land, including two federally protected wilderness zones.

THE BIG PICTURE

Distance: 223 miles (360 km)

Elevation Change: approx. 32,000 feet (9,750 m)

Time: 2–3 weeks

Difficulty: Strenuous

Best Time: Spring and fall

More Info: friendsoftheouachita .org and fs.usda.gov/recarea/ ouachita/recarea/?recid=10804

portions that traverse two federal wilderness areas.

In addition to dispersed camping in the national forest, hikers can overnight at 21 wooden shelters along the route that are maintained by Friends of the Ouachita Trail.

Renowned for its vibrant fall foliage, **Talimena State Park** anchors the western end of the trail with a visitors center and small campground. The route doesn't stray far from scenic **Skyline Drive** over its first 10 miles (16 km). **Winding Stair Campground** marks the start of the real wilderness and a climb into the **Upper Kiamichi River Wilderness** with its mixed beech-pine-oak forest.

Forty-six miles (74 km) from the start, the OT crosses from Oklahoma into Arkansas near the **State Line Shelter.** Up ahead, **Queen Wilhelmina State Park** offers a respite from the wilderness that includes a historic lodge, restaurant, campground, showers, and laundry. Perched atop **Rich Mountain,** the second highest point in Arkansas, the lodge is named for the Dutch monarch who was crowned the year it opened (1898).

Sliding down from Rich Mountain, the route crosses the **Ouachita River** and begins a deep dive into **Ouachita National Forest.** Other

Tucked-away waterways and rock formations grace the pristine Ouachita National Recreation Trail.

than the overnight shelters and occasional road crossing, this middle section of the OT is nearly devoid of human touch and the best part of the route on which to keep an eye out for wildlife.

The trail summits **Fourche Mountain, Blowout Mountain,** and **Big Round Top** on its undulating route across the range. Reaching **State Highway 27,** hikers can dig into burgers, fried chicken, and other hot meals at **Bluebell Café and Country Store.** Returning to the woods, the route features a 10-mile (16-km) transit of the **Flatside Wilderness** and a chance to camp, swim, and shower at **Lake Sylvia Recreation Area.**

Beyond **State Highway 9,** the OT drops into the **Maumelle River Valley** and an easy hike along **Lake Maumelle. Pinnacle Mountain State Park** and its pyramid-shaped peak punctuate the eastern end of the trail. From there, hikers can trek surface streets and the **Arkansas River Trail** roughly 15 miles (24 km) into downtown **Little Rock.** ■

SHORT CIRCUITS

These sections of the OT are ideal for day hikes:

• **Pinnacle Mountain State Park:** Striking out from the visitors center, hikers can follow the eastern end of the OT for 3.2 miles (5.1 km) to Lake Maumelle and a tiny town called Natural Steps and its colorful history.

• **Flatside Pinnacle:** A trailhead beside Forest Road 94 marks the start of a short (0.7-mile/1.1-km) hike along a remote portion of the OT to the Flatside summit and its panoramic views of the Ouachita Range.

• **Highway 27 Trailhead:** After a meal at the Bluebell Café, explore Irons Fork Scenic Area on an out-and-back hike along the OT to John Archer Shelter.

• **Queen Wilhelmina State Park:** This four-mile (6.4-km) out-and-back hike on the OT heads from the history lodge to a pioneer cemetery founded in 1860 by the mountain's first Euro-American settlers.

• **Winding Stair:** From the campground, this easy 3.8-mile (6.1-km) hike runs along the OT to Horsethief Springs picnic ground and the remains of a 1930s Civilian Conservation Corps springhouse.

San Antonio River Walk

Texas

One of the nation's earliest urban trails is updated for the 21st century with user-friendly extensions that ramble up and down the San Antonio River.

THE BIG PICTURE

Distance: 15 miles (24 km)

Elevation Gain: approx. 140 feet (40 m)

Time: 1 day

Difficulty: Easy

Best Time: Winter, spring, or fall

More Info: thesanantonio riverwalk.com

Given its extreme popularity with both locals and visitors, it's hard to believe that San Antonio's celebrated waterfront walkway started life as a flood-control measure rather than the city's foremost attraction (after the **Alamo,** of course).

Although the 15-mile (24-km) **San Antonio River Walk** was started in the 1930s, it didn't become an "overnight sensation" until hordes of visitors invaded the Texas city for the HemisFair '68 international exposition. And it wasn't until the early 21st century that the River Walk hit its stride as a full-fledged recreation route.

The original U-shaped downtown section has long flourished on water-side restaurants, shops, bars, and hotels complemented by boat cruises and special events like an annual mariachi festival, holiday light parade, and artisan shows. But the addition of two sections of the Museum Reach, in 2009 and 2011, made the River Walk much more amenable to hikers, bikers, runners, and even kayakers.

Peeling off to the north, the **Museum Reach** follows the **San Antonio River** roughly 4.5 miles (7 km) upstream to **Brackenridge Park** and the **San Antonio Zoo.** Along the way are cultural icons like the **Tobin Center for the Performing Arts, San Antonio Museum of Art,** the **Witte Museum** of natural history, and the interactive family-friendly exhibits and workshops of the new **DoSeum.**

The Museum Reach also runs along the riverfront of the **Pearl District,** a former brewery converted into a popular pedestrian precinct with restaurants, shops, and other entertainment outlets tucked inside vintage industrial buildings. Nearby, as many as 50,000 Mexican free-tailed bats roost beneath the **Camden Street Bridge** (I-35) above the River Walk during the summer.

Snaking south from downtown, the **Museum Reach** stretches downriver through historic neighborhoods like the King William Historic District and Southtown to **San Antonio Missions National Historical Park.** With 10 miles (16 km) of paved trail to hike or bike—or 20 miles (32 km) for those going out and back—this section of the River Walk offers a serious workout.

But it's not all sweat. Trekkers can dive deep into Texas history at the riverside **Villa Finale** (built in 1876)

San Antonio's bustling River Walk is a lively spot to grab a bite and catch a leisurely ride down the San Antonio River.

Diners and tour boats alike enjoy the River Walk, the most popular tourist draw in the state.

and **Steves Homestead** (1877), or browse the eclectic galleries of the **Blue Star Arts Complex,** located in another old beer factory adapted for modern uses.

The only UNESCO World Heritage site in Texas, the historical park that punctuates the southern end of the River Walk preserves four Spanish missions founded between 1690 and 1720. Still an active place of Roman Catholic worship, **Mission San José** offers a **Mariachi Mass** every Sunday at noon, as well as National Park Service ranger–guided tours.

Two other trails offer extensions of the River Walk. Starting near **Mission Concepción,** the **San Pedro Creek/Apache Creek Greenways** offers hikers and bikers a 6.2-mile (10-km) route through neighborhoods like Lone Star and Prospect Hill. The **Medina River Greenway,** which kicks off beside **Mission Espada,** meanders through 17 miles (27 km) of farms, fields, and wetlands along San Antonio's southern edge. ■

LAY YOUR HEAD

• **St. Anthony Hotel:** Located just blocks from the River Walk's downtown and Museum Reach sections, this opulent overnight spot was founded in 1909 by ranchers who wanted a posh place to crash when they visited the city; from $314; thestanthonyhotel.com.

• **Hotel Emma:** The Pearl District offers industrial-style digs with gourmet eateries and a cozy bar beside the San Antonio River; from $645; thehotelemma.com.

• **Noble Inns:** This trio of B&Bs housed in historic mansions in King William District includes the Aaron Pancoast Carriage House and the 1894 Texas Victorian–style Jackson House; from $179; nobleinns.com.

• **Hotel Havana:** The Cuban colonial architecture of this charming riverside boutique channels the spirit of the avid Caribbean traveler who built the mansion in 1914; from $217; havanasanantonio.com.

Tallulah Gorge
Georgia

Often called the "Grand Canyon of the South," Tallulah Gorge cleaves a deep trench into the southern Appalachians, a geological wonder best explored along a steep ravine trail and two rim routes.

THE BIG PICTURE

Distances: Hurricane Falls Loop, 2 miles (3.2 km); Sliding Rock, 0.25 mile (0.4 km)

Elevation Gains: Hurricane Falls Loop, approx. 380 feet (120 m); Sliding Rock, approx. 500 feet (150 m)

Time: 1–3 hours

Difficulty: Strenuous

Best Time: Spring or fall

More Info: gastateparks.org/ TallulahGorge

The focus of a popular Georgia state park, Tallulah Gorge was carved over thousands of years by a swift-flowing river of the same name, a canyon that features waterfalls, rock pools, and several short but precipitous hiking trails.

Hurricane Falls Loop is the most sought-after route, but it's not for anyone with vertigo or acrophobia. Starting from **Jane Hurt Yarn Interpretive Center** on the North Rim, the path plunges 200 feet (60 m) via hundreds of metal stairs to a pedestrian suspension bridge above **Hurricane Falls.** After crossing the river, the trail ascends to the South Rim along another series of steep, metal steps. Complete the loop by using the **South Rim Trail,** the Highway 441 suspension bridge above Tallulah Falls Dam, and the **North Rim Trail** to return to the visitors center.

An alternative way to access the gorge floor is **Sliding Rock Trail,** which starts from the South Wallenda Tower, erected for Karl Wallenda's epic 1970 tightrope walk across Tallulah Gorge. Sliding Rock is only a quarter mile (0.4 km) one way, but it descends 500 feet (150 m) at a 45-degree angle. At the bottom are **Bridal Veil Falls** and a natural rock pool that's the only place in the gorge that's safe for swimming.

Hikers descending into the gorge must obtain a free permit from the Interpretive Center before striking off. Only 100 first-come, first-served permits are issued each day as a precaution against overuse. Hikers must have proper footwear to obtain a permit (no flip-flops, sandals, or Crocs). Given the sketchy surface conditions—metal steps on the Hurricane, boulders on Sliding Rock—the gorge trails are closed in rainy or snowy weather.

Those who aren't game for the vertical challenge can stroll the rim trails to numerous viewpoints that

Skilled paddlers take on the churning rapids of the Chattooga River during an aesthetic water release.

Hike the Hurricane Falls Trail at Tallulah Gorge State Park for epic views from the suspension bridge.

afford spectacular views down into the chasm. Tallulah Gorge State Park also features campsites, picnic areas, archery, tennis, and swimming or fishing in **Tallulah Falls Lake** behind the dam. There's also boating on big **Lake Tugalo** below the gorge, and radical white-water rafting on the nearby **Chattooga River,** the first federally designated wild and scenic waterway east of the Mississippi.

One of the best times to hike the gorge is during **"aesthetic water releases"** and **"whitewater boating weekends,"** when water is released from the dam and the river runs at full, raging capacity below the suspension bridge. Only highly skilled paddlers are allowed to kayak the river during these special events.

Tallulah Gorge is also awesome for hikers with an interest in rare plants and animals. The canyon's distinctive topography sustains several ecosystems and rare, protected species like the persistent trillium, hairy mock orange, monkey-face orchid, and green salamander.

The campaign to save northern Georgia's wild rivers inspired James Dickey to write *Deliverance,* later made into a movie (starring Burt Reynolds and Jon Voight) with key scenes filmed at Tallulah Gorge. ■

OTHER GREAT TRAILS

• **Raven Cliffs Falls:** Chattahoochee National Forest provides the setting for a five-mile (8-km) out-and-back hike up Dodd Creek to a 40-foot (12-m) cascade plunging down a granite face.

• **West Rim Loop:** Tucked in the state's northwest corner near Lookout Mountain, this 4.8-mile (7.7-km) lollipop trail runs along the edge and into a 1,000-foot (300-m) gorge in Cloudland Canyon State Park.

• **Parallel Trail:** Shaded by a canopy of ancient oaks, the 15.2-mile (24-km) main path across Cumberland Island National Seashore features wildlife-rich ponds and palmetto thickets, and access to unspoiled Atlantic beaches.

Visit Tallulah Falls, Georgia, during autumn for a vibrant show of peak fall color.

Mountains-to-Sea Trail
North Carolina

From the Appalachians to the Atlantic, this ambitious cross-state trail covers just about every type of North Carolina landscape, from remote mountain hollows and charming Piedmont villages to the high-tech Triangle, the state's agricultural heartland, and wave-splashed Outer Banks.

It's surprising that more coastal states haven't jumped on the bandwagon of blazing a long-distance trail from their inland mountains all the way to the sea. Because North Carolina has given them the perfect template: a route stretching nearly 1,200 miles (1,930 km) between Great Smoky Mountains National Park in the west and Cape Hatteras National Seashore in the east.

Only around 700 miles (1,130 km) of the **Mountains-to-Sea Trail** (MST) are completed. Between the already finished sections, the route rambles down back roads and bicycle paths that may not be as traffic-free as footpaths, but in many cases they're just as scenic.

Hikers can start at either end. But setting off from the west affords a glaringly obvious advantage: Much

more of the trek is downhill. And you're setting off from one of the most spectacular places on the East Coast—**Clingmans Dome.** The 6,643-foot (2,025-m) peak in **Great Smoky Mountains National Park** is the third highest point in eastern North America. As if that's not enough, hike to the modern, flying saucer–shaped observation tower to gaze at the misty landscape that gives the mountains their smoky name.

Clingmans is also the highest point along the entire **Appalachian Trail.** The MST tags along with that more famous trail for only a short while before plunging downhill on a 22.8-mile (36-km) trek through the Smoky Mountain wilderness that's the longest stretch of the entire trail without vehicle access. Past the park's **Oconaluftee Visitor Center,** the trail passes through the **Qualla Boundary** lands of the Cherokee people at the start of a long and winding segment that it shares with the **Blue Ridge Parkway.**

Continuing along the parkway, the MST climbs into **Pisgah National Forest** and its famous mountaintop restaurant before skirting around the eastern edge of **Asheville.** The artsy city is a great place to break the journey for a couple of days before another climb brings hikers to the base of **Mount**

The 156-foot (48-m) Bodie Island Lighthouse is one of only a dozen brick tower lighthouses remaining in the entire United States, complete with an original Fresnel lens.

Take the Mountains-to-Sea Section 4 route for this glimpse of Linville Gorge in Pisgah National Forest.

Mitchell, highest point east of the Mississippi River at 6,684 feet (2,037 m).

Yet the vertical challenge is far from over. After navigating the lower end of **Linville Gorge** (one of several southern chasms that call themselves the "Grand Canyon of the East"), the trail soars up and over **Beacon Heights.** Reaching **Boone,** hikers can dive deep into Appalachian lore at **Hickory Ridge Living History Museum** or bluegrass music at **Jones House, Mast General Store,** and other venues.

Finally bidding adieu to the Blue Ridge Parkway in **Stone Mountain State Park,** the MST descends into the **Piedmont** region via the **Yadkin Valley** and North Carolina's first American Viticultural Area. **Stony Knoll, Haze Gray,** and **Carolina Heritage** are three of the vineyards

that trekkers can visit between **Elkin** and the riverside portion of **Pilot Mountain State Park.**

Rather than following a straight line that would take hikers through the relatively flat but highly urbanized

terrain of **Winston-Salem** and **Greensboro,** the trail curves around the northern edge of the cities via the **Sauratown Mountains** and **Hanging Rock State Park.** Much of the 124-mile (200-km) stretch

DETOURS

- **Biltmore Estate:** The first Gilded Age comes into full focus at this Asheville mansion, built in the 1890s and still the nation's largest privately owned home.

- **Guilford Courthouse National Military Park:** Yorktown may have ended the American Revolution, but the Battle of Guilford Courthouse near Greensboro was the clash that laid the groundwork for the final British defeat.

- **NASCAR Hall of Fame:** From Red Byron and Richard Petty to Dale Earnhardt, Sr. and Jr., the legends of American stock car racing are honored in Charlotte.

- **Raleigh Museums:** North Carolina's capital city boasts excellent collections of art, nature, and state history.

- **Kitty Hawk:** Wright Brothers National Memorial preserves the seaside spot where Wilbur and Orville achieved the first heavier-than-air powered flight in 1903.

between Hanging Rock and **Durham** is along road shoulders and sidewalks through small towns, farmland, and satellite cities of the big urban areas.

Eno River State Park marks the start of a long foot-only path that meanders along the south shore of **Falls Lake.** The trail uses the 27.5-mile (44-km) **Neuse River Greenway** to slip between **Raleigh** and **Wake Forest.** Leaving the big cities in the proverbial dust, the MST is once again flanked by pastoral countryside.

Reaching **Smithfield,** hikers have an opportunity to shortcut their way to the Carolina coast by paddling down the **Neuse River** on a 170-mile (273-km) water trail that flows past **Cliffs of the Neuse State Park** and throwback towns like **New Bern** with its four historic districts. During the six days it takes to canoe or kayak the route, the river evolves from a narrow, swift-flowing watercourse into a wide, slow-moving tidal estuary. The paddle trail ends near **Havelock** and an easy segue back onto the land portion of the MST.

Frog Hollow Outdoors in Durham offers a complete start-to-finish Neuse Paddle Trail package that includes shuttle service, canoes or kayaks, and other equipment necessary to make the water passage. In future years, the trail overseers hope to complete a hiking path running alongside the Neuse between Smithfield and Havelock.

South of Smithfield, the terrestrial MST runs through **Howell Woods Environmental Learning Center** and **Bentonville**

Carolina rhododendrons cling to the cliffside in the Linville Gorge Wilderness.

Battlefield, where North Carolina's largest clash of the Civil War played out. Beyond is the state's agricultural heartland, the trail flanked by soybean, sweet potato, tobacco, and cotton fields. Starting a slow bend toward the coast, the route runs through **Carolina Bay Country,** an unusual landscape dotted with elliptical ponds and depressions called "bays" oriented in northwest-southeast rows. Tucked among the bays is **White Lake,** an old-fashioned resort town with water sports, carnival rides, miniature golf, and a **Water Festival** each May.

The MST finally reaches the ocean at **Surf City,** the start of a nine-mile (14.5-km) beach walk beside the Atlantic whitecaps. However, this flirtation with the sea is short lived because the route swings inland through **Croatan National Forest.** Although fairly small as national forests go, Croatan boasts an incredible variety of ecosystems,

including piney woods and pocosin wetlands. Beyond Havelock (and the downstream end of the paddle trail), the route joins the long-established **Neusiok Trail** across a patch of Croatan National Forest to another rendezvous with the sea at **Oyster Point.**

Hikers reach the **Outer Banks** on a 2.5-hour vehicle and passenger ferry from Cedar Point to folksy Ocracoke village. Most of the final 82 miles (132 km) of the MST is along beaches in **Cape Hatteras National Seashore.** There's another ferry between Ocracoke and Hatteras Islands, and a couple of bridges to cross, but otherwise it's a flat, breezy walk beside the sea with numerous chances to take a dip or overnight. The Mountain-to-Sea comes to a dramatic end at **Jockey's Ridge State Park,** where the tallest dunes on the Atlantic coast rise above the place where the **Wright brothers** made their famous first flight. ∎

LAY YOUR HEAD

- **Bon Paul & Sharky's Hostel:** Having accomplished the tough roller-coaster hike through the Smoky Mountains, chill out for a couple of days and meet other young travelers at this international backpacker hostel on Asheville's west side; from $22; bonpauland sharkys.com.

- **Stone Mountain State Park:** Find primitive backpack camping beside Widow's Creek and tent camping in a developed campground with tent pads, picnic tables, fire rings, shade, and hot showers; from $12; ncparks.gov/stone-mountain-state-park/camping.

- **Hanging Rock State Park:** Cozy two-bedroom cabins that can sleep as many as six hikers include fully

equipped kitchen, barbecue grill, private bathroom, heating and air conditioning; from $98; ncparks.gov/hanging-rock-state-park/camping.

- **Eno River State Park:** Take a dip in the slow-flowing Eno and sack out at dedicated backpacker campgrounds at Fanny's Ford and Cole Mill in a state park near Durham and Chapel Hill; from $12; ncparks.gov/eno-river-state-park/camping.

- **Howell Woods Environmental Learning Center:** Sleeping four to 16 people, these cabins with kitchens, private bathrooms, and front porches are tucked into pine woods near Bentonville and its Civil War battlefield; from $60; johnstoncc.edu/howellwoods.

Kennesaw Mountain Loop
Georgia

One of the nation's best battlefield trails loops through a mixed oak, hickory, and pine forest to historic sites that recall General Sherman's unrelenting "March to the Sea."

THE BIG PICTURE

Distance: 17.4 miles (28 km)

Elevation Gain: approx. 2,220 feet (680 m)

Time: 5–7 hours

Difficulty: Moderate to strenuous

Best Time: Year-round

More Info: nps.gov/kemo

The clash took place in the summer of 1864, more than 30,000 troops thrown together on a wooded ridge in northwest Georgia. It was a last chance for Rebel forces to keep Gen. William Tecumseh Sherman from capturing Atlanta and driving a stake into the heart of the Confederacy.

Although the South prevailed at Kennesaw Mountain, it was a pyrrhic victory because shortly after they were forced to abandon the city as Sherman continued his brutal scorched-earth march across Georgia. By the early 20th century, the battle-scarred forest had largely regenerated and the ridge became **Kennesaw Mountain National Battlefield Park.**

The nation's second most visited battlefield park after Gettysburg, Kennesaw offers a rich variety of native plants and both resident and migratory songbirds. A dense network of trails penetrates a landscape that alternates between thick woods, grassy meadows, and rocky mounts where the battle played out in 1864.

Ten of the park's trails are less than three miles (4.8 km) in length and ideal for walks of a couple hours or less. But hikers who want to maximize their experience in terms of exercise, history, and terrain opt for the 17.4-mile (28-km) **Kennesaw Mountain Loop,** which ranges all the way across the elongated park and back. Anyone trekking the route for the first time should start at the northern end, where the National Park Service **visitors center** provides maps and the latest trail and weather conditions.

Hikers can strike off along either side of the loop. But the western side is the one that starts with a bang: a 650-foot (200-m) climb to the summit of **Kennesaw Mountain** with its views across the battlefield and northwest Georgia. Artillery pieces and information boards show where the Rebel troops were dug in.

The trail rambles over **Little Kennesaw Mountain** and **Pigeon Hill,** where Confederate forces repelled one of the Union's major attacks on June 27, 1864. Today's thick woods and steep rocky slopes reflect the inhospitable terrain that must have been as

Union and Confederate soldiers clashed at this spot on Kennesaw Mountain in 1864.

A cannon from the Civil War overlooks Kennesaw Mountain National Battlefield Park.

much of a challenge as Rebel guns.

Crossing Burnt Hickory Road, the trail continues across **Noses Creek** and ambles down **Old John Ward Road** to the former site of Sherman's headquarters during the battle. Marking the southern end of the loop are **Kolb's Farm** and a small cemetery. The stout farmhouse served as a Union field hospital and is the only structure in the park that survives from the Civil War.

Making an about-face at Kolb's Farm, hikers return to their starting point via an eastern leg that includes a climb up **Cheatham Hill,** where the fiercest fighting of the entire battle took place. Rebel earthworks and memorials like the **Illinois Monument** mark the so-called "Dead Angle," where so many Union troops perished. ∎

APRÈS HIKE

• **Gone With the Wind Museum:** Marietta's historic Brumby Hall pays homage to the classic tale through Margaret Mitchell memorabilia, the bengaline honeymoon gown worn by Vivien Leigh (as Scarlett O'Hara), and other relics of the book and movie.

• **Earl and Rachel Smith Strand Theatre:** Movie sing-alongs, silent films, live musicals, comedy, and tribute bands are the delights of a restored Marietta picture house that opened in 1935.

• **Aviation History & Technology Center:** Perched on the edge of Dobbins Air Reserve Base and the Lockheed Martin factory, this small but fascinating aviation collection exhibits vintage fighter jets, cargo planes, and civilian aircraft.

• **Zuckerman Museum of Art:** Wrapped inside a modern glass shell at Kennesaw State University, the museum highlights the sculptures of Ruth V. Zuckerman and houses the college's permanent collection.

• **Cobb Antique Mall:** More than 100 vendors hawk a vast array of goods both old and new at this indoor warren of crafts and keepsakes just 15 minutes from the battlefield visitors center.

Fiery Gizzard Trail
Tennessee

This red-hot hiking route in south-central Tennessee offers a rugged journey along a gorge shaded by old-growth forest and cooled by numerous waterfalls, pools, and streams.

The name alone is enough to pencil this Tennessee trail on your bucket list. What exactly is a fiery gizzard? It's the name of the creek that carved the gorge that carries the trail through a slice of primeval wilderness in **South Cumberland State Park.**

Various stories purport to explain how the creek got its name, ranging from a cantankerous 19th-century blast furnace and Cherokee legend to a tall tale about frontiersman Davy Crockett burning his tongue on a turkey gizzard and tossing the offending organ into the gorge.

If that's not enough to lure potential hikers, consider that *Backpacker* magazine has rated the **Fiery Gizzard Trail** as one of

THE BIG PICTURE

Distance: 12.5 miles (20 km)

Elevation Gain: approx. 1,500 feet (460 m)

Time: 1–2 days

Difficulty: Strenuous

Best Time: Any time of year

More Info: tnstateparks.com/parks/info/south-cumberland

the nation's top 25 hiking trails.

The nearby Smoky Mountains may have higher summits and deeper valleys, but few of its trails (including the Appalachian) can match the utter ruggedness of the Fiery Gizzard. Strewn with waterfalls, caverns, springs, rock formations, and 500-year-old trees, it's easy to imagine the Cherokee or Crockett tramping the gorge in days of yore.

Thru-hikers can start at either end. However, the route also lends itself to two out-and-back hikes with Raven Point as the turnaround spot. It's also possible to undertake the trail as a two-day hike with an overnight at several primitive campsites along the route. No matter what: Be sure to pack a swimsuit (or not) for a dip in the refreshing pools beneath several falls.

About a 40-minute drive from **Chattanooga,** formidable **Foster Falls** marks the southern end of the trail with a 60-foot (18-m) plunge off the escarpment and a zigzag descent into the gorge. Those who want to get an ultra-early start can overnight at the campground above the falls.

The first few miles of the hike follow **Little Gizzard Creek** through a **Small Wild Area** that was earmarked for environmental preservation by the Tennessee Valley Authority (TVA) in the 1970s. In

Hikers will find the 60-foot (18-m) drop of Foster Falls at the southern end of Fiery Gizzard Trail.

The gentle waters of Sycamore Falls along the Fiery Gizzard Trail in South Cumberland State Park

addition to its hemlock and mountain laurel trees, the area safeguards rare plants like the monkey-face orchid *(Platanthera integrilabia)* and fame flower *(Talinum teretifolium).*

Beyond the **Small Wild campground** on **Laurel Branch** creek, the path rises to the **Cumberland Plateau** and a long stretch beside the gorge's east rim. Roughly 7.5 miles (12 km) from the start, the trail reaches **Anderson Falls** and a short spur to the lofty overlook at **Raven Point.**

From Raven Point, hikers have a choice of continuing another three miles (4.8 km) along the rim via the **Dog Hole Trail** or descending to the bottom of the gorge for a tough, rock-strewn

ramble up **Big Fiery Gizzard Creek.**

The two routes converge at the swimming hole beneath **Sycamore Falls.** It's a great place to chill out before a final push up **Little Fiery**

Gizzard Creek and its almost endless series of rapids and small waterfalls to the **Grundy Forest** trailhead at the north end of the Fiery Gizzard. ■

OTHER GREAT TRAILS

- **Virgin Falls Trail:** Another deep gorge in the Cumberland Plateau harbors a strenuous route to the trail's 110-foot (33.5-m)-high namesake.

- **Volunteer Trail:** Located on the eastern outskirts of Nashville, this 10.7-mile (17-km) out-and-back route hugs the shore of Percy Priest Lake in Long Hunter State Park.

- **Honey Creek Loop:** Don't let the short length (5.5 miles/8.8 km) fool

you—even the rangers think this steep, narrow, boulder-strewn trail is the toughest hike in Big South Fork National River and Recreation Area.

- **Cumberland River Greenway:** This 10.2-mile (16-km) route through central Nashville winds along the south bank between Ted Rhodes Park and Lower Broadway, where it leaps the river on a pedestrian bridge to Cumberland Park and Nissan Stadium.

Florida Trail
Florida

Crank back the clock to the Sunshine State of long ago on a trail that shies away from bays and beaches but plunges deep into the forests, glades, prairies, and ranchlands that infuse so many of Florida's inland areas.

THE BIG PICTURE

Distance: approx. 1,500 miles (2,410 km)

Elevation Gain: Negligible

Time: 2–3 months

Difficulty: Moderate to strenuous

Best Time: Late fall to early spring

More Info: floridatrail.org and fs.usda.gov/fnst

With one of the nation's longest coastlines, it seems almost impossible that hikers could trek clear across Florida and only briefly walk along a beach. But the 1,500-mile (2,410-km) **Florida Trail** proves the Sunshine State is a lot more than just sea and sand.

Stretching from the subtropical Everglades to the pinelands and wiregrass wilderness of the panhandle, the route offers a throwback to the Florida of long ago, when wetlands, woodlands, and ranches—rather than theme parks, subdivisions, and beach resorts—ruled the landscape.

One of 11 national scenic trails, the sinuous track was cobbled together from existing footpaths, rail trails, unpaved country roads, and levees, as well as street, highway, and sidewalk connectors, when it was first established in the 1960s. Since then, a basket of public and private entities, working closely with the Florida Trail Association, have endeavored to blaze new sections with the aim of making the entire route motor free.

Weather is one of the biggest considerations for thru-hikers. Winter offers the best temperatures for hiking the entire route, but there can also be the occasional freeze (of the type that spoils orange crops). Given humidity and daytime temperatures in the 90s along the entire route, summer is best avoided. Not to mention the fact that hurricane season runs from June to November. That means late winter and spring are undoubtedly the best times to trek the Florida Trail from start to finish.

Like many other long-distance routes, the Florida Trail is blessed with "trail angels" eager to aid and abet thru-hikers and official gateway communities (like St. Marks, White Springs, Inverness, and Okeechobee) where trekkers can find hotels, restaurants, and stores to recharge and resupply.

Situated 60 miles (96 km) west of **Miami** along the Tamiami Trail (U.S. 41), the southern end of the trail lies beside **Oasis Visitor Center** in **Big Cypress National Preserve.** Sprawling across an area larger than Rhode Island, the preserve safeguards a massive freshwater swamp and associated ecosystems. Among the many inhabitants are the Florida panther, black bear, alligators, river otters, sandhill cranes, and ghost orchid. This most remote stretch of the entire Florida Trail runs 36 miles

Traditional basket weaving is just one of Florida's historic crafts that visitors can learn about at Stephen Foster Folk Culture Center State Park.

Winding some 1,300 miles (2,090 km) through the state, Florida's Big Cypress National Preserve protects the freshwater swamp and its ecosystems.

(58 km) across the heart of the preserve through hardwood hammocks, pinelands, and subtropical prairie. During the wet season between May and November, parts of the trail can be flooded.

Exiting the preserve, hikers follow the trail's distinctive orange blazes across the **Big Cypress Seminole Indian Reservation** and then elevated levees through the grassy wetlands south of **Lake Okeechobee.**

Reaching tiny Lake Harbor, the route splits into east and west branches of the **Lake Okeechobee Scenic Trail** (LOST). Much of the lakeside path sits atop the **Herbert Hoover Dike,** a massive earthen barrage that surrounds the state's largest lake. Both paths are roughly the same length (about 54 miles/87 km)

but the western route includes the gateway communities of **Clewiston** and **Moore Haven.** When portions

of the dike are closed for renovation, check for alternate road routes at floridatrail.org.

DETOURS

• **Everglades National Park:** Due south of Big Cypress, Florida's largest nature reserve offers hiking and paddling trails, coastal campgrounds, and plenty of swamp critters.

• **Orlando:** Whether your favorite character is Mickey Mouse or Harry Potter, hikers with a guilty passion for theme parks can connect with their inner child at half a dozen fantasy worlds in O-Town.

• **Palatka:** This Florida Trail gateway community on the St. Johns River is renowned for its many murals, the rustic tropical architecture of Ravine

Gardens, and the North Historic District with its 76 vintage structures.

• **Olustee Battlefield:** The state's largest clash of the Civil War played out among the pines of this historic state park near Lake City in far northern Florida.

• **St. Marks National Wildlife Refuge:** Just outside the eponymous town, this pristine preserve revolves around salt marshes and Florida's second oldest lighthouse; among its many denizens are alligators, bald eagles, frosted flatwoods salamanders, and monarch butterflies.

Beyond Okeechobee, the trail follows the **Kissimmee River** into the lake district of central Florida. Ironically, the region is also home to the nation's second largest expanse of dry prairie. Arriving at the **Three Lakes Wildlife Management Area,** hikers are confronted with another fork in the road, branches of the Florida Trail that offer distinctly different terrain and adventures.

The **Western Corridor** slips into **Kissimmee** on the southern edge of Orlando and the huge **Disney** complex. Skirting around the metro area, the route goes wilderness again in the wetlands and pinelands of the great **Green Swamp** while snaking through the copious water bodies of **Withlacoochee State Forest** before a walk along the **Cross Florida Greenway** to Ocala National Forest.

Heading the other way around Orlando, the **Eastern Corridor** uses a combination of footpaths and roads to reach the **St. Johns River** watershed near **Cape Canaveral.** Tacking to the northwest, the trail passes through **Little Big Econ State Forest** before breezing into **Oviedo,** a trail gateway community with free-range chickens and a popular farmers market that offers a charming small-town alternative to thrill-packed Orlando.

Not long after gliding into **Ocala National Forest,** the eastern and western arms of the Florida Trail meet again. With numerous campgrounds and recreational opportunities—and a chance to cool off at several freshwater springs—the national forest is a great place to sojourn before striking out on the second half of the trail.

Watch for alligators sunning themselves amid the foliage at Big Cypress National Preserve.

SHORT CIRCUITS

- **Big Cypress Round-Trip:** Tramp the southernmost portion of the Florida Trail on a 19.4-mile (31.2-km) out-and-back path through pine groves and sawgrass prairie to 10 Mile Camp in Big Cypress National Preserve.

- **Lake Okeechobee Scenic Trail:** Hike the dike that encircles Florida's largest inland water body on a multiuse path that can be accessed at dozens of spots around the lakeshore.

- **Cross Seminole Trail:** The onetime route of the Sanford and Indian River Railroad is now a popular 23-mile (37-km) rail trail along a portion of the Florida Trail between Oviedo, Winter Springs, and Lake Mary.

- **Alexander Springs-Juniper Springs:** Ocala National Forest provides a woodsy setting for a 17.4-mile (28-km) section of the Florida Trail that connects to two Forest Service recreation areas with freshwater swimming holes.

- **Blackwater South:** A 30-mile (48-km) spur of the Florida Trail near Pensacola runs through the wetlands, woodland, and clay hills of Blackwater River State Park and State Forest.

Beyond the national forest, the trail swings west along the 47-mile (76-km) **Palatka-Lake Butler** (PLB) rail trail. Just below the Florida-Georgia border, the route traverses the flatwoods and swamps of **Osceola National Forest** on its way to **White Springs.** One of the state's oldest American towns (founded in 1831), it flaunts a wealth of Victorian architecture from the days when White Springs was a fashionable health and wellness resort. Dedicated to the composer of "Old Folks at Home" (aka "Swanee

River"), the town's **Stephen Foster Folk Culture Center** hosts the world's largest tubular bell carillon and the Florida Folk Festival over Memorial Day weekend.

After crossing the **Suwannee River** into the **Florida Panhandle,** the trail follows a series of country roads to the **Wacissa-Aucilla** watershed, a marine protected area that's also popular with paddlers. A nonmotorized trail across this stretch is on the drawing board, an alternative that would follow the **Steinhatchee River** to the **Gulf Coast** and the remote **Big Bend** region.

West of the **Wacissa River,** the trail ambles through the town of **St. Marks,** renowned for both its autumn **Stone Crab Festival** and the manatees that migrate up the nearby **Wakulla River** each winter. Sneaking inland again just south of **Tallahassee,** the route crosses **Apalachicola National Forest** with its longleaf pines, hardwood hammocks, sandy flatlands, and black-water streams stained by tannins.

The **Blountstown Greenway** takes the route deeper into the panhandle, where it crosses **Econfina Creek** on the **Two Penny and Fender** suspension bridges before a long trek around the outer edge of **Elgin Air Force Base.** A whiff of salt water and seaweed alerts hikers to the fact that the ocean looms just ahead.

Leaping **Santa Rosa Sound** on the **Navarre Beach Causeway,** the trail begins a 27-mile (43-km) homestretch through **Gulf Islands National Seashore** that offers plenty of scope for sun, sea, and sand. **Fort Pickens** (completed in 1834) marks the northern end of the Florida Trail. From there, it's just a short hike into **Pensacola** and its transportation links to the rest of the nation. ■

The Florida Trail skirts the state line at Osceola National Forest, winding through swamplands on its way to the historic town of White Springs.

Bartram Trail
North Carolina & Georgia

This under-the-radar trail over the mountains and through the backwoods of North Carolina and Georgia pays tribute to one of the country's first naturalists.

THE BIG PICTURE

Distance: 115 miles (185 km)

Elevation Change: approx. 21,000 feet (6,400 m)

Time: 5–6 days

Difficulty: Strenuous

Best Time: Year-round

More Info: blueridgebartram .org/the-bartram-trail and gabartramtrail.org

Long before John James Audubon wandered the region with paint and easel or John Muir made his "Thousand-Mile Walk" to the Gulf of Mexico, another American naturalist roamed the American South. His name was William Bartram, a Philadelphia botanist and ornithologist who spent the better part of four years (1773–77) traveling lands that would later become eight southern states.

Despite penning one of the 18th-century's classic travel books, Bartram's name was largely lost in history until the 1970s. That's when a group of modern admirers decided the best way to preserve his legacy—and introduce Bartram's feats to a nation that was just starting to discover long-distance hiking—was to blaze and name a trail in his honor.

Bartram's most epic feat was a solo exploration of the Cherokee Nation at a time when it was dangerous for even a group of Europeans to venture into the western wilds of Britain's Carolinas and Georgia colonies. The **Bartram Trail** traces a portion of his risky but rewarding journey, a 115-mile (185-km) route through the southern Appalachians.

Readers of *Backpacker* magazine once chose it as the nation's best long-distance trail for solitude, an honor that made one veteran Bartram trekker wonder who had voted for it, because so few people even knew about its existence. These days the route isn't quite so obscure. Still, anyone who thinks that hiking the **Appalachian Trail** (AT) is a lonely pursuit should spend a few days tramping the Bartram.

Hikers actually need to walk a short section of the AT through **Nantahala National Forest** in western North Carolina to reach the northern terminus of the Bartram Trail at the summit of **Cheoah Bald.** The route kicks off with a 3,000-foot (910-m) plunge into the **Nantahala River Gorge** and big **Nantahala Lake,** where a cluster of lakeside cabins provides a temporary respite from dispersed camping along the route.

Leaving the lake behind, the

Hikers yearning for rejuvenating solitude should seek out the Bartram Trail, accessible via a short trek through the Appalachian Trail.

The splendor of sunrise is worth the early morning efforts to reach Wayah Bald and Tower in Nantahala National Forest.

trail climbs to **Wayah Bald,** the highest point along the Bartram at 5,385 feet (1,641 m). Erected in 1937 by the Civilian Conservation Corps, the summit's **stone lookout tower** affords broad views across the southern Appalachians. The trail drops into the farm-filled **Little Tennessee River Valley** and slips through **Franklin** on city streets before ascending again into the roadless highlands.

Hopscotching across **Wolf Rock, Fishhawk Mountain, Jones Knob,** and half a dozen other peaks, the Bartram makes its way down to the Georgia state line. The border also marks the route's transition from the Nantahala to **Chattahoochee National Forest.** The trail climbs up and over **Rabun Bald**—where hikers can peer down on the mountains from another tall fire tower—before a final segment via **Warwoman Dell** that takes the route to **Russell Bridge** on the **Chattooga River.** ■

OTHER GREAT TRAILS

Bartram Canoe Trail

Meandering 200 miles (320 km) through the Mobile-Tensaw Delta of southern Alabama, the **Bartram Canoe Trail** is one of the nation's longest and most intriguing paddle routes. The delta embraces a wide array of typical southern ecosystems, from cypress-tupelo swamps and hardwood-shaded bottomlands to bayous, estuarine marshes, and oxbow lakes.

Trail namesake William Bartram explored these same waters during the summer of 1775, visiting the Creek people and sketching flora and fauna. Some of those species are now among the area's 50 rare and endangered plants and animals.

The watery route features six separate day-use and six overnight routes with floating platform shelters that can accommodate up to eight people each. Six landings along the eastern side of the delta between Stockton and Tensaw provide easy canoe/kayak access to the trail. Platform reservations are available on the Alabama State Lands Division website (alabamacanoetrails.com/bartram).

Florida Keys Overseas Heritage Trail
Florida

Cruise the length of the Florida Keys along a new hiking/biking trail with overnight stops at island state parks along a historic route between Key Largo and Key West.

This sun-splashed route across the **Florida Keys** gives a whole new meaning to island-hopping, a way to hike or bike your way between Key Largo and Key West without battling the notoriously heavy traffic on U.S. Highway 1.

The "heritage" in the name derives from the fact that the multiuse trail follows the route pioneered by the Florida Overseas Railroad between 1912 and 1935 and the Florida Overseas Highway that opened in 1928. Making its way down the chain, the **Florida Keys Overseas Heritage Trail** (FKOHT) flows across 23 historic railroad bridges.

THE BIG PICTURE

Distance: 90 miles (145 km)

Elevation Gain: approx. 180 feet (60 m)

Time: 4–6 days

Difficulty: Easy

Best Time: Winter, spring, or fall

More Info: floridastateparks
.org/parks-and-trails/florida
-keys-overseas-heritage-trail

Roughly 90 miles (145 km) of the proposed 106-mile (170-km) length is finished. Because so much of the trail runs right beside **Highway 1,** bikers might find the route more user-friendly than hikers. There's also the question of where to overnight. The islands are flush with motels, hotels, and rental units. But there are only half a dozen spots to erect a tent.

One of those camping spots—**John Pennekamp Coral Reef State Park** on Key Largo—is a great place to start for those doing the trail from north to south. Consider scuba diving or snorkeling the reef to see awesome tropical fish before setting off down the trail.

The first leg of the FKOHT between Key Largo and **Long Key State Park** is the longest and toughest of the entire route, 35 miles (56 km) between campgrounds, which is easy enough for bikers but a very long day for those on their feet. Hikers can cut the leg in half by hopping on a shuttle or ride-share farther down the chain or splurging on a motel room or vacation rental on one of the **Matecumbe Keys.** Overnighting affords the option of a guided boat tour to **Lignumvitae Key Botanical State Park** with its lush native vegetation, or of renting a kayak for a half-day paddle to

After conquering the Bahia Honda to Key West route of the Florida Keys Overseas Heritage Trail, thirsty hikers can recuperate with a drink along Duval Street.

Jellyfish are just one marine creature protected as part of Florida Keys National Marine Sanctuary.

Indian Key Historic State Park and the remains of an island town that once thrived on treasure hunting and shipwreck salvaging.

Much of the trail between Long Key and **Curry Hammock State Park** (11.7 miles/18.8 km) rides bridges and causeways between Florida Bay and the Florida Strait. One of the largest protected areas in the archipelago, Curry is renowned for bird-watching in the shoreline mangroves or tropical hardwood "hammocks" that give the island its name.

Another waterfront campground awaits at **Bahia Honda State Park** (19 miles/32 km) but not before you traverse busy **Marathon** town and across the new **Seven Mile Bridge.** At some point, gaps in the historic old bridge will be filled,

making it much easier for hikers and bikers to make the passage. Bahia Honda preserves a hurricane-battered railroad bridge and several white-sand beaches.

Bahia Honda to Key West is another brutal stretch for hikers (35 miles/56 km) that can be divided into two days by overnighting

at **Sugarloaf Key KOA** or a **Cudjoe Key** vacation rental. The FKOHT gets increasingly urban as it approaches **Key West.** Thirsty hikers and bikers can make a beeline for the bars along **Duval Street** or opt for a siesta at **Boyd's Key West Campground,** the city's only tent-friendly digs. ■

APRÈS HIKE

• **Dry Tortugas:** Ride the *Yankee Freedom* ferry or Key West Sea-planes to one of the nation's most remote national parks for a day of beach, bird-watching, and historic Fort Jefferson.

• **Sailing the Keys:** Spend a few hours under canvas on a day sail

or sunset cruise aboard a modern Sebago catamaran or the vintage two-masted schooner *Appledore*.

• **Mangrove Discovery:** Launch into a guided kayak or paddleboard tour of the thick mangroves around Geiger Key with Key West Eco Tours.

High Bridge Trail
Virginia

March across an architectural landmark and through a small but significant slice of Civil War history on a trail through Virginia's heartland.

THE BIG PICTURE

Distance: 31 miles (50 km)

Elevation Change: approx. 1,000 feet (300 m)

Time: 1–2 days

Difficulty: Easy

Best Time: Year-round

More Info: dcr.virginia.gov/state -parks/high-bridge-trail

America's rail trails cross thousands of bridges and trestles, but how many can claim they were the focus of a crucial Civil War battle?

Not just history attracts hikers and bikers to this route. There's also the glorious countryside of south-central Virginia, a spectacle that's especially handsome in the spring and fall. With an influx of Amish migrants from Pennsylvania in recent decades, the region also offers cultural appeal. Being a rail trail, it's universally flat and easy.

Users don't even have to travel the whole route to cross the lofty **High Bridge.** Rising 125 feet (38 m) above the **Appomattox River** and spanning half a mile (0.8 km), the bridge was completed in 1854 as part of a Southside Railroad line connecting **Lynchburg** and **Petersburg.** During the Civil War, it was part of a vital supply line for Confederate forces.

As the Rebels staged their final retreat in April 1965, Union forces tried to destroy the bridge to prevent Robert E. Lee's army from fleeing across the span. Confederate troops saved the viaduct during a bloody skirmish that resulted in hundreds of casualties. The following day the Confederates themselves were ordered to burn the span to keep the enemy from advancing, but a furious Union charge across the bridge once again saved the High Bridge for posterity.

A 15-minute drive from **Farmville,** the historic wooden viaduct is part of **High Bridge Trail State Park.** Those who just want to stroll the span should park at **Camp Paradise trailhead.** From there, it's just a 0.3-mile (0.5-km) walk to the bridge's east end. Benches beneath a shade structure are perched about halfway across. A short side trail leads to the remains of Civil War–era **Camp Paradise,** earthwork fortifications manned by the 43 Louisiana Creole Canonniers during the Battle of High Bridge.

There are several options for anyone who wants to hike all or part of the trail. One of the easiest is a 9.4-mile (15-km) out-and-back trek from **Main Street** in downtown Farmville via the forested **Rochelle Tract** with its own network of hiking/biking trails.

Another option is trekking the

Visitors have numerous options for starting points on their way to the half-mile (0.8-km) High Bridge over the Appomattox River.

Listed on the National Register of Historic Places, High Bridge is the longest recreational bridge in the state of Virginia.

western and eastern ends of the High Bridge Trail on either side of Farmville. The western half extends 16.2 miles (26 km) to **Pamplin,** where **Mr. Bubbles Snack and Ice Cream Stand** offers milk shakes, sundaes, and other frozen treats for those who complete the march. The town is also home to the remains of the old **Pamplin Pipe Factory,** founded in 1879 and once the nation's largest clay pipe maker.

The eastern half of the trail includes the High Bridge and stretches 15 miles (24 km) from downtown Farmville to just above **Burkeville.** The **Rice Trail** is around the halfway point, near **Sailor's Creek Battlefield State Park,** where the last major engagement of the

Civil War unfolded at the same time as the High Bridge clash.

Those who crave a deeper dive into the history of the railroad that birthed the modern trail can visit the **Burke-ville Depot** and the nearby **Crewe**

Railroad Museum, which offers the chance to climb on a diesel engine, caboose, or steam engine, as well as see railroad artifacts and a display of the Crewe Roundhouse and trains of the steam era. ■

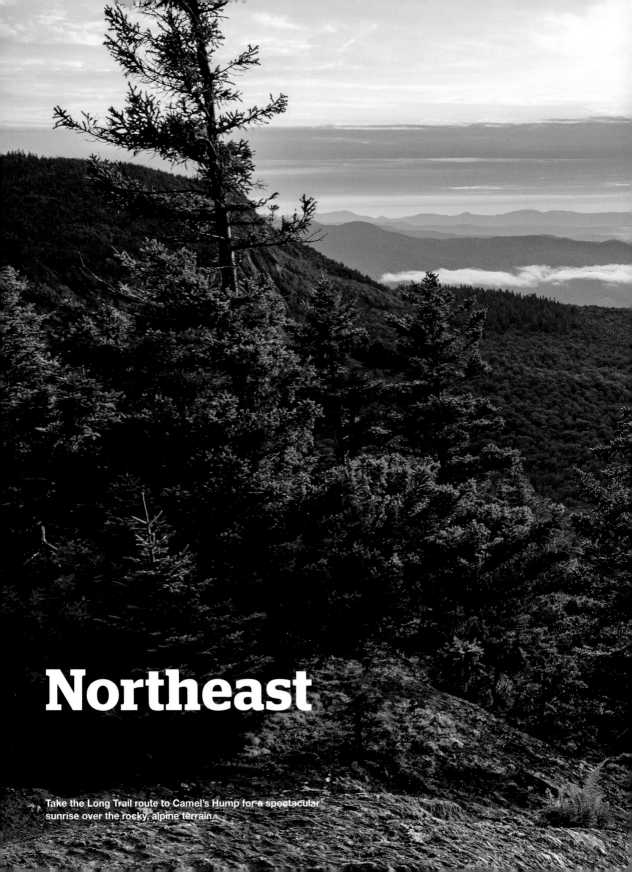

Northeast

Take the Long Trail route to Camel's Hump for a spectacular sunrise over the rocky, alpine terrain.

Great Allegheny Passage
Pennsylvania & Maryland

The Allegheny Highlands of western Pennsylvania and the Maryland panhandle provide the rugged terrain and historical backdrop for a mega-popular rail trail.

Much like Monopoly, this journey from Pittsburgh to the Potomac involves four railroads (one of them the Baltimore and Ohio of board game fame)—or rather their former right-of-ways. Because four rail trails provide the backbone of a popular route through the Allegheny Highlands.

The **Great Allegheny Passage** (GAP) is helping revitalize a region built on coal, steel, and timber that fell on hard times as those industries declined. That legacy is reflected in *The Deer Hunter*, the 1978 Oscar-winning film shot in Clairton, two miles (3.2 km) off the GAP near Pittsburgh.

Nearby McKeesport is one of 12 official trail towns along the route that welcome bikers and hikers with hot meals, cold drinks, overnight

THE BIG PICTURE

Distance: 150 miles (240 km)

Elevation Gain: approx. 7,500 feet (2,300 m)

Time: 6–10 days

Difficulty: Easy to moderate

Best Time: Late spring, summer, or early fall

More Info: gaptrail.org

digs, and a chance to learn a little about what makes these rural towns and cities tick.

The trail starts its southward journey at **Point State Park,** the triangular green space where the **Monongahela** and **Allegheny Rivers** meet to form the mighty **Ohio River** in downtown **Pittsburgh.** The park's **Fort Pitt Museum** and remnants of bastions built during the French and Indian War are reminders that the GAP runs through a region that was once a remote frontier area engulfed in a global struggle between two European empires.

Heading upstream through the heart of Pittsburgh, the trail uses the **Hot Metal Bridge** (built in 1887) to jump the Monongahela to **Homestead,** a onetime steel town that has reinvented itself in modern times as an entertainment hub with abundant bars and restaurants, a water park, a comedy club, and the **Rivers of Steel** heritage sites.

Reaching **McKeesport**—where future presidents John F. Kennedy and Richard Nixon famously debated as young politicos in 1947—the trail turns along the **Youghiogheny River.** After passing through the supposedly haunted **Dead Man's Hollow Conservation Area,** the GAP continues upstream to the **West Newton Visitor Center** in a rebuilt train depot and

The Great Allegheny Passage takes hikers on a historic journey from western Pennsylvania down south past the Mason-Dixon Line that once denoted the geographical separation of states with and without legalized slavery.

Twelve official routes welcome cyclists on the Great Allegheny Passage.

Connellsville, a coal boomtown that once had more millionaires per capita than any other U.S. city.

The GAP reaches a scenic crescendo in **Ohiopyle State Park,** an area with numerous waterfalls, regenerated woodlands, and two Frank Lloyd Wright masterpieces—**Fallingwater** and **Kentuck Knob.** Meanwhile, plentiful white water makes the **Youghiogheny River Gorge** ripe for paddling adventures.

The town of **Confluence** marks the trail's transition from the Youghiogheny to the **Casselman River** and a transit across the **Eastern Continental Divide** near **Meyersdale.** Three miles (4.8 km) ahead lies another geographic boundary, the **Mason-Dixon Line** that once marked the divide between states with and without slavery as well as the Pennsylvania-Maryland border.

The **Borden Tunnel** shuttles the GAP into **Frostburg** with its lively college-town bars and restaurants. A final leg through the Maryland panhandle leads past the **Cumberland Bone Cave,** where scores of Pleistocene fossils were unearthed, then down to **Cumberland** on the banks of the **Potomac River,** where bikers and hikers can segue onto the **C&O Canal Towpath** for an onward journey to **Washington, D.C.** ∎

LOCAL FLAVOR

• **Driscoll & Sons Café:** Trailside surf, turf, and pasta dishes are complemented by Yough Twister Ice Cream; 2101 Douglas Run Road, Elizabeth, PA; driscollandsonscafe.com.

• **Connellsville Canteen:** A combination café and museum serves breakfast, lunch, and World War II mementos in equal portions; 131 West Crawford Avenue, Connellsville, PA; connellsvillecanteen.org.

• **Falls City Pub:** Take in burgers, burritos, and craft beer with live music and outdoor seating near Ohiopyle State Park; 112 Garrett Street, Ohiopyle, PA; www.fallscitypub.com.

• **Lucky Dog Cafe:** From mojitos and craft beers to pulled pork pizza and smoked brisket tacos, this riverside restaurant defines eclectic eating; 849 River Road, Confluence, PA; facebook.com/LuckyDogCafe.

• **Princess Restaurant:** Opened in 1939, this college town eatery offers soups, salads, and sandwiches to power up for the last leg of the GAP; 12 West Main Street; Frostburg, MD; princessrestaurant.com.

Batona Trail
New Jersey

Unusual landscapes, unexpected wilderness, and obscure history make this route through the legendary Pinelands the best long-distance hike in the Garden State.

THE BIG PICTURE

Distance: 50 miles (80 km)

Elevation Gain: approx. 960 feet (290 m)

Time: 3–4 days

Difficulty: Easy to moderate

Best Time: Year-round

More Info: state.nj.us/dep/parksandforests/parks/docs/batona14web.pdf

Whether you're a fan of *The Sopranos,* fascinated by legendary monsters, or merely in the mood for a good hike, the **Batona Trail** offers a surprisingly wild escape in south New Jersey.

Located about halfway between **Philadelphia** and **Atlantic City,** the 50-mile (80-km) trail links several state forests as it snakes across **New Jersey Pinelands National Reserve.** Also called the Pine Barrens, the region was once renowned for nefarious mob activities and as the home of a legendary winged creature called the Jersey Devil.

However, its origins are much less ominous. Batona is an acronym of BAck TO NAture, adopted by a Philadelphia hiking club when it was founded in 1928. Their group hikes took place throughout the region, including the Pinelands. But it wasn't until the early 1960s that club members began blazing the trail that would bear their name.

Camping is available at five state forest campgrounds. Dispersed camping along the trail is strictly forbidden. Bikes, horses, and anything with a motor are also banned, which means the Batona is reserved for hikers, snowshoers, and Nordic skiers.

Mile zero is a parking lot on Turkey Buzzard Bridge Road in **Ongs Hat,** New Jersey, about an hour's drive from downtown Philly. Although users can obviously start from either end, kicking off from the north means that you finish beside a swimmable lake and only a short distance from beaches along the Jersey Shore.

From Ongs Hat, the trail's distinctive pink blazes lead hikers through the pine-oak woods and white cedar wetlands of **Brendan T. Byrne State Forest,** named after the New Jersey governor who helped save the Pinelands from suburban development and a controversial supersonic jetport project.

Veering to the south, the Batona ambles across **Apple Pie Hill,** highest point along the route at 205 feet (62 m) and the only spot where hikers can relish a panoramic view across the Pinelands. The hill's iconic fire tower is open to visitors whenever forest fire observers are on duty.

The 32-room mansion at Batsto Village is just one fascinating stop in this historic village with roots reaching back to 1766.

The Mullica River winds its way through the Pine Barrens along the Batona Trail.

Coming down from the hill, the trail slips into **Wharton State Forest** and a secluded section of the route that features **Batona** and **Lower Forge campgrounds** as well as the **Carranza Memorial,** which marks the site where famed Mexican aviation pioneer Emilio Carranza died in a 1928 plane crash.

More history awaits at **Batsto,** a onetime bog iron and glassmaking center. Hikers can take a break from the trail to chat with blacksmiths and other historical reenactors or tour the village's 33 historic structures with a smartphone app.

Swinging around to the east, the Batona crosses the wide **Wading River** and reaches its southern terminus on the edge of **Bass River State Park.** Established in 1905 as New Jersey's first state forest, the park includes **Lake Absegami** (swimming, boating, fishing) and a rare **pygmy forest** comprising miniature pitch pines and blackjack oaks stunted by the sandy soil. ∎

OTHER GREAT TRAILS

• **Watchung Reservation History Trail:** The remains of a deserted village, sawmill, and farmhouse are scattered along this six-mile (9.6-km) route through a large nature preserve in Union County.

• **North Wildwood Boardwalk and Seawall:** Carnival attractions and ocean views are the lures of a six-mile (9.6-km) route along Hereford Inlet and the main beach of this popular resort town near Cape May.

• **Rahway Fairy Trail:** New Jersey's best family-friendly trail, this half-mile (0.8-km) hike in South Mountain Reservation near Newark is decorated with miniature homes and other fairy paraphernalia.

• **Henry Hudson Trail:** This 24-mile (38-km) rail trail between Highlands and Freehold near the southern shore of Lower New York Bay honors the English sea captain who explored the region in 1609.

• **Mount Tammany Loop:** Just off the Appalachian Trail in northwest New Jersey, the loop offers bird's-eye views of the Delaware Water Gap from Tammany's 1,527-foot (465-m) summit in the Kittatinny Mountains.

New England Trail

Connecticut & Massachusetts

It may ramble across only two of the region's six states, but the New England National Scenic Trail personifies many of the natural wonders people cherish about the nation's northeast corner.

Picture a quintessential New England scene in your mind—a whitewashed church, big red barn, traprock ridge, old stone bridges, maples reflected in a forest pond—and you're sure to find it somewhere along the **New England Trail** (NET).

Launched in 2009, the NET is a relatively new national scenic trail with roots that stretch back to a mid-20th-century trailblazing campaign that created three long-distance trails—the **Mattabesett, Metacomet,** and **Monadnock**—across Connecticut and Massachusetts.

The vintage "M-M-M" network forms the backbone of the modern New England Trail on a 215-mile (346-km) journey between Long

THE BIG PICTURE

Distance: 215 miles (346 km)

Elevation Change: approx. 31,000 feet (9,450 m)

Time: 2–4 weeks

Difficulty: Moderate to strenuous

Best Time: Late spring, summer, or fall

More Info: newenglandtrail.org

Island Sound and New Hampshire. Hikers can overnight at 10 primitive cabins, lean-tos, and tent sites along the route. Otherwise, they must seek off-trail accommodations because dispersed/stealth camping is not permitted.

With the northern end of the trail only about 940 feet (286 m) above sea level, there's no great advantage in starting at the top end of the NET and working your way down to the coast. Striking off from **Jacob's Beach** on **Long Island Sound,** the trail cuts across the lawn of the historic **Henry Whitfield House** (built in 1639) before disappearing into the woods of the **East River Preserve** and **Cockaponset State Forest.**

Reaching the craggy gray schist of the **Broomstick Ledges** and **Bluff Head,** hikers have a choice between veering right onto the **Mattabesett Trail** or a trek that leads through **Millers Pond State Park** to **Middletown.** Or keep left along the NET as it rises to viewpoints on **Trimountain, Higby Mountain,** and **Ragged Mountain** on a sweep around the western outskirts of **New Britain** and **Hartford.**

After peering down at the state capital from the Bavarian-style **Heublein Tower** in **Talcott Mountain State Park,** trekkers continue their northward march atop the

Established in 2009, the New England Trail is a scenic pathway through the varied topographies that characterize this charming corner of the United States.

South of the town of Hadley, Section 7 of the trail crests the Seven Sisters hills of the Mount Holyoke Range.

long, wooded **Metacomet Ridge.** You know you've crossed into Massachusetts at **Rising Corner** because the trail markers change from blue to white.

West of **Springfield,** hikers can carefully wade across the **Westfield River,** walk a three-mile (4.8-km) detour along surface streets, or hail a rideshare. Rising back up the Metacomet Ridge, the trail skirts around **Holyoke** and through **Mount Tom State Reservation** to its second large water crossing: the deep and swift-flowing **Connecticut River.** Anyone who wants to continue their stroll on the other side must arrange road transport or walk a 10-mile (16-km) detour via **Northampton.**

Resuming on the east bank, the NET rambles across the **Holyoke Range** and through the woods between redbrick **Amherst College** and **Quabbin Reservoir.**

Shutesbury village marks the start of a 47-mile (76-km) jaunt to the Massachusetts–New Hampshire border through **Lake Wyola State Park** and four state forests.

Royalston Falls and the **TTOR Shelter** punctuate the official end of the NET. However, many hikers cross the border and continue for 18 miles (29 km) along the **Metacomet-Monadnock Trail** to the summit of 3,165-foot (964-m) **Mount Monadnock** in southern New Hampshire. ■

DETOURS

• **Eric Carle Museum:** Treasured by grown-ups and children, this collection offers a whimsical journey into the world of picture book art on the Hampshire College campus.

• **Northampton Main Street:** Visit lively bars, restaurants, and one-off shops frequented by students from the area's five colleges and universities.

• **Naismith Memorial Basketball Hall of Fame:** Housed inside a giant silver ball in Springfield, this holy grail of hoops features Michael Jordan,

Kobe Bryant, Bill Russell, and all the other greats.

• **Old New-Gate Prison & Copper Mine:** The colonial officials who created the prison in 1773 figured the warren of old mine tunnels would make a perfect place to incarcerate prisoners; the underground guided tours are captivating.

• **Mark Twain House:** The great American bard wrote *Adventures of Huckleberry Finn, A Connecticut Yankee in King Arthur's Court,* and other classics during his 17-year residency in Hartford.

The High Line
New York

Transformed into a marvelous modern park, a vintage railroad viaduct on Manhattan's west side offers a breath of fresh air and outdoor art in crowded New York City.

The engineers and steelworkers who created the **High Line** viaduct for the New York Central Railroad in the 1930s could have never imagined that their pragmatic solution to Manhattan traffic congestion would someday provide a platform for the city's most intriguing trail.

There are lots of great walks around the Big Apple, but none that so successfully blend architecture, public art, wildflowers, people-watching, and an effortless way to rack up 10,000 daily steps (when you complete two round-trips).

The High Line was an immediate hit when it opened in 2009 after a three-year makeover from railroad to recreation. Thru-hikers can start at the **Hell's Kitchen/Hudson Yards** "trailhead" on 34th Street at the trail's north end or the **Chelsea/Meatpacking District** entrance on Gansevoort Street in the south.

Starting from the north end renders immediate views of the Hudson River and **Penn Station**-bound passenger trains. Past the **Pershing Square Beams** play area, a huge S-bend takes the elevated trail past two of Manhattan's latest architectural icons, including **The Shed** arts center. Hovering above the intersection of 10th Avenue and 30th Street, an offshoot of the High Line called **The Spur** doubles as a stage for large, contemporary artworks.

The next 10 blocks of the High Line (28th to 19th Streets) run through the heart of Chelsea's vaunted **art district** and dozens of galleries that showcase painting, sculpture, photography, and more by the global stars of modern art. Between 22nd and 21st Streets is the **Chelsea Thicket,** a portion of the trail where original railroad tracks run through the lush vegetation.

Hikers who've worked up an appetite can duck into **Chelsea Market** for gelato, tacos, doughnuts, chowder, noodles, and what seems like an infinite selection of other fast but tasty foods. Just past the market, the Hudson River suddenly appears again from the **Diller–von Furstenberg Sundeck** with its kid-friendly water feature. In the late afternoon, this stretch of the High Line is a great place to catch the sunset over the river while chillaxing on one of the wooden benches or chaise

The Diller–von Furstenberg garden and water feature are a favorite for escaping the summer heat along New York City's High Line.

Reimagined in 2009, the old railroad viaduct is now a spectacular park in Manhattan's west side. Stop at the Diller–von Furstenberg sundeck for a memorable sunset.

loungers. If it's evening, duck into the **14th Street Passage** for video programs on a giant screen.

The final southbound section below 14th Street parallels a shop-aholic stretch of **Washington Street** that harbors designer clothing, shoe, and perfume outlets. Or you can skip the shops and continue through the **Donald Pels and Wendy Keys Gansevoort Woodland,** the most densely landscaped portion of the High Line.

Descending the steps or elevator onto Gansevoort, hikers should hang a right for the entrance of the cutting-edge **Whitney Museum of American Art.** Alternatively, they can traverse the busy westside highway at the Horatio Street pedestrian crossing and continue their walk north or south along the waterfront **Hudson River Greenway.**

The High Line is accessed by elevators and/or stairs at more than 15 spots along its length.

Check the High Line website for outdoor dance, music, and performance art events that take place throughout the year. ∎

LOCAL FLAVOR

• **Death Avenue Brewing Company:** Find craft beer and Greek American cuisine on 10th Avenue near The Spur; 315 10th Avenue; deathave.com.

• **Ovest Pizzoteca:** Enjoy Naples-style pizza, panini, and pasta in an industrial brick setting on West 27th Street right below the High Line; 513 W. 27th Street, New York, NY; ovestnyc.com.

• **Intelligentsia:** This upscale coffee bar in the historic High Line Hotel offers a shaded patio, freshly baked pastries, and a good tea selection; 180 10th Avenue; intelligentsia.com.

• **Hearth on the High Line:** This trailside wine bar and café with modern American and Italian fare has an outdoor deck overlooking 10th Avenue; 10th Avenue and W. 15th Street; restauranthearth.com.

• **Top of the Standard:** This elegant drinking establishment has killer views, live jazz, and innovative cocktails on the 18th floor of the Standard Hotel; 848 Washington Street; standardhotels.com.

This repurposed railroad track is part of New York City's
High Line.

Freedom Trail & Battle Road
Massachusetts

America was born along these historic routes in and around Boston, where the ideals of liberty were tried and tested in churches, meeting halls, and city streets, leading to a "shot heard round the world" and revolution.

THE BIG PICTURE

Distance: Freedom Trail, 2.5 miles (4 km); Battle Road, 5 miles (8 km)

Elevation Gain: Freedom Trail, approx. 130 feet (40 m); Battle Road, approx. 240 feet (70 m)

Time: Half day each

Difficulty: Easy

Best Time: Year-round

More Info: nps.gov/bost and nps.gov/mima

There's an argument to be made that if the actions and ideals that transpired along the **Freedom Trail and Battle Road** between 1770 and 1775 had never played out, this book might be about hiking routes in 13 small independent nations (that were once British colonies) rather than the 50 states of a united nation that we know today.

The Boston Tea Party and Boston Massacre, Sons of Liberty and minutemen, the battles of Concord and Lexington, John Hancock, Sam Adams, and Paul Revere—two and a half centuries later, the events and personalities associated with these routes remain the cornerstones of the American nation.

Despite their historical link, the two routes are dramatically different. The Freedom Trail is unabashedly urban, a wander along narrow streets through some of **Boston's** oldest neighborhoods. Battle Road, on the other hand, flows through forest and fields on the city's western outskirts, not far from where Henry David Thoreau laid the groundwork for the modern environmental movement.

Both are fully paved, easy to walk, and an absolute rush for anyone who loves exploring the places where history was made.

FREEDOM TRAIL

Marked by red bricks embedded in the sidewalk, the Freedom Trail follows a circuitous 2.5-mile (4-km) route between Boston Common and Bunker Hill. There are 16 official stops, some of them significant before the buildup to the Revolution and some that didn't become significant until the early 1800s, but all of them played important roles in the creation and early development of American culture and politics.

Along the way are numerous other places that will surely grab your interest. Some of them historic, others scenic, and still others culinary (for those who want to bookend or break up their Freedom Trail walk with a meal or beverage).

Most folks start from the **Boston Common Visitor Center,** where maps of the trail and information on other Boston attractions are readily available. But don't be shy about jumping in somewhere else along the route. The National Park Service offers visitors centers with

American flags adorn Boston Common during a Memorial Day commemoration.

Old North Bridge drapes over the Concord River near the well-known Minute Man statue.

similar info at Faneuil Hall and Charlestown Navy Yard.

Boston Common—founded in 1634 as the nation's first and oldest public park—boasts several landmarks, including **Brewer Fountain** and the memorial to one of the first Black regiments that served in the Civil War. Across Beacon Street is the golden-domed **Massachusetts State House,** and just beyond Park Street Church is the **Old Granary Burying Ground,** where Paul Revere, Sam Adams, John Hancock, and other Founding Fathers are buried.

A zigzag route through the skyscrapers of downtown Boston takes the Freedom Trail to the **Old South Meeting House** and the spot where the Boston Massacre occurred in 1770. Although not an official part of the trail, the **Boston Tea Party Ships & Museum** is worth a detour down Kirby and Oliver Streets to the waterfront where colonials

protested "taxation without representation" in 1773.

A little farther along is **Faneuil Hall,** where the Sons of Liberty spoke out against British oppression. With its numerous indoor and outdoor eateries and food stalls, neighboring **Quincy Market** is a great

place to stop for lunch or a snack.

Crossing over the Big Dig freeway tunnels via the **Rose Kennedy Greenway,** the trail plunges into the fabled **North End.** Tucked between historic sites like the **Paul Revere House** and the **Pierce/Hichborn House** are popular restaurants and

OTHER GREAT TRAILS

Black Heritage Trail

The abolition of slavery, the Underground Railroad, and the civil rights movement are a few of the ideas that took root and flourished in a historic African American neighborhood on Boston's Beacon Hill. Established by the National Park Service as part of Boston African American National Historic Site, the 1.6-mile (2.5-km) **Black Heritage Trail** takes walkers on a 220-year journey through local history. Starting from the northeast corner of Boston Common, the trail passes the homes of Black Americans and community structures where key events took place. The walk culminates with visits inside the Abiel Smith School (opened in 1835), where the community's struggle against school segregation played out, and the African Meeting House (built in 1806), the nation's oldest surviving Black church structure. The Park Service offers ranger-guided walks of the route at 10 a.m. Wednesday to Sunday.

bakeries left over from the era when the North End was a die-hard Italian American neighborhood. Fronted by an equestrian statue of Revere, the **Old North Church** remains a lively place of worship that offers concerts by the resident chamber choir, underground crypt tours, and a historical speaker series.

Descending from **Copp's Hill Burying Ground,** the Freedom Trail crosses the **Charles River** into **Charlestown.** Founded by Puritan settlers in 1628, the waterfront witnessed the first major engagement between the British and the Continental Army.

The Freedom Trail makes a beeline for historic **Charlestown Navy Yard** and the **U.S.S. *Constitution,*** a three-mast frigate launched in the 1790s that became one of the most storied ships in American naval history. Turning away from the water, the trail makes its way through a warren of classic Boston brownstone homes to **Bunker Hill,** where a

In 1776, Bostonians gathered at the Old State House to hear the very first reading of the Declaration of Independence.

June 17, 1775, battle proved a pyrrhic victory for a British Army that realized the colonials were going to be much tougher foes than they had ever expected.

BATTLE ROAD

Battle Road once stretched all the way from Boston to Concord, but urban sprawl over the past two centuries has obscured most of the original route. However, you can still drive or hike the approximate path of the redcoats' march by following **Massachusetts Avenue** from **Harvard Bridge** to Fiske Hill. Roughly 12 miles (19 km) in length, the route passes through the **Massachusetts Institute of Technology (MIT)** and the **Harvard University** campus as well as **Massachusetts National Cemetery** and **Lexington Common National Historic Site.**

Just past Interstate 95, the route glides into **Minute Man National Historical Park,** where a woodsy five-mile (8-km) multiuse trail follows remnants of the original Battle Road between **Fiske Hill** and Concord village. Monuments and information boards mark places where key events unfolded on April 19,

1775, including the spot where redcoats captured Paul Revere, the **Bloody Angle** where the American militia ambushed retreating British troops, and the graves of British soldiers who fell on that pivotal day.

Even if you're not into history, Battle Road doubles as a nature trail through meadows, farm fields, wetlands, and woods that are especially attractive come fall. A dozen 18th-century structures—most of them homes, but also a tavern and a barn—preserve the architecture of the era. And be on the lookout for wildlife that ranges from deer, beaver, and fox to salamanders, frogs, and 160 bird species.

Battle Road Trail ends at **Meriam's Corner,** but hikers and bikers can continue another two miles (3.2 km) along Lexington Road and Monument Street to the **Old North Bridge** and famous **Minute Man statue.** Passing through the middle of **Concord** village, it's also a walk through American literary history, a route that passes homes where the likes of authors Louisa May Alcott, Nathaniel Hawthorne, and Ralph Waldo Emerson once lived and wrote. ■

LAY YOUR HEAD

- **Bed & Breakfast Afloat:** Throw your own tea party on Boston Harbor while overnighting aboard one of the private boats in this rental flotilla at Constitution Marina. The marina can also arrange sighting cruises, fishing charters, sunset sails, and water taxis to other spots along the Boston waterfront; from $215; *bedandbreakfast afloat.com.*

- **Omni Parker House:** Opened in 1855, the luxurious Parker House offers rooms overlooking Boston

Common and the Freedom Trail. From John F. Kennedy and Charles Dickens to Ho Chi Minh and Malcolm X, many historical figures have links to the hotel; from $249; *omnihotels.com/ hotels/boston-parker-house.*

- **Inn at Hastings Park:** No two rooms are the same at this designer-savvy boutique hotel just footsteps from Lexington Common, where the first shots (and casualties) of the American Revolution took place on April 19, 1775. The inn also has an excellent

farm-to-table restaurant; from $221; *innathastingspark.com.*

- **Colonial Inn:** Welcoming travelers to Concord since 1715, the inn lies at the eastern end of Battle Road within walking distance of the North Bridge and Concord Battlefield. It served as an ammunition store during the Revolution and as the permanent abode of Henry David Thoreau for two years; from $159; *concords colonialinn.com.*

Pine Creek Rail Trail
Pennsylvania

Hikers and bikers take to this popular path in the Pennsylvania Wilds region for a jaunt through regenerated wilderness in an area once ravaged by clear-cut logging.

THE BIG PICTURE

Distance: 62 miles (100 km)

Elevation Gain: approx. 100 feet (30 m)

Time: 3–4 days

Difficulty: Easy

Best Time: Spring, summer, or fall

More Info: pinecreekvalley.com/pine-creek-rail-trail

More than any other route in this book, the **Pine Creek Rail Trail** in north-central Pennsylvania is proof that—given enough time and nurturing—nature can rebound from terrific devastation. Black-and-white photos taken more than a century ago show nothing but stumps on both sides of Pine Creek, the result of clear-cutting during the region's 19th-century timber boom.

Once the trees were gone, the local economy collapsed and the region fell into a prolonged depression that lasted well into the next century when outdoor recreation came to the rescue. Ironically, it was lumber baron Leonard Harrison who, nearing the end of his life, donated much of the land along the trail right-of-way to the Commonwealth of Pennsylvania to reforest and transform into a park.

Decades later, the Jersey Shore, Pine Creek and Buffalo Railway line that transported so much of that timber far away from Pine Creek was converted into a trail that's been listed among the top 10 places in the world to bike tour.

Much of the wildlife that lived along the original Native American trails through the region—black bears, lynx, wolves, and even bison—never returned. But a century of reforestation has lured white-tailed deer, wild turkeys, and river otters. Meanwhile, more than 120 bird species have been spotted in the skies above the trail or perched in the sugar maples and sycamores, oaks and aspens, beeches, birches, and other trees that flank the route.

With an average grade of only 2 percent, the trail is easy to hike or bike in either direction. But starting from **Wellsboro Junction** at the north end does mean the journey is basically downhill all the way. Beyond **Ansonia** junction, the route glides into **Tioga State Forest** and **Pine Creek Gorge.** With walls towering 800 feet (240 m), the "Grand Canyon of Pennsylvania" cuts a

Pine Creek Rail Trail is an easy, enjoyable hike or bike for those seeking a scenic escape.

The expansive view of Pine Creek Gorge as seen from Leonard Harrison State Park

47-mile (76-km) gash across the **Allegheny Plateau** and is without doubt the highlight of any hiking or biking trek along the trail.

Flanking the gorge are **Leonard Harrison State Park** and **Colton Point State Park.** The steep **Turkey Path** offers access to campgrounds in both parks, as well as the **Environmental Interpretive Center** in Leonard Harrison, which organizes ranger walks, talks, campfire programs, and occasional cider squeezing sessions.

If the state park campsites are taken, trail users can continue downstream to **Tiadaghton Campground** or rental cabins in **Blackwell** village. Because the wilderness portion of the route wanes in Blackwell, a lot of hikers and bikers bail on the trail at that point.

Downstream from the village, the trail shares the gorge with Highway 414. Vehicle access means more homes, hamlets, and overnight options, including campgrounds at **Pettecote Junction, Tomb Flats, Black Walnut Bottom,** and **Bonnell Flats.**

There's also more trailside grub. **Wolfe's General Store** in tiny **Slate Run** offers provisions and deli meals. Catering to gorge travelers since 1825, **Waterville Tavern** serves hearty meals before the last stretch of the Pine Creek path to **Jersey Shore** on the **Susquehanna River.** ∎

APRÈS HIKE

• **Cherry Springs State Park:** This official International Dark Sky Park offers overnight star parties, astronomer talks, and an observation field with telescope pads and power outlets for telescopes and laptops.

• **Pennsylvania Lumber Museum:** Interactive exhibits and a re-created lumber camp in Galeton illuminate the golden age of logging in the Allegheny Highlands.

• **Kinzua Bridge:** Once hailed as the "Eighth Wonder of the World," this Victorian-era engineering marvel was once the world's tallest and longest railway viaduct.

• **The Wildlife Center at Sinnemahoning:** State-of-the-art exhibits complement outdoor viewing platforms and blinds where visitors scout for elk, eagles, black bears, waterfowl, and other critters.

Gordons Pond to Poodle Beach
Delaware

This eclectic walk along the Delaware shore runs a broad gamut from wild beaches and coastal lagoons to the carnival attractions of the Rehoboth Beach Boardwalk.

Over the last 400 years, the beaches and dunes of **Cape Henlopen** have evolved from the southernmost point of Dutch New Amsterdam into a military stronghold that protected Delaware Bay during two world wars and is currently Delaware's premier state park.

The park's most popular hiking/biking path is the **Gordons Pond Trail,** a leisurely route that starts near the 80-foot (24-m) **Great Dune** and the **Fort Miles Historical Area.** A blend of boardwalk, paving, and crushed stone, the trail makes its way south past the **Biden Environmental Training Center** and historic six-inch (15-cm) gun batteries and dune-top picnic area above the beach at **Herring Point.**

THE BIG PICTURE

Distance: 5.7 miles (9.1 km)

Elevation Gain: approx. 50 feet (20 m)

Time: 3–4 hours

Difficulty: Easy

Best Time: Year-round

More Info: destateparks.com/ Beaches/CapeHenlopen and cityofrehoboth.com/visitors/ beach-and-boardwalk

Tacking inland, the trail wraps around three sides of **Gordons Pond,** a 900-acre (364-ha) lagoon sprinkled with tiny islands and flanked by a large salt marsh called **Holland Glade.** Boardwalk overlooks along the shore provide benches and information boards on some of the creatures that frequent the pond. Among the many avian seasonal visitors and year-round residents are snow geese, great blue herons, greater yellowlegs, northern pintail ducks, and willet sandpipers.

The trail ends at **Gordons Pond Beach,** where hikers and bikers can take a dip in the sea or examine a vintage artillery fire observation tower constructed during World War II. The hike continues along a series of three sandy strands—**Whiskey Beach, North Shores Beach,** and **Deauville Beach**—to the north end of the celebrated **Rehoboth Beach Boardwalk.**

Rehoboth Beach was just a lonely stretch of the Delaware coast until 1873, when a Methodist Episcopal camp was established. By the end of the decade, the railroad had reached the shore, which blossomed into a full-blown holiday resort. Although much changed over the years, the boardwalk traces its roots to that Victorian-era church camp.

Rehoboth Beach's family-run Funland amusement park shines with lights and laughter at dusk.

The Rehoboth Beach boardwalk lets cyclists weave amid the dunes and waves along the Delaware coastline.

Name your culinary guilty pleasure and you're bound to find it somewhere along the boardwalk: **Thrasher's French Fries** (founded in 1929), **Zelky's Donut Rings, Starkey's Funnel Cake Factory, Kiwi's Tiki Hut** tropical cocktail bar, **Obie's** clam strips and crab balls, and the 100-flavor **Ice Cream Store.**

Hikers and bikers can pop into the **Rehoboth Toy and Kite Company** to browse a wide variety of objects for playing on or flying above the adjacent sands. The **Rehoboth Beach Bandstand** has staged a summer concert series for more than 60 years. There's also miniature golf, game arcades, and a "haunted" seaside mansion.

However, the boardwalk's landmark attraction is **Funland,** a vintage indoor/outdoor amusement park established in 1962 and still

managed by the founding Fasnacht family. The park features 11 circus midway games and 17 carnival rides, including five classic rides that have been there since Funland opened.

Or you can ignore the food and fun, and just keep heading south. The boardwalk ends beside **Poodle Beach** at the foot of Prospect Street. But the beach keeps going for another seven miles (11 km), a route that takes hikers down **Dewey Beach** and **Delaware Seashore State Park** to **Coin Beach,** where the **Indian River Inlet** flows into the Atlantic. ■

DETOURS

• **Fast Cars:** Pilot a go-kart yourself at Delaware's Midway Speedway or watch NASCAR's stars compete for the checkered flag at Dover International Speedway.

• **Cape May–Lewes Ferry:** Hop an early morning boat across Delaware Bay for a walking or cycling tour of the Victorian-era beach resort in south New Jersey.

• **Prime Hook National Wildlife Refuge:** Paddle the seven-mile (11-km) canoe trail, hike six miles (9.6 km) of terrestrial trails, catch a nature lecture, angle for largemouth bass, or scan the skies for more than 300 bird species at this Delaware Bay preserve.

• **Salted Vines Vineyard:** Sip a locally produced Chardonnay or Cabernet on the patio while listening to live tunes on the back lawn.

Delaware Bay greets the Atlantic at the Point Overlook of
Cape Henlopen.

North South Trail

Rhode Island

Back roads and backwoods are the allure of a long-distance trail that runs along the western edge of Rhode Island, connecting the Ocean State's breezy shore and densely wooded inland areas.

THE BIG PICTURE

Distance: 78 miles (125 km)

Elevation Gain: approx. 3,620 feet (1,110 m)

Time: 3–5 days

Difficulty: Moderate

Best Time: Spring, summer, or fall

More Info: rockgeist.com/routes/north-south-trail and trailsandwalksri.wordpress.com/category/north-south-trail

How long does it take to hike across the nation's smallest state? Anywhere from three to five days if you're trekking the **North South Trail.**

Relatively unknown outside the region, the trail wanders through forest reserves and farmland along the state's west side, dipping briefly into Connecticut twice on a route that stretches between **Block Island**

Sound and the Massachusetts border.

The North South is marked by blue-green blazes and the occasional mileage sign, but that's about all in terms of services and amenities. Backcountry or trailside camping is forbidden. However, hikers and bikers can overnight at several developed state campgrounds and a handful of private camping spots along the way.

Around half of the path rambles up and over the wooded hills of western Rhode Island, but overall, the North South is pretty easy walking. The route can get a little muggy in summer, but nothing too oppressive because so much of the trail is shaded. Although the trail technically runs north to south (hence the name), striking off from the south offers the advantage of continuing your trek into Massachusetts and even New Hampshire.

Trekkers can start from several spots along the **Charlestown** coast, but the best is **East Beach** with its surfside state campground. From there, the route wraps around the west end of **Ninigret Pond** and crosses the historic **Post Road** (U.S. 1) into **Burlingame State Park** with its general store and woodsy lakeside campground.

As one of Rhode Island's most popular state parks, Burlingame can get awfully crowded in summer. But beyond **Watchaug Pond,** the crowds start to thin out to the point where you sometimes wonder if anyone else is hiking the trail. After traversing the **Carolina Management Area,** the route swings through **Richmond,** founded in the 1660s and now home to

Visit the Moses Taft House, built in 1786, in Burrillville for an example of Federal architecture.

A quaint trail marker guides hikers ahead.

Rhode Island's largest county fair (held in August).

Ducking beneath Interstate 95 in the **Arcadia Management Area,** the trail passes close to **Stepstone Falls** before crossing the state line into **Oneco,** Connecticut, with its convenience store, pizza pub, and **River Bend Campground.**

Back in Rhode Island, the route passes the 19th-century country churches of **Rice City Historic District** before rising into the gently rolling hills of northwest Rhode Island. Up ahead, **Ginny-B Campground** features a camp store, swimming hole, and tavern at the adjacent **Foster Country Club.** Around 10 miles (16 km) farther north, hikers can summit **Jerimoth Hill,** highest point in Rhode Island at 812 feet (247 m).

The trail has another brief flirtation with Connecticut—this time through **Killingly Pond State Park**—before reverting to Rhode Island for the rest of its run. **Oakleaf Family Campground** and **George Washington State Campground** offer two more overnight options before a final push through **Buck Hill Management Area** in the state's extreme far northwest corner.

The North South ends among the multiple wooden mileage posts at the Rhode Island-Massachusetts border. However, hikers can continue northward along the 92-mile (148-km) **Midstate Trail,** which leaps across central Massachusetts to the 21-mile (34-km) **Wapack Trail** in southern New Hampshire. ■

OTHER GREAT TRAILS

Block Island Hiking

Floating nine miles (14 km) off the Rhode Island mainland, Block Island offers a rare slice of New England maritime nature.

More than 40 percent of the island is covered by parks, farm preserves, wildlife refuges, and other conservation areas that hikers can explore on 28 miles (45 km) of Greenway Trails.

Block Island trail maps and guidebooks on the trail and wildlife are available at the Nature Conservancy office on High Street and the Island Bound Bookstore on Water Street, both within easy walking distance of the ferry landing in New Shoreham village.

Erie Canalway
New York

Once the heartbeat of the American industrial revolution, the Erie Canal now provides hikers, bikers, and paddlers with a scenic route between the Great Lakes and the Hudson Valley with plenty of history, culture, and nature along the way.

THE BIG PICTURE

Distance: 360 miles (580 km)

Elevation Gain: approx. 4,800 feet (1,460 m)

Time: 3–5 weeks

Difficulty: Easy to moderate

Best Time: Spring, summer, or fall

More Info: eriecanalway.org and ptny.org/cycle-the-erie-canal

It's hard to imagine nowadays while hiking or biking beside the serene waterway in upstate New York, but the **Erie Canal** was once an American superhighway. At any given time, hundreds of barges—pulled by mules or horses and laden with all sorts of cargo—were making their way along a canal linking Lake Erie and the Hudson River.

Spanning more than half a century between 1790 and 1855, the canal age coincided with the advent of the industrial revolution on American soil as well as one of the engines that helped fuel the rise of manufacturing and capitalism. Hundreds of canals were dug in the Northeast and Midwest to transport bulk commodities to factories and whisk finished goods in the other direction.

But the 524-mile (843-km) Erie Canal between Buffalo and Albany was the queen of them all. At its peak, the waterway conveyed more than 30,000 barges and 40,000 passengers a year, minuscule by today's standards but a huge impact on eastern commerce and westward migration in the early 1800s. The canal also sparked the rise of great cities like Buffalo, Rochester, and Syracuse.

Railroads, interstates, and cargo planes eventually upstaged the canals. But the Erie found new life in the late 20th century as a popular biking, hiking, paddling, and powerboating route called the Erie Canalway. Threading its way through and around more than 230 upstate communities and 23 counties, scores of state and local parks, and three dozen national historic landmarks, the trail provides a valuable outdoor escape for locals and visitors alike.

The main waterway is the longest and most celebrated part of the **Erie Canalway National Heritage Corridor,** which also includes the 92-mile (148-km) **Cayuga-Seneca Canal** that heads south into the exquisite **Finger Lakes Region;** the 23-mile (37-km) **Oswego Canal** that meanders north through the **Oswego River Valley** to **Lake Ontario;** and the 63-mile (101-km) **Champlain Canal** that connects the Hudson River and **Lake Champlain** near **Saratoga Springs.**

Now part of the New York State Canal System, the Erie Canal runs 524 miles (843 km) from Albany to Buffalo.

The late 20th century brought new life to the Erie Canal as a pathway for cyclists, hikers, paddlers, and boaters.

Although the elevation does spike here and there along the route when the trail veers away from the canal, starting from the **Lake Erie** end means less overall elevation gain. Starting in Buffalo's **Canalside District,** the first few steps lead past the **Explore & More Children's Museum,** the **U.S.S.** *Little Rock,* and along the **Buffalo** waterfront and **Niagara River.** Reaching **Tonawanda,** the trail intersects with the westernmost part of the Erie Canal.

Featuring historical homes and living history programs, **Buffalo Niagara Heritage Village** offers a glimpse of frontier life when the canal was completed in the 1820s. Farther along, the **Erie Canal Discovery Center** in **Lockport** demonstrates how the canal works beside the historic **Flight of Five**

Locks—the first of 57 locks that thru-paddlers must navigate.

Transitioning from pavement to stone dust, the route continues

across western New York through the canalside towns of **Medina, Albion,** and **Brockport** before a broad sweep around the southern

DETOURS

* **Saratoga Springs:** Legendary spring water, a famous Thoroughbred horse-racing track, and a Revolutionary War battlefield are just a few of the attractions of a town that also offers copious dining and shopping options.

* **International Boxing Hall of Fame:** Muhammad Ali, Joe Louis, Rocky Marciano, and Floyd Mayweather, Jr., are just a few of the many pugilists honored at this Canastota collection.

* **George Eastman Museum:** The world's oldest photo museum showcases the wide world of

photography, cinema, and camera technology at the Eastman Estate in Rochester.

* **Sunset Drive-In:** During the summer months, three high-definition digital projectors and high-fidelity stereo FM sound screens feature films at a vintage 1950s outdoor movie theater in Middleport.

* **Landmark Theatre:** Touring Broadway shows, headliner concerts, and cutting-edge comedians are now the forte of a historic art deco movie palace in downtown Syracuse that opened in 1928.

edge of **Rochester.** The "Young Lion of the West" (as Rochester was called during the canal era) offers an **REI** outlet right beside the trail for those who need to reequip, as well as half-day canoe and kayak rentals at **Genesee Waterways Center.**

The first of several cities along the Erie Canal that take their name from ancient cities, **Palmyra** preserves numerous early 19th-century buildings and a fair amount of Mormon history. If you're passing through **Newark** on a summer Thursday, browse the **farmers market** for fresh provisions before

Beautiful views of the water follow the Erie Canalway Trail near Herkimer, New York.

traversing a rare road section between **Clyde** and **Weedsport.**

Unlike the bend around Rochester, the canal passes right through the middle of **Syracuse,** the largest city along the route. The **Great New York State Fairgrounds**—which host the state fair during the last three weeks of August—run by the trail before passage along **Water Street** in downtown Syracuse that includes the **Erie Canal Museum and Heritage Area Visitor Center** and the elegant Romanesque Revival **City Hall.** Syracuse also offers the convenience of three canalside bike shops.

Roughly 16 miles (26 km) east of Syracuse, the route passes an old Erie Canal drydock area that now harbors the **Chittenango Landing Canal Boat Museum.** As the birthplace of author L. Frank Baum, Chittenango is also home to the **All Things Oz Museum** and more than 15,000 items from the various *Wonderful World of Oz* books, plays, and movies.

Tacking to the northeast, the route slips into **Rome** and a rendezvous with historic sites like **Erie Canal Village,** the reconstructed **Fort Stanwix** of Revolutionary War renown, and **Oriskany Battlefield,** where American and British troops faced off in August 1777.

Learn about the canal at Lockport Locks, and catch a canal tour while you're there.

Starting its way down the **Mohawk River Valley,** the route soon reaches **Utica.** If you're running the trail, be sure to duck into the city's **National Distance Running Hall of Fame.** Otherwise, you can catch a ride into the mountains on the **Adirondack Scenic Railroad** or quaff a prize-winning IPA at the imposing redbrick factory home of **Saranac Brewery** (founded in 1888). Beyond Utica, the route is paved for much of its remaining mileage.

Continuing along the Mohawk, the Canalway passes historic **Fort Herkimer stone church** (erected in 1767) and a row of 19th-century waterfront factories in **Little Falls.** Repurposed into an entertainment and cultural complex called **Canal Place,** the vin-tage structures host the weeklong **Canal Celebration** in August as well as the annual **Mohawk Valley Garlic and Herb Festival** in September.

The arts, societies, and cultures of the Mohawk Valley are the focus of the modern **Arkell Museum** in **Canajoharie,** while **Schoharie Crossing State Historic Site** offers Erie Canal exhibits and historic canal structures like the ruined **Schoharie Aqueduct.** On the outer edge of the **Capital District, Mabee Farm Historic Site** preserves the oldest European house still standing in the Mohawk Valley (built in 1705).

Thomas Edison founded General Electric in **Schenectady** in 1892. Nowadays, the once gritty industrial city lights up the stage for performances at **Mopco Improv,** the **Schenectady Light Opera Company,** and Broadway summer stock at **Proctors Theatre** (opened in 1926).

The route continues along the Mohawk River to **Cohoes Falls** and the city of **Cohoes** on the **Hudson River.** Hikers and bikers can take the **Green Island Bridge** across the river to **Troy** and its numerous well-preserved historic district and 19th-century buildings used as backdrops for movies (*Scent of a Woman, Ironweed, The Age of Innocence*) and TV shows (*The Gilded Age*).

Dropping south along the Hudson, the Canalway reaches a grand finale at the waterfront **Corning Preserve** park in **Albany,** about a mile (1.6 km) from the **New York State Capitol Building.** ■

Long Trail
Vermont

The nation's oldest long-distance hiking trail rambles over the peaks and through the heavily forested wilderness areas of the Green Mountains.

THE BIG PICTURE

Distance: 272 miles (438 km)

Elevation Gain: approx. 65,000 feet (20,000 m)

Time: 3 weeks

Difficulty: Strenuous

Best Time: Summer or fall

More Info: greenmountainclub .org/the-long-trail

From the Green Mountain Boys of the American Revolution to Ben and Jerry of ice-cream fame, Vermonters have always marched to the beat of their own drum. That independent spirit also featured in the formation of the **Long Trail,** blazed in the early 20th century as a path where locals could commune more easily with Vermont nature.

Conditions were ideal for the creation of the nation's first long-distance hiking path. A mountainous spine runs the entire length of Vermont from north to south with plenty of wilderness along the way. The **Green Mountain Club,** which maintains the trail, has established more than 70 campsites and shelters along the route, so hikers have many overnight options.

The early success of the Vermont path is one of the factors that inspired the creation of the **Appalachian Trail** (AT) a decade later, and it now shares its initial 100 miles (160 km) with the AT. In fact, the best way to reach the southern terminal of the Long Trail is hiking 4.1 miles (6.6 km) of the northbound AT from Massachusetts Avenue in **North Adams,** Massachusetts.

Sherman Brooks Campsite provides digs near the state line, or hikers can continue into Vermont for a first overnight at **Seth Warner Shelter** or **Congdon Shelter** in **Green Mountain National Forest.** Skirting around the east side of **Bennington** and its Revolutionary War battlefield, the trail slides into heavily forested **Glastenbury Wilderness,** a critical habitat for black bears and an area that was actually clear-cut prior to the 1930s.

Stratton Mountain offers a chance to sojourn at a popular winter/summer resort before resuming the hike through **Lye Brook Wilderness** and a section that rambles across peaks overlooking **Manchester Center.** After passing through **Mad Tom Notch,** the trail takes its sweet time meandering through **Peru Peak Wilderness** and **Stafford White Rocks National Recreation Area.**

Coolidge State Forest and **Killington** resort provide a connector between the south and north sections of Green Mountain National Forest. Reaching **Middlebury Gap,** hikers can detour down into the eponymous college town or plunge into a lengthy walk through **Breadloaf Wilderness Area.**

Watch the conditions near Jay Peak on the Long Trail. Mud is so ubiquitous on Vermont's hiking trails that the state has garnered the nickname "Vermud."

The ski lifts offer sky-high views of the sunrise at Middlebury Snow Bowl on the Long Trail.

Beyond **Camel's Hump State Park,** the route rendezvouses with Interstate 89 and a short road journeys into **Montpelier** to see the golden-domed state capitol, **Burlington** for a glance at **Lake Champlain,** or historic **Waterbury** village and its **Ben & Jerry's Factory Tour.** The hike through **Mount Mansfield State Forest** includes a summit of 4,393-foot (1,339-m) **Mount Mansfield,** the highest point in Vermont.

North of State Route 15, slender **Long Trail State Forest** was created in 1996 for the specific purpose of ushering the route on its homestretch to **Jay Peak** and the Vermont-Québec border. From there, it's about a five-mile (8-km) walk into **North Troy** village. ■

LOCAL FLAVOR

• **Papa Pete's:** Reload your carbs with the giant, pizza-size pancakes and other breakfast and lunch goodies at this roadside café near Bennington; 1104 Woodford Road, Woodford, VT; facebook.com/ Papa-Petes-of-Bennington-VT -Home-of-the-Giant-Pancakes -189049503043.

• **The Warren Store:** Restock your backpack with deli cheese, meat, and bakery items—and grab a breakfast burrito or gourmet sandwich—at a provisions store founded in 1839; 284 Main Street, Warren, VT; warrenstore.com.

• **Liquid Art Coffeehouse & Eatery:** Yummy breakfast sandwiches and lunchtime soups,

salads, and wraps make this a worthwhile downhill detour off the trail; 37 Miller Brook Rd, Killington, VT; liquidartvt.com.

• **Moogs Joint:** Splurge on apple cider chicken, penne Florentine, or honey barbecued pork at a laidback eatery with live music and plenty of outdoor seating in the Lamoille Valley; 1015 Highway 15, Johnson, VT; moogsjoint.com.

• **Miso Hungry:** Ramen noodles and miso soup are the forte of a vintage tramcar turned food cart (with summer sand volleyball) at Jay Peak Resort; 1136 Jay Peak Road, Jay, VT; jaypeakresort.com/ things-to-do/restaurants-dining/ miso-hungry.

Go a short distance past the rock garden to experience a panoramic view at White Rocks overlook on the Long Trail near Wallingford, Vermont.

C&O Canal Towpath
Maryland, Virginia & D.C.

An ambitious 18th-century transportation project laid the groundwork for a popular hiking and biking path along the Potomac River upstream from Washington, D.C.

In addition to winning the American Revolution and presiding over the transition from British dependency to an independent democratic republic, George Washington also gets credit (at least in part) for one of the most popular hiking and biking routes in the mid-Atlantic states.

Four years before he was elected the first president, Washington helped found a company to improve navigation along the **Potomac River** and spur waterborne trade between the Atlantic and the Great Lakes. A cornerstone of that plan was a series of canals beside the Potomac that later evolved into the **Chesapeake and Ohio Canal.**

The dirt and stone towpaths where mules once pulled canal boats along the route are now the realm of hikers and bikers propelling themselves along a 184-mile (296-km) trail between the Maryland panhandle and Washington, D.C. Campgrounds spaced five to

THE BIG PICTURE

Distance: 184.5 miles (297 km)

Elevation Gain: Negligible

Time: 1–2 weeks

Difficulty: Easy

Best Time: Year-round

More Info: canaltrust.org and nps.gov/choh

seven miles (8 to 11 km) apart along the towpath serve backpackers and bikepackers.

Picking up where the **Great Allegheny Passage** leaves off, the **C&O Canal Towpath** starts its downward journey at the Park Service's **Cumberland Visitor Center** and **C&O Canal Museum** inside an imposing redbrick depot shared with the **Western Maryland Scenic Railroad.** On the outskirts of **Cumberland,** the trail crosses the **Evitts Creek Aqueduct,** the first of 11 bridges that carried the canal over streams flowing into the Potomac.

Twenty-nine miles (46 km) from Cumberland, the canal and towpath make their way through the **Paw Paw Tunnel,** an engineering feat that cut six miles (9.6 km) off the C&O's total length. Ramblers have a choice of disappearing into the aperture or hiking the open-air **Tunnel Hill Trail** to the other side.

A sinuous passage through **Green Ridge State Forest**—Maryland's largest tract of public land—takes the trail past the ruins of **Round Top Cement Mill** into **Hancock** in the narrowest part of the Maryland panhandle. Sample luscious local apples at **Blue Goose Market** before moving down the trail to **Fort Frederick State Park** and a reconstructed 18th-century bastion that was active during three wars. Nearby

Picturesque Georgetown offers joggers a quaint path along the Chesapeake and Ohio Canal.

The Chesapeake and Ohio Canal Towpath owes its creation in part to a company that was founded by George Washington and went on to create the canal system.

Lockhouse 49 is one of seven lock-keeper cottages where visitors can spend the night.

Williamsport harbors a cluster of historic C&O buildings around the **Cushwa Basin** and canal boat rides over **Conococheague Aqueduct.** The Civil War looms ahead on a possible side trip to **Antietam National Battlefield,** a railroad bridge across the Potomac to **Harpers Ferry,** and relics of John Brown's 1859 raid on the federal armory.

After sharing 2.6 miles (4 km) of towpath with the **Appalachian Trail,** the C&O continues its downstream journey through **Brunswick** and the outer edge of the **National Capital Region** to **Great Falls Park.** Managed by the National Park Service, the big green space offers three different **Billy Goat Trails** and canal cruises in mule-pulled packet boats.

A grand finale walk or ride past the canalside **Abner Cloud House** (built in 1801) and **Fletcher's Boathouse** (rental rowboats, kayaks, and paddleboards) ends in the heart of fashionable **Georgetown.** ∎

Presidential Traverse
New Hampshire

Ponder the lives of seven presidents—and other noteworthy Americans with namesake peaks—while trekking this iconic rough-and-tumble route across the White Mountains.

THE BIG PICTURE

Distance: 23 miles (37 km)

Elevation Gain: approx. 9,000 feet (2,740 m)

Time: 2–3 days

Difficulty: Strenuous

Best Time: Summer or early fall

More Info: summitpost.org/the -presidential-traverse/796154

New England's most celebrated hike rambles up and over seven peaks in the **Presidential Range** of northern New Hampshire. Although it's just 23 miles (37 km) in length, the hike involves around 9,000 feet (2,740 m) of elevation gain and potentially some of the gnarliest weather on planet Earth.

The region's Native Americans never climbed the peaks because they considered them sacred, the abode of gods. The first known ascent was by English colonist Darby Field in 1642, and it's been a thing ever since. Locals started renaming the peaks after U.S. presidents shortly after the Revolutionary War, starting with Mount Washington when he was still a general rather than the chief executive.

The ultimate challenge is bagging all seven presidents in a single day, a quest best left to experienced long-distance hikers. Some also try conquering the route in winter, largely a fool's errand considering that more than 150 people have perished while hiking the Presidential Range (mainly from hypothermia and avalanches) since 1849.

Ordinary mortals undertake the **Presidential Traverse** as a multiday hike. Dispersed camping above the tree line is forbidden in the range, but a string of mountain huts and campgrounds offer overnight digs.

Veteran trekkers recommend starting from the north end, a trailhead off U.S. Highway 2 near **Randolph.** Several trails climb **Mount Madison**—including a path beside **Snyder Brook** with several waterfalls—but all involve around 4,000 feet (1,220 m) of elevation gain to reach the first presidential summit.

Mount Adams looms a little farther along the vertiginous **Star Lake Trail,** which features a sheer drop-off into the **Madison Gulf.** The route soon segues onto a leg of the **Appalachian Trail** for the hike to **Mount Jefferson** and **Mount Washington.**

After navigating 10 miles (16 km) of solitary wilderness, many hikers find themselves overwhelmed by Mount Washington's three-ring circus. Thousands of people reach the highest point in New England (6,288 feet/1,917 m) each day during

Colorful train cars park on the Mount Washington Cog Railway lines in White Mountain National Forest.

What the Presidential Traverse Trail lacks in length (it's just 23 miles/37 km long), it makes up for in 9,000 feet (2,740 m) of elevation gain and challenging weather systems.

the summer season via a vintage **cog railway** (opened in 1868) and a **scenic auto road** (finished in 1861).

Among the summit's eclectic attractions are a cafeteria, gift shops, post office, interactive extreme weather exhibit, and a **weather observatory** where a longtime, world-record wind speed of 231 miles (372 km) an hour was recorded in 1934. Take a load off, grab a meal, scribble a postcard to the folks back home, or quickly escape into the wilderness again. Your choice.

Although the traverse isn't quite all downhill from there, the hardest part is now history. It's a relatively easy walk along the **Crawford Path**—blazed in 1819 and considered the nation's oldest continuously

maintained hiking trail—to the summits of the last three presidents **(Monroe, Eisenhower,** and **Pierce)**

and a final steep descent to the route's southern terminus in **Crawford Notch.** ■

LAY YOUR HEAD

- **Valley Way Campground:** Located around three miles (4.8 km) from the north trailhead, this primitive Forest Service tent site near Snyder Brook offers the only free digs along the traverse; fs.usda.gov/recarea/whitemountain/recarea/?recid=74537.

- **AMC Madison Spring Hut:** Built in 1888, this historic cabin on Mount Madison offers hot meals, potable water, bunk beds, weather reports, and naturalist talks from early June to late September; from $256 all-inclusive; outdoors.org.

- **Randolph Mountain Club:** The RMC maintains three rustic cabins with kitchen, outhouse, and sleeping pads at around 4,200 feet (1,280 m), just below the tree line to the west of Mounts Madison and Adams; $8–$25 per person; randolphmountainclub.org.

- **AMC Lakes of the Cloud Hut:** Although much newer than the other AMC cabin in the Presidential Range, this overnight stop between Mounts Washington and Monroe offers hikers similar facilities and services; from $256 all-inclusive; outdoors.org.

Cutler Coast Loop
Maine

Maine's Bold Coast offers an audacious location for a short but spectacular hike along the pristine shoreline between Acadia and the Canadian border.

THE BIG PICTURE

Distance: 10.3 miles (16.6 km)

Elevation Gain: approx. 970 feet (300 m)

Time: 1–2 days

Difficulty: Moderate

Best Time: Spring, summer, or fall

More Info: maine.gov/dacf/ parksearch/PropertyGuides/ PDF_GUIDE/cutlercoastguide .pdf

Any list of the best hiking trails in Maine is invariably packed with walking routes in Acadia. And rightly so: The first national park east of the Mississippi is drop-dead gorgeous. But just a two-hour drive north of **Bar Harbor** is a trail with equally stunning shoreline scenery and just a fraction of fellow hikers.

The **Cutler Coast Loop** is part of a state public land reserve that safeguards more than 12,000 acres (4,856 ha) of beaches, bluffs, forest, bogs, and blueberry barrens along the **Bold Coast** between **Winter Harbor** and **Lubec.** More than 200 bird species have been recorded in the reserve, while the offshore waters in the Bay of Fundy provide safe harbor for seals, whales, and porpoises. Whale-watching is at its best from early summer to early fall; bird-watching is best from spring to fall.

The coast's other claim to fame—something that late fall or winter hikers can experience by camping along the Cutler Coast Loop—is the earliest sunrise in the United States on mornings between October and March. The park's five campsites are situated along the shore, 3 to 5 miles (4.8 to 8 km) from the parking lot and trailhead on State Highway 191.

Trekkers can tackle the loop in either direction, but most are anxious to reach the coast before venturing inland. Which means walking the trail in a clockwise direction. The first hint of sea—the sound of crashing waves, an onshore breeze ruffling the trees, and perhaps a hint of salt water in the air—comes around half an hour from the trailhead. And suddenly you're there, at **Ocean Overlook,** standing at the top of jagged cliffs staring out at the **Bay of Fundy.**

From that initial vantage point, the trail heads south—along the top of igneous bedrock deposited 450 million years ago by ancient volcanoes—to **Black Point Cove** and the first overnight spot—just three miles (4.8 km) into the hike. Below the cliffs is a small rocky beach, reached via a log ladder for those who dare take a dip in the chilly (even in summer) North Atlantic.

There's another campsite at **Long Point Cove,** the next big

An Atlantic puffin on Machias Seal Island off the coast of Maine

With an otherworldly beauty all its own, the Bold Coast Trail transports hikers to a land of moss-covered forests and beckoning beaches.

inlet along the coast, and three more near **Fairy Head** at the reserve's southern extreme. Be sure to pack binoculars, because no matter where you camp, there's a good chance of seeing wildlife. A variety of shorebirds nest or migrate along the Bold Coast. Four whale species have been spotted offshore, including humpbacks, minkes, and very rare fin and northern right whales.

Just beyond Fairy Head, the loop veers away from the coast for an inland portion that weaves through alternating forest, grassy barrens, and freshwater bogs. The area's maritime forest comprises mainly spruce, larch, and fir trees.

There's copious birdlife, including six different types of owl, as well as a beaver pond. The inland section stretches just over five miles (8 km) between Fairy Head and the starting point. ■

OTHER GREAT TRAILS

• **Eastern Promenade and Back Cove Trails:** Starting from the top of Maine State Pier, Portland's premier walking route (5.6 miles/9 km) passes through historic Fort Allen Park and across Tukey's Bridge before a huge loop around Back Cove.

• **Cutts Island Loop:** Environmental icon Rachel Carson would no doubt appreciate this short but scenic coastal woodland trail (1.8 miles/2.9 km) in the national wildlife refuge that bears her name.

• **Mount Battie Trail:** It's only a half mile (0.8 km) to the top and its historic stone tower, but the view of Penobscot Bay and the Camden coast makes this steep, rocky climb worthwhile.

• **The Beehive:** Cadillac Mountain may have the global rep, but many insiders think the most stunning trail in Acadia National Park is the near-vertical trek across narrow rock ledges and iron rungs to the summit of Beehive Mountain above Sand Beach.

Ocean bluffs carry hikers alongside sunshine and waves on the stunning Cutler Coast Loop.

The Long Path
New York

Meandering through the wilds of the Empire State between New York City and the Adirondacks, the Long Path takes in the lovely Hudson Valley and rugged Catskills along routes once tramped by Native Americans, frontiersmen, and great American writers.

THE BIG PICTURE

Distance: 358 miles (576 km)

Elevation Gain: approx. 68,080 feet (20,750 m)

Time: 3–4 weeks

Difficulty: Moderate to strenuous

Best Time: Late spring, summer, or early fall

More Info: nynjtc.org/region/long-path

The 175th Street subway station in Manhattan may seem like an odd spot to start a wilderness hike. But it's perfect for a trail that exposes the remarkable extremes of the Empire State, from skyscrapers and mighty bridges to ancient trees and early American towns.

Beyond the great metropolis, the **Long Path** offers a trip back in time to an age when upstate New York was mostly wilderness. The trail takes its name from *Song of the Open Road* by 19th-century American poet and fresh-air advocate Walt Whitman: "The long brown path before me, leading wherever I choose . . ."

New York's long brown path heads north from the Big Apple through the **Hudson Valley,** the **Catskill Mountains,** and the **Mohawk Valley** to the southern edge of the **Adirondacks.** Although there's plenty of farmland along the way, the trail sticks as much as possible to heavily wooded and often rugged state parks and forest preserves.

Catering to casual trekkers as well as thru-hikers, the route is divided into 40 segments, each of them perfect for day hikes.

The Long Path was born in the mind of a Renaissance man—meteorologist, scientist, archaeologist, historic preservationist, winter sportsman, and avid walker Vincent Schaefer. After helping to create the Mohawk Valley Hiking Club in 1929, he proposed a long-distance path across New York to a journalist friend who began advocating for the path in his newspaper column.

Together with friends and family members, Schaefer scouted the initial route in the early 1930s. But he was adamant that it shouldn't be signposted or otherwise marked. According to the New York–New Jersey Trail Conference, which oversees the path today, Schaefer wanted hikers to use a map, compass, and dead reckoning to navigate between landmarks along the way.

But things didn't turn out that way. By the 1940s, hikers were blazing a marked route between New York City and the Catskills. The northern half of the Long Path took decades to complete, and its evolution continues as vehicle-free footpaths replace rural roadway portions.

Hikers ride the A train to Upper **Manhattan** to commence a

The Long Path reaches its peak (literally) in the Catskill Mountains, with views of the Blackhead Range from Burnt Knob.

At 728 feet (222 m), Hook Mountain is the second highest peak in the Hudson Valley.

northward journey on the Long Path. But the trail doesn't linger long in the city, for almost at once you're walking across the **George Washington Bridge.**

Opened in 1931 as the world's longest suspension bridge, the span is still the world's busiest motor vehicle bridge, with an average of 3.5 million cars and trucks passing each day. The pedestrian walkway along the south side of the upper deck renders awesome views of the **Hudson River** and **Manhattan skyline.**

Reaching the far side, the trail hangs a sharp right and follows the celebrated **Palisades** cliffs through 14 miles (22.5 km) of **New Jersey** before reentering New York via **Tallman Mountain State Park.** Creeping up the river's west bank, the trail passes through several historic villages like **Nyack,** a boatbuilding hub

where visitors can charter a sailboat on the Hudson.

North of Nyack, the route turns inland for an ascent of **High Tor,** a

bald-topped mountain with views of the Hudson Valley and (on a clear day) the far-off New York City skyline. Beyond Palisades Parkway is

---

DETOURS

• **West Point:** Located near Section 7 of the Long Path, the riverside heights offer views of the U.S. Military Academy campus and Revolutionary War strongholds Fort Clinton and Fort Putnam.

• **Storm King Art Center:** America's largest outdoor sculpture garden—including works by Alexander Calder, Henry Moore, and Richard Serra—sprawls across 500 acres (202 ha) near Section 8.

• **Delaware Water Gap National Recreation Area:** Located just seven miles (11 km) down the Delaware River from Port Jervis, the NRA

renders water sports, horseback riding, rock climbing, and 28 miles (45 km) of the Appalachian Trail.

• **Woodstock:** Although the legendary 1969 music fest took place in nearby Bethel, this Catskills burg retains its counterculture galleries, theater, concerts, a popular flea market, and Buddhist monastery.

• **Schenectady:** Cinema and stage plays at the restored Proctor's Theatre (opened in 1926), the Museum of Innovation and Science, and Via Aquarium offer an urban break in the Mohawk Valley near Section 38.

one of the Long Path highlights: **Harriman State Park.** Founded in 1910 on land donated by the Harriman family of railroad fame, the park embraces more than 30 lakes and several campsites and trailside shelters. It's also the only place where the Long Path intersects with the **Appalachian Trail.**

Edging along the boundary of the **U.S. Military Academy** at West Point, the trail runs up and over **Schunemunk Mountain** and follows the **Orange Heritage Trailway** through the pastoral countryside to **Goshen.** A horse-racing hub since the 18th century, Goshen is home to the **Harness Racing Museum & Hall of Fame** and the **Historic Track** (opened in 1838), where racing still takes place every summer.

The route comes within five miles (8 km) of the **Delaware River** near **Port Jervis,** New York, before tacking to the northeast and following lengthy **Shawangunk Ridge** into the **Catskill Mountains,** where the Long Path reaches its literal peak.

Much of the range is protected within the confines of **Catskill Park.** Established in 1885 as one of America's first state parks, the reserve offers 10 segments and more than 100 miles (160 km) of the Long Path, including many of the **Catskill High Peaks** (mountains that rise above 3,500 feet/1,067 m). Astride the trail and nearly dead center in the park is artsy-craftsy **Phoenicia,** a hamlet renowned for its **International Festival of the Voice** (August) and the **Empire State Railway Museum.**

Schoharie Valley gives the trail a natural route down out of the

Follow the Peekamoose-Table Trail to Table Mountain for views of the Catskills along the Long Path.

Dense old-growth forests line the Northville-Lake Placid and North Country Trails in the Adirondacks.

Catskills into the farmland of central New York. All is peaceful now, but during the Revolutionary War the valley was the scene of bloody fighting between the British-allied Iroquois and American farmers.

The Long Path traverses yet more wilderness, with lakeside **Mine Kill State Park** and several state forests on its way to Vroman's Nose, a rocky outcrop above the Schoharie Valley. It then traces the historic **Indian Ladder Trail** through **John Boyd Thacher State Park** before descending into the **Mohawk Valley.**

Just west of the **Albany-Troy-Schenectady** metro area, the town of **Altamont** was the traditional end of the trail until the 1990s, when the Long Path North Hiking Club endeavored to extend the route across the Mohawk Valley.

Following mostly rural roads, this northward extension crosses the **Mohawk River/Erie Canal** on the **Lock 9 bridge** before marching through the backwoods of **Saratoga County** to the southern edge of **Adirondack Park.** The Long Path finally peters out in **Northville** on **Great Sacandaga Lake,** with plenty of options to continue trekking into the Adirondacks. ■

OTHER GREAT TRAILS

Into the Adirondacks

The Long Path gets even longer for those who continue into the Adirondack Mountains of northern New York. Founded in 1892—and framed by the famous Blue Line boundary drawn on their original map of the park—it's the largest nature reserve of any kind east of the Mississippi.

Capable of equaling or surpassing just about any national park in its majesty, the Adirondacks embrace more than 10,000 lakes, thousands of campsites, 46 peaks near or more than 4,000 feet (1,220 m), and the scenic shorelines along Lake Champlain and Lake George.

The Adirondacks also offer more than 2,000 miles (3,200 km) of walking routes, including the

Northville-Placid Trail (NPT) through the heart of the park.

Starting from the northern terminus of the Long Path, the NPT rambles through some of the region's most remote corners, generally straying away from the heavily visited (in summer) tourist areas. Campsites and hiker shelters are well spaced along the route.

Here and there along its 138-mile (222-km) length, the NPT offers opportunities for non-hiking adventures, like white-water rafting the Hudson Gorge and scenic flights in vintage floatplanes from Long Lake. The trail eventually climbs into the fabled High Peaks Wilderness and its 40-plus summits before ending in the winter sports haven of Lake Placid.

Niagara Gorge Trails
New York

The bluffs, cliffs, and rocky slopes downstream from Niagara Falls provide a dramatic setting for a series of trails that reveal the area's natural and human history.

THE BIG PICTURE

Distance: 1 to 6.2 miles (1.6 to 10 km)

Elevation Gain: Various

Time: 1–2 hours

Difficulty: Easy to strenuous

Best Time: Late spring, summer, fall, or early winter

More Info: niagarafallsstatepark .com

Although long overshadowed by Niagara Falls—and justly so, given the natural and historical significance of the celebrated cascades—the **Niagara Gorge** is awe-inspiring all on its own. Like the falls, the gorge was formed over thousands of years by the world's largest pool of fresh water (the Great Lakes) seeking the easiest outlet to the Atlantic.

Stretching 7.1 miles (11.4 km) between the bottom of the falls and Lake Ontario, the gorge harbors a dozen species of rare and endangered plants on its cliffs and rocky talus slopes. From bald eagles and peregrine falcons to 19 gull species, the gorge also provides shelter for many birds, as many as 50,000 individuals from a single species during the peak of autumn migration.

Eight trails along the American side of the gorge connect five New York state parks. Rambling across an array of terrain, they range from flat and extremely easy to steep and difficult. Park authorities suggest that hikers avoid the more challenging route in winter and early spring, when rockfalls are more likely to occur during or following inclement weather.

The **Niagara Gorge Rim Trail** (6.2 miles/10 km) is far and away the most popular, used by around eight million people each year. For good reason. Starting from a spectacular overlook of **Horseshoe Falls** on **Goat Island,** the route offers access to the **Cave of the Winds,** the 282-foot (86-m) **Observation Tower** and entrance to *Maid of the Mist* boat tours, the state park's **Orin Lehman Visitor Center,** the **Aquarium of Niagara,** and two bridges across the gorge to the Canadian side.

Those who want to explore farther along the gorge should pop into the **Niagara Gorge Discovery Center,** which features a museum with hands-on exhibits and a trail information hut where hikers can snatch maps or join guided hikes from late spring through fall. Right outside the discovery center is the start of the easy **Robert Moses Recreation Trail** (3.2 miles/5.1 km) through the woods behind the rim to

Old Fort Niagara has been occupied by three different nations during its long history: France, Great Britain, and the United States.

Named after a now collapsed rock overhang, the incredible Cave of the Winds is accessed via the Niagara Gorge Rim Trail.

Deveaux Woods and **Devil's Hole State Parks.**

Beneath the rim, the hiking becomes much more challenging. The short but moderate **American Falls Gorge Trail** (1 mile/1.6 km) meanders through the ruins of the old **Schoellkopf Power Station**—largely destroyed by a massive 1956 landslide—while the **Whirlpool Rapids Loop** (1.3 miles/ 2.1 km) involves multiple stairs and boulder hopping along the **Niagara River.**

Steep stairs descend to the **Devil's Hole Trail** (2.5-mile/4-km round-trip) for a close encounter with the cave and rapids of the same name, at a place where a Seneca war party ambushed a British Army convoy in 1763. Farther down the gorge, **Artpark State Park** hosts two additional trails as well as outdoor summer concerts and alfresco art projects.

At the bottom of the gorge, **Fort Niagara State Park** offers five trails along **Lake Ontario,** the Lower Niagara River, and around a largely restored 17th-century citadel that saw action in the French and Indian War, American Revolution, and War of 1812. ■

OTHER GREAT TRAILS

Niagara River Recreation Trail

Across the border in Ontario, hikers and bikers can journey along the **Niagara River Recreation Trail,** a 33-mile (53 km) paved path along the Niagara corridor between Lake Ontario and Lake Erie.

The trail divides into northern and southern halves separated by the city of Niagara Falls, Ontario. Hikers, runners, and cyclists are welcome during the warmer times, snowshoers and Nordic skiers in winter.

Starting from Niagara-on-the-Lake, the trail includes Fort George, Queenston Heights, Niagara Glen Nature Centre, and the Whirlpool Aero Car. The route resumes above Horseshoe Falls along a path that includes Chippewa Battlefield and the Willoughby one-room schoolhouse museum to Fort Erie.

Wissahickon Valley Park Trail

Pennsylvania

Philadelphia's brotherly love extends to the Wissahickon Valley, a favorite wilderness escape since the 17th century and still a favorite nature walk.

Inspired by an 1844 journey through the Wissahickon Valley, horror maestro Edgar Allan Poe set aside his bread-and-butter work for a brief venture into travel writing that extolled the vale's primal beauty in no uncertain terms.

"The Wissahiccon [*sic*] is of so remarkable a loveliness that, were it flowing in England, it would be the theme of every bard, and the common topic of every tongue," Poe gushed in an essay called "Morning on the Wissahiccon." "Its banks are . . . clothed with noble shrubbery near the water, and crowned at a greater elevation, with some of the most magnificent forest trees of America."

Nearly two centuries later, the valley and its namesake creek retain their magic allure. They are now protected within the confines of **Wissahickon Valley Park,** just a 20-minute drive from downtown Philly but light-years in mood from the huge urban area that now surrounds it.

The park harbors more than 50 miles (80 km) of hiking, biking, and equestrian paths, including the **Wissahickon Valley Park Trail** (WVPT), which runs just over seven miles (11 km) down the middle of the gorge to the creek's confluence with the **Schuylkill River.**

Much of the route flows along **Forbidden Drive,** a crushed gravel path that hugs the western side of **Wissahickon Creek.** Originally constructed before the Civil War, the onetime carriage toll road and motorcar route became "forbidden" in 1924, when it was closed to wheeled traffic.

Starting from the top end, the route begins beside a small parking lot at the intersection of Thomas Road and Northwestern Avenue in the city's **Andorra** neighborhood. Quickly disappearing into the trees, the trail soon reaches **The Cedars House** restaurant and the slow-flowing creek.

Several bridges jump the creek, including the stone **Bells Mill Road Bridge** (1820) and the dark red **Thomas Mill Covered Bridge** (1855). About a third of the way

Wissahickon Creek meanders under a picturesque covered bridge in Wissahickon Valley Park.

Autumn returns to Forbidden Drive in Wissahickon Valley Park with a vibrant blanket of fall color.

down the trail, the **Valley Green Inn** offers brunch and lunch in a lovely, whitewashed structure opened in the 1850s as the valley's first tourism enterprise.

Having satisfied their appetite, hikers can continue down Forbidden Drive or hop across the creek to the **Orange Trail,** a narrow dirt footpath down the east bank past the **historic Glen Fern Farm** (ca 1725) and **The Monastery** house and stable, erected in 1747, near the spot where a German mystic and his doomsday cult awaited the end of the world in 1694.

Both Forbidden Drive and the Orange Trail peter out near **Rittenhouse Town,** where six historic structures recall the village's papermaking days (1690–1732). One of the old stone buildings houses the **Paper**

Trail Bike Café, which serves hot and cold drinks and baked goods.

Shifting onto **Lincoln Drive Trail,** the route continues along the creek to busy **Ridge Avenue.** To

continue the hike, cross the street and follow the **Schuylkill River Trail** downstream to **Fairmount Park,** the **Philadelphia Museum of Art,** and downtown **Philadelphia.** ■

APRÈS HIKE

• **Morris Arboretum:** More than 13,000 plants—including very rare dawn redwoods from China—flourish in this University of Pennsylvania botanical park, which doubles as the state's official arboretum.

• **Wissahickon Brewing Company:** Craft beer, cider, and wine are served at an establishment conveniently located near the southern end of the trail in the East Falls neighborhood.

• **Chestnut Hill:** Perched along the valley's east side, Philly's historic

"Garden District" overflows with trendy restaurants, bars, and boutiques.

• **Woodmere Art Museum:** The homegrown art and artists of Philadelphia are the focus of a collection tucked inside a 19th-century stone mansion near the trail's northern end.

• **Manayunk Main Street:** This onetime working-class neighborhood along the Schuylkill River is popular for bar-hopping and Philadelphia's biggest summer arts festival.

Canada

Cloud cover hides the peaks surrounding Moraine Lake in Banff National Park.

Cape Chignecto Coastal Loop

Nova Scotia

World-record high tides and even higher cliffs adorn a hiking route that wanders along a remote, rugged coast on the Nova Scotia peninsula.

It doesn't take a *Jeopardy!* champion to answer one of the world's enduring geography questions: Where are the world's greatest tides? The **Bay of Fundy,** of course.

While millions of people flock to the easily accessible **New Brunswick,** the tides along the **Nova Scotia** side are just as extraordinary, especially those along the shore of **Cape Chignecto Provincial Park.**

Located about a two-hour drive

THE BIG PICTURE

Distance: 34 miles (55 km)

Elevation Gain: approx. 6,500 feet (2,000 m)

Time: 3–6 days

Difficulty: Moderate to strenuous

Best Time: Spring, summer, or fall

More Info: parks.novascotia.ca/cape-chignecto-hiking-trails

from **Amherst** on the Trans-Canada Highway, the remote reserve boasts 40-foot (12-m) tides that ebb and flow beneath the highest cliffs on the **Nova Scotia peninsula.** Adding to its allure is the park's inclusion in **Cliffs of Fundy UNESCO Global Geopark.**

The hydrographic phenomenon is easily viewed from the beach beside the **Cape Chignecto Visitor Centre** near **Advocate Harbour.** But the only way to explore the park's entire coast—and its 600-foot (180-m) palisades—is hiking the **Cape Chignecto Coastal Loop.**

More or less triangular, the route runs along beaches and cliff tops, and through a lush "fog forest" inhabited by mature red spruce, endemic wildflowers, and a few of the only moose that survive on mainland Nova Scotia. Campsites and a bunkhouse provide the overnight digs.

You can walk the loop in either direction. But it's almost impossible to resist the temptation to start out along the park's spectacular coast rather than the inland leg. At low tide, hikers can trek the first mile (1.6 km) along a rocky beach past the rust-colored **Red Rocks.**

Steep wooden stairs lift the route to the forested heights and an up-and-down walk along the coast to

An eastern cottontail *(Sylvilagus floridanus)* in Cape Chignecto Provincial Park, Nova Scotia

The Bay of Fundy follows the New Brunswick coastline, with the entirety of the route within the UNESCO Fundy Biosphere Reserve.

Mill Brook Cove and the campsite at **Refugee Cove,** about a 7.5-mile (12-km) hike from the visitors center. The latter cove draws its name from French-speaking Acadians who tried to avoid the 18th-century British forced relocation from Nova Scotia by hiding out at Cape Chignecto.

Day two starts with a short hike along the cliff to **Cape Chignecto** and its striking views across the Bay of Fundy. Tacking right, the trail makes its way up the park's west coast past **Little Bald Rock, Big Bald Rock,** and **Carey Brook** to the beachside campsite at **Seal Cove.**

If you're not tired and doing the trail as a quick three-day walk, carry on along the shore to the historic **Eatonville** area. During the 19th and early 20th centuries, a shipyard and sawmill sat beside **Eatonville Harbour.**

Hike short spur trails to the **Three Sisters** sea stacks—the focus of an ancient Mi'kmaq legend—and the rocky red-sand beach at **Andersons Cove** before settling in for the night at the Eatonville campground or bunkhouse. On the final day, it's a 9.6-mile (15.5-km) trek back to Advocate Harbour through the coastal rainforest. ■

OTHER GREAT TRAILS

• **Rum Runners Trail:** Stretching 74 miles (119 km) down the Atlantic shore from Halifax, the all-weather Rum Runners route weaves around bays, coves, and beaches along a coast renowned for illicit alcohol smuggling during Prohibition.

• **Sentier de Clare:** The Acadian heritage of southwest Nova Scotia inspired this 26-mile (42-km) multiuse rail trail between Weymouth and Hectanooga, with the possibility of continuing along the Yarmouth County Rail Trail.

• **Skyline Trail:** Nova Scotia's most celebrated hike is small in distance (4 miles/6.5 km) but big on wildlife and awesome views across the Cape Breton Island coast and Gulf of St. Lawrence.

• **Cape Split Loop:** Find more great views of the Bay of Fundy along an 8.2-mile (13.2-km) circuit across palisades on the provincial park's Scots Bay and Minas Basin Trails.

• **Liberty Lake Loop:** This 45-mile (72-km) hike around the periphery of Kejimkujik National Park offers a rare glimpse of wilderness and glacial landforms in the heart of the Nova Scotia peninsula.

Fundy Footpath
New Brunswick

Extreme tides and intense wilderness are the focus of a no-nonsense trail that rambles along a remote stretch of Canada's east coast.

THE BIG PICTURE

Distance: 25 miles (41 km)

Elevation Gain: approx. 9,010 feet (2,750 m)

Time: 3–5 days

Difficulty: Strenuous

Best Time: Spring, summer, or fall

More Info: hikingnb.ca/Trails/FundyEast/FundyFootpath.html

The whimsical name and its relatively short distance make the **Fundy Footpath** sound like an easy stroll in the park. But make no mistake: This trail along the New Brunswick coast is a pretty tough customer.

The allure is a walk along a rugged and remote stretch of the Bay of Fundy, a branch of the Atlantic that boasts the world's most extreme tides—an average 52 feet (16 m)

between the diurnal highs and lows. The entire route lies within the **Fundy Biosphere Reserve.**

What makes the trail so challenging is steep coastal terrain, an exhausting series of ravines and bluffs with an overall elevation gain equal to climbing more than 9,000 feet (2,700 m) straight up a mountainside.

The route also crosses two tidal

rivers that can only be forded at low tide, so trekkers need to consult an accurate tidal table. The **Fundy Trail Parkway Interpretive Centre** in **Salmon River** village (near the trail's west end) sells a footpath kit that includes a map and tide chart.

Those who can't or don't want to walk the entire footpath can sample the remote shore by walking short stretches at either end. Those who undertake the thru-hike are rewarded with a slice of the Canadian coast that seems virtually unchanged from when the Norsemen, Basque fishermen, and French explorers landed hundreds of years ago.

Starting from the Interpretive Centre parking lot, the Fundy Footpath crosses the **Salmon River** on a pedestrian bridge and then points for the coast. The opening five miles (8 km) are relatively easy, some of it beside the scenic **Fundy Trail Parkway.** Among the waypoints is **Tufts' Point,** where hikers can access the beach via wooden steps. **Seely Beach** (above the high tide line) is a popular spot to spend the first night on the trail.

Beyond Seely Beach the hike gets strenuous, creeping along the cliff tops and through several steep ravines with grades that are occasionally so steep the route requires cable stairs. The payoff is a second overnight in

Stop for a photo op at the Point Wolfe covered bridge over the Wolfe River Gorge.

Point Wolfe marks the final leg of the Fundy Footpath with an eight-mile (13-km) stretch in Fundy National Park.

the gorgeous **Little Salmon River Valley.** After making camp, trekkers can explore the shore or follow a spur trail through the narrow **Eye of the Needle** ravine to **Walton Glen Gorge Falls.**

Day four evolves into another tough roller-coaster hike, but plenty distracts trekkers from their aching muscles, including several waterfalls and the **Rapidy Brook suspension bridge.** Beyond **Telegraph Brook Beach,** the trail veers inland to a camping spot beside the **Quiddy River.** At low tide, hikers can cross a gravel bar to jagged **Martin Head** and fossilized sand dunes.

The final stretch is an eight-mile (13-km) hike from Quiddy River

to **Point Wolfe** in **Fundy National Park.** Once again, there's plenty of up and down. But the biggest challenge is timing your arrival at **Goose Creek** so it's shallow enough to ford

at low tide. Those who want to linger along the coast can crash at **Point Wolfe Campground** with its tent sites, laundry facilities, and hot showers. ■

LOCAL FLAVOR

• **Alma Lobster Shop:** Reward yourself for a successful traverse of the Fundy Footpath with lobster rolls, lobster tacos, or steamed whole lobsters at this eating institution on the edge of Fundy National Park; 36 Shore Lane, Alma, NB; almalobster.live.

• **Holy Whale Brewing Company:** Devil's Half Acre IPA, Keller Whale, and Grandy's Shandy are just a few of the locally crafted beverages on tap at a microbrewery located in an

old blue church that also serves killer coffee; 8576 Main Street, Alma, NB; facebook.com/buddhabearcafe.

• **An Octopus' Garden:** From breakfast poutine smothered in hollandaise sauce to smoked salmon Alfredo and duck confit, the café offers new takes on Canadian comfort foods plus live music and a brookside patio; 8561 Main St, Alma, NB; facebook.com/anoctopusgardencafe.

A scenic stop along the Point Wolfe River estuary on the Shiphaven Trail

Confederation Trail
Prince Edward Island

Prince Edward Island may be Canada's smallest province, but the Atlantic outpost has one of the nation's oldest and longest rail trails.

One of Canada's first rail-to-trail conversions takes its name from the 1867 merger of the three British North American colonies into a single nation called Canada (although it should be pointed out that Canada didn't receive full autonomy from Great Britain until the 1980s).

The **Confederation Trail** comprises nearly all the former Canadian National Railway (CN) networks on Prince Edward Island (PEI). The main trail stretches 170 miles (274 km) from east to west across Canada's smallest province. But various spurs off the primary route take the total distance to 270 miles (435 km). Only hiking and biking are allowed between April and November, but snowmobilers are also permitted during the winter.

The Confederation Trail turns inland at O'Leary village, where you can learn about the humble potato at the Canadian Potato Museum.

THE BIG PICTURE

Distance: 170 miles (274 km)

Elevation Gain: approx. 11,600 feet (3,540 m)

Time: 7–9 days

Difficulty: Easy to moderate

Best Time: Spring, summer, or fall

More Info: tourismpei.com/pei-confederation-trail

In addition to its pastoral scenery, the trail features 250 bilingual interpretive panels and 1,900 hidden geocache sites. Most of the main route runs down the middle of the island rather than along the coast. In fact, it only reaches the sea at three points: Alberton, Summerside, and St. Peter's Bay. However, the six spur trails all lead to coastal settlements.

Mile zero is located in the public park behind the historic redbrick post office building in **Tignish** village near the island's northwest corner. From there, the trail meanders through a mix of forest and field to **Alberton,** a fishing village on the **Gulf of St. Lawrence** near the spot where French explorer Jacques Cartier landed in 1534. Turning inland again, the trail rambles through a region renowned for the tasty PEI potatoes that flourish in its orange, iron-rich soil. Learn more about local spuds at the **Canadian Potato Museum** in **O'Leary** village.

A huge S-bend takes the trail through the French-speaking **Evangeline Region** around Wellington, settled by Acadians in the early 19th century and still a stronghold of Acadian culture. **Summerside** and its lively waterfront are just down the road. On its journey through downtown, the trail runs past eclectic shops and eateries of **Spinnakers' Landing** and the equally diverse

Cyclists will find lots to enjoy on the waterside portion of the Confederation Trail in Montague, Prince Edward Island.

Eptek Art and Culture Centre.

At **Emerald Junction,** the Confederation Trail merges with the **International Appalachian Trail,** bringing hikers from the mainland via the **Confederation Bridge** in Borden-Carleton. The two trails tag along for 25 miles (40 km) before the IAT splits off at **Royalty Junction** and follows a spur trail into **Charlottetown,** the provincial capital and the place where the first assembly that led to Canada's Confederation was held.

Tacking to the northeast, the Confederation Trail threads an isthmus that separates the **Hillsborough Estuary** from **Tracadie Bay** and its mussel farms. The route's longest seaside segment starts at **Morell,** a 7.1-mile (11.5-km) meander along the southern shore of

St. Peter's Bay. The homestretch is an easy trek through farmland and forest to **Elmira** village near the island's eastern end. **Elmira Railway Museum** in the old station marks

the end of the trail. For hikers and bikers who need to punctuate their trek with a sea view, **East Point Lighthouse** lies around 6.3 miles (10 km) away via two road routes. ■

LOCAL FLAVOR

• **The Albert & Crown Pub & Eatery:** Find fresh fish, cold suds, and live music along Main Street in Alberton; 480 Main Street, Alberton, PE; facebook.com/AlbertandCrownPub.

• **Deckhouse Pub & Eatery:** Drunken PEI mussels, Eh burgers, poutine, and an *Anne of Green Gables* martini are some of the Canadian-themed treats at this Spinnakers' Landing seasonal hangout in Summerside; 150 Heather Moyse Drive, Summerside, PE; facebook.com/deckhousepub.

• **St. Peter's Landing:** This quaint waterfront cluster has three taste treats: DJ's Dairy Bar, Maritime Marzipan, and the Black & White Café & Bakery; 5549 St Peters Road, St. Peter's Bay, PE; stpeterslanding.ca.

• **North Lake Boathouse Harbour Eatery:** Finish the trek with an awesome seafood meal (lobster, scallops, fish tacos, clam chowder) at this popular restaurant on the Gulf of St. Lawrence; 67 Cape Road, Elmira, PE; facebook.com/boathouseeatery.

Cavell Meadows Loop
Alberta

It may be named for a British war hero, but this stunning trail in Jasper National Park flaunts the best of the Canadian Rockies.

THE BIG PICTURE

Distance: 5.2 miles (8.3 km)

Elevation Gain: approx. 1,900 feet (580 m)

Time: 2–4 hours

Difficulty: Easy to moderate

Best Time: Late spring, summer, or early fall

More Info: pc.gc.ca/en/pn-np/ab/jasper

It's hard to imagine that a fairly short and easy trail could offer nearly everything that's special about **Jasper National Park** in the Canadian Rockies. But that's what makes this particular route so extraordinary—close encounters with mountains, glaciers, forest, flowers, wildlife, and even an alpine lake along a lollipop loop that runs 4 to 5 miles (6.4 to 8 km) depending on how far up the incline you decide to tread.

The trail ascends the northern flank of **Mount Edith Cavell,** named for a British nurse who was executed by the Germans during World War II for aiding and abetting the escape of 200 Allied soldiers from behind enemy lines. The Norman-style tower of **St. Mary & St. George Church** in **Jasper** village is also named for Cavell.

The trailhead lies around 17 miles (27 km) south of the village via the **Icefields Parkway** and Edith Cavell Road. Find out more about the heroic British nurse on an information board near the parking lot and then set off along the paved **Path of the Glacier Trail.**

Around a third of a mile (0.5 km) along, hang a sharp left onto the **Cavell Meadows Trail,** which zigzags up a steep moraine that shows just how far glaciers once extended down the mountain. As the trail skirts the pristine subalpine forest that crowns the moraine, hikers catch a great glimpse of **Angel Glacier,** a pair of giant white "wings" spread across a hanging valley high on the mountainside.

Inside the forest, the trail evolves into a loop that climbs above the tree line to the **Cavell Meadows** and their carpet of summer wildflowers. Beyond the far

Alpine meadows and rocky terrain mingle at the Cavell Meadows Trail in Jasper National Park.

Mount Edith Cavell and Angel Glacier are on full display as you hike the Cavell Meadows Trail.

end of the loop, hikers can continue 0.4 mile (0.6 km) along a steep trail into the rocky tundra zone and the second most astonishing viewpoint along the Cavell route.

Backtracking to the meadows, hike the lower part of the loop to several more awesome viewpoints before it slips back into the dark forest and a steep descent back to the paved trail. But it's not time to return to your vehicle just yet. Hang a left onto the Path of the Glacier Trail and follow it a short distance to the hike's ultimate "Wow!" experience—a terrace with a view upward to Angel Glacier and downward to little **Cavell Glacier** and milky jade-colored **Cavell Pond,** a classic alpine tarn sprinkled with icebergs that have calved from the

two glaciers. From the terrace, it's 0.6 mile (1 km) along the paved path to the parking lot.

Those who want to linger longer on the mountainside can book a stay at the **HI Mount Edith Cavell**

Wilderness Hostel (reservations required). Accommodation is in 16-bed cabins with no electricity or running water, but the hostel does offer cooking facilities and a warm, comfy living/dining area. ■

OTHER GREAT TRAILS

• **The Whistlers Trail:** Ride the Jasper Skytram to the 7,320-foot (2,231-m) mountaintop and hike down along a steep 3.9-mile (6.3-km) path with killer views of the valley and surrounding Rockies.

• **Valley of the Five Lakes Trail:** This woodsy route from Jasper village can be tackled as a 6.6-mile (10.7-km) one-way with a takeout point on Icefields Parkway or an 11.4-mile (18.3-km) out-and-back with two loops.

• **Lower Sunwapta Falls:** Feel the spray in your face on a short (2-mile/3.2-km) return trail that leads along the Sunwapta River to the three cascades that make up the lower falls.

• **Maligne Canyon Loop:** Hikers can gaze down at the rapids and waterfalls of this narrow gorge from four wooden suspension bridges along a 2.3-mile (3.7-km) loop from the Wilderness Kitchen parking lot.

West Coast Trail

British Columbia

Wooden ladders, boardwalks, suspension bridges, and two-person, hand-powered cable cars complement beaches and forest trails on this historic hike along the British Columbia coast.

THE BIG PICTURE

Distance: 47 miles (75 km)

Elevation Gain: approx. 6,000 feet (1,830 m)

Time: 5–8 days

Difficulty: Strenuous

Best Time: Late spring, summer, or early fall

More Info: www.pc.gc.ca/en/pn-np/bc/pacificrim/activ/SCO-WCT and hikewct.com

One of Canada's bucket-list hiking routes, the **West Coast Trail** (WCT) stretches 47 miles (75 km) across the **Pacific Rim National Park Reserve** and eight First Nations enclaves. The rigorous shoreline path is open only between May 1 and September 30 but closed the rest of the year when torrential rains and strong wind lash the Vancouver Island coast.

Parks Canada manages the trail in partnership with the **Huu-ay-aht, Ditidaht,** and **Pacheedaht** peoples whose ancestors blazed the original coastal path. Members of those First Nations communities volunteer as **West Coast Trail Guardians,** interacting with hikers, monitoring flora and fauna, repairing trail structures, and making sure that sacred sites are respected.

The WCT's southern trailhead lies near **Port Renfrew,** a two-hour drive from **Victoria.** All hikers need to register and attend a WCT orientation session at the **West Coast Trail Information Centre** at the **Pacheedaht First Nation,** which also offers camping and ferry passage across the **Gordon River** to start the trek.

Scaling the cliffs along **Port San Juan,** the trail reaches its highest point (700 feet/213 m) before **Thrasher Cove** and the **Owen Point** sea caves. From **Camper Bay,** a series of ladders, boardwalks, wooden bridges, hand-pulled cable cars, and a cool new **Logan Creek** suspension bridge take hikers to the red-and-white **Carmanah Point Light Station** (founded 1891).

Dare Beach offers a nice walk across sand before a long, wooden bridge across the **Cheewhat River** to the floating dock at **Nitinat Narrows.** Hikers can grab inexpensive meals and WCT T-shirts at **Carl's**

Stretching 47 miles (75 km), the West Coast Trail tests climbers with a challenging shoreline route and gusty winds rolling in off the open sea.

The West Coast Trail weaves through the Pacific Rim National Park Reserve and the enclaves of eight First Nations.

Crab Shack before hopping the ferry across the estuary. Around two miles (3.2 km) farther along, the **Ditidaht First Nation**'s glamping camp at **Tsuquadra Point** features tents and cabins equipped with cots, stoves, and decks.

Trekkers have a choice of beach or forest paths on the stretch to **Tsusiat Falls,** a cascade that tumbles 108 feet (33 m) onto a black-sand strand and a freshwater swimming hole. The rusted anchor of the **steamship** *Woodside* that wrecked in 1888, as well as a derelict donkey steam engine and grader used to construct the telegraph line along the coast, are among the relics of pioneer days near **Trestle Creek.**

Valencia Bluffs is the spot where the **S.S.** *Valencia* ran aground, triggering the creation of the precursor to the West Coast Trail. Just up the coast, **Pachena Point Lighthouse** (built in 1907) was another outcome of that tragedy. First Nations hunters once used one of the waterside rocks below the lighthouse to spear whales that strayed too close to the shore.

Beyond the lighthouse, it's just a 6.2-mile (10-km) walk to **Pachena Bay** and the northern terminus of the WCT beside an A-frame ranger station where southbound hikers register and get their orientation. The **Huu-ay-aht Nation** offers a campground in nearby **Anacla** village, and nearby **Bamfield** has accommodations and restaurants. ∎

OTHER GREAT TRAILS

Dominion Lifesaving Trail

Back in the day they called it the "Graveyard of the Pacific," the capricious west coast of Vancouver Island that devoured more than 500 ships between the late 18th and early 20th centuries. Many wrecked without loss of life. But in 1906, when the American steamer S.S. *Valencia* ran aground near Pachena Bay, more than 100 people perished.

Shocked by the tragedy, the Canadian government and U.S. president Teddy Roosevelt ordered inquiries to investigate the ongoing danger and offer solutions. One result was creation of the **Dominion Lifesaving Trail,** a series of shelters equipped with wireless transmitters, blankets, and food for shipwreck survivors and rescuers.

With the advent of modern shipping and maritime safety procedures, the lifesaving route eventually morphed into the West Coast Trail, created in 1973 after the establishment of the Pacific Rim National Park Reserve.

Be sure to time your hike correctly to avoid high tide when venturing to the Hole in the Wall arch on the West Coast Trail.

Bruce Trail
Ontario

The Niagara Escarpment provides a natural high-rise way for a trail that weaves through the rustic countryside, waterfall-flanked canyons, and ancient old-growth forests of southern Ontario.

THE BIG PICTURE

Distance: 550 miles (885 km)

Elevation Gain: approx. 70,000 feet (21,340 m)

Time: 4–6 weeks

Difficulty: Moderate

Best Time: Late spring or early fall

More Info: brucetrail.org

Canada's oldest and longest marked trail owes its existence to creatures that populated a vast tropical sea covering much of the Great Lakes region around 450 million years ago.

The remains of those creatures, mixed with sediment and other organic material, formed a sedimentary bed that was eventually uplifted and eroded into the **Niagara Escarpment,** the ridge that carries the **Bruce Trail** all the way across southern Ontario.

It's just not the views that elevate a trek along the Bruce Trail into something more than a run-of-the-mill long-distance hike. The escarpment's dolomitic limestone flaunts an incredible number of caves, canyons, and waterfalls. And because the terrain was too deep for farming, grazing, or human habitation, much of the original vegetation has survived.

In fact, the Niagara Escarpment is so unique it was declared an international biosphere reserve in 1990 based on its biodiversity, topographic variety, and widespread old-growth forest.

Because the Bruce runs through more than 1,000 private properties, dispersed camping along the route is strictly forbidden and considered trespassing. But there are enough designated campgrounds, hotels, motels, cabins, bed-and-breakfasts, and other accommodations along the way to more than compensate.

The trail starts in rather dramatic fashion in **Queenston Heights Park,** renowned for both its views into the deep **Niagara Gorge** and as the site of a British victory over the invading Americans during the War of 1812.

Meandering west across the **Niagara Peninsula,** the trail passes over the **Welland Canal,** through the **Brock University** campus, and almost all the way around **Lake Moodie** before slipping in the backside of **Short Hills Provincial Park.** The "short hills" are actually the

Experience a reproduction of an Iroquoian longhouse at Crawford Lake in Ontario.

Follow the Bruce Trail through the Niagara Escarpment for a dramatic environment filled with canyons, waterfalls, and caves ready for exploring.

Niagara Escarpment, and the park's dense forest and myriad cascades strongly hint at what's ahead.

If you make it past the wineries. Because the next section of the Bruce passes through the heart of the **Niagara Wine Country,** especially the countryside around **Jordan** and **Beamsville,** which nurtures more than 30 visitor-friendly vineyards along or near the trail. The heights above **Grimsby** offer awesome views of **Lake Ontario** before the trail makes its way across the Hamilton metropolitan area, home to more than 770,000 Canadians.

The passage through **Hamilton** is one of the more crowded segments of the Bruce, but also one of the more interesting, because the trail manages to snake right through the middle of the city using parks, forest preserves, rail trails, and wooded ridges along the crest of the escarpment. Hamilton rightly calls itself the "waterfall capital of the world," and the trail passes landmark cascades like the **Devil's Punchbowl, Tiffany Falls,** and **Tews Falls.**

After traversing through suburban **Dundas**—which hosts the **Dundas International Buskerfest** each June—the Bruce slips back into the

Ontario countryside. The route ambles across the escarpment above **Burlington** and Lake Ontario before veering inland on a leg that takes the trail along the northwestern edge of the huge Toronto metro area.

Making its way around Toronto, the trail runs along country roads between a string of local conservation areas—**Crawford Lake, Kelso/ Glen Eden, Limehouse, Silver Creek,** and **Terra Cotta**—where wilderness reigns again. Crawford Lake boasts a replica 15th-century **Iroquoian village** with three reconstructed longhouses where hikers can learn about the region's First Nations inhabitants.

The Bruce uses provincial parks and nature reserves to hopscotch across the **Caledon Hills, Mono Cliffs,** and **Dufferin Hi-Land** between Toronto and Georgian Bay. Unlike Ontario's largest parks, these smaller reserves don't have campgrounds, and in some cases few amenities or activities other than hiking the Bruce Trail.

Georgian Bay finally comes into view from the **Blue Mountains.** Trekkers can descend from the heights and access the lakeshore at **Craigleith Provincial Park.** In addition to a waterfront campground, the park also offers hot showers, laundry, and a store to restock for the rest of the journey.

Rather than cut straight across the **Beaver Valley,** the Bruce stays true to its calling and sticks to the escarpment all the way down to **Eugenia** and its towering waterfall and back up the other side of a dale renowned for its apples and apple cider.

Owen Sound marks the end of the trail's middle section and the

start of what most folks consider the highlight of the entire hike: a walk up the **Bruce Peninsula.** Town camping is available at waterfront **Kelso Beach Park** and **Harrison Park,** adjacent to the excellent **Grey Roots Museum** and its **Moreston Heritage Village.**

Rising into the heights again, the Bruce follows the **Georgian Bluffs** around **Cape Commodore** to **Wiarton,** a onetime timber town and fishing village that now makes a living from tourism and the annual **Wiarton Willie Festival,** Canada's version of Groundhog Day. Making its way through town, the trail runs right past a lakeside statue of the weather-predicting woodchuck.

Beyond Wiarton, the Niagara Escarpment inches closer and closer to the shoreline until it eventually becomes the western edge of Georgian Bay.

The escarpment guides the trail through a portion of the **Neyaashiin- igmiing Reserve 27** of the Chippewas of Nawash Nation to a stunning overlook at **Jones Bluff.** Farther along are **Greig's Caves,** a network of

10 limestone caverns where much of the prehistoric saga *Quest for Fire* was filmed in the 1980s.

Around the next big bend is the distinctive **Lion's Head** rock formation that hovers high above Georgian Bay. Nearby **Lion's Head village** is the only town for nearly 100 miles (160 km) along this stretch of the Bruce. Farther along are a spiral staircase that leads down to the beach near **Smokey Head** and a large limestone flowerpot formation called the **Devil's Monument.**

The tail end of the trail is a lengthy section across the cliff tops and through the ancient cedar trees of **Bruce Peninsula National Park,** which safeguards the largest remaining old-growth forest in southern Ontario. The park offers several campgrounds and easy shore access for a swim in Georgian Bay or a giant sea cave called **the Grotto.**

From there, the town of **Tobermory** at the top end of the peninsula is an easy jaunt, and a ferry crosses to **Manitoulin Island** for those who want to keep going. ∎

DETOURS

• **Royal Botanical Gardens:** Canada's largest flora reserve features more than 2,400 plant species in formal gardens, wetlands, and nature reserves beside Lake Ontario near Hamilton.

• **Blu Wave SUP Academy:** Find stand-up paddleboard rentals, lessons, guided tours, and yoga sessions at Collingwood and Wasaga Beach on the Georgian Bay.

• **Blue Mountain Resort:** Take a total break from the Bruce at a year-round resort that segues from snow sports in winter to a warm-weather menu that includes swimming pools,

zip lines, golf course, bars, restaurants, and a private beach on Georgian Bay.

• **Historic Roxy Theatre:** Opened in 1913 as an opera house, the 400-seat venue is now home to the Owen Sound Little Theatre, which stages four musicals, comedies, or dramas each year.

• **Fathom Five National Marine Park:** Located off the northern tip of the Bruce Peninsula, this scuba diving mecca preserves 22 shipwrecks along a submerged portion of the Niagara Escarpment between Georgian Bay and Lake Huron.

A breathtaking view of the coast along Tobermory, Canada

Long Range Traverse

Newfoundland

Make like the ancient Norsemen and march across a blustery island landscape in eastern Canada where hikers are more likely to come across moose than other humans.

Around A.D. 1020, the Vikings established their only known North American settlement along the west coast of Newfoundland. And they must have felt right at home. With dramatic fjords, glacial lakes, and tundra vegetation, the geography is downright Nordic.

Which makes the **Long Range Traverse** (LRT) of **Gros Morne National Park** feel more like a trek across Scandinavia than your traditional Canadian hike.

The other thing that makes this walk unique is an almost total lack of maintained trail. Bushwhacking is the name of the game on a route that's marked largely by cairns rather

THE BIG PICTURE

Distance: 21 miles (35 km)

Elevation Gain: approx. 5,000 feet (1,520 m)

Time: 4–5 days

Difficulty: Strenuous

Best Time: Summer

More Info: pc.gc.ca/en/pn-np/ nl/grosmorne/activ/experiences/ backcountry/longrange

than blazes or signposts. No one should set off without a compass, topographic map, GPS device, and detailed descriptions of the route from previous users.

Before even traveling to Newfoundland, hikers should secure an online reservation and pay the park's wilderness hiking fee. No more than a dozen people are allowed to start the trek each day. Arriving at Gros Morne, hikers must attend a mandatory Parks Canada orientation session and backcountry briefing—that emphasize the route's rugged and potentially risky nature—at the **Rocky Harbour Visitor Centre.**

Despite its lack of maintained trail, the LRT does offer six campsites along the route, with wooden tent platforms because of the boggy terrain. Moose are common, and bear boxes at campsites means that bruins are lurking even if you can't see them.

The journey kicks off in sublime fashion with a boat trip across **Western Brook Pond,** a freshwater fjord flanked by colossal rock escarpments. Dropped on a remote dock near the pond's east end, hikers have a choice of waterfront camping with panoramic views of **Pissing Mare Falls** or continuing upward to the **Big Level Plateau.**

Reaching the plateau involves 1,800 feet (550 m) of elevation gain

Tour boats take visitors back in time as they navigate the waters of Western Brook Pond and the ancient, glacier-carved fjord.

A rocky path propels hikers to the stunning view of Western Brook Pond via the Long Range Traverse trail.

through thick vegetation. This first leg often feels more like rock climbing—scrambling over boulders and often using your hands to find purchase—than hiking. The payoff is a jaw-dropping view down the U-shaped fjord that you just sailed across. From there, it's around 1.5 miles (2.5 km) to a campsite beside **Little Island Pond.**

With the great wall conquered, the remainder of the traverse seems relatively easy, a ramble through the **Long Range Mountains** to overnight spots beside **Marks, Harding,** and **Green Island Ponds.** The path weaves around dozens of glacial lakes through vegetation that varies from grassy moorlands and low-alpine scrub to thick "tuckamore"—dense, stunted spruce and fir forest deformed by the wind and subarctic winter.

A final campsite at the top of **Ferry Gulch** has an option to summit rocky, tundra-topped **Gros Morne** peak on the final

morning—before a steep descent into the forest and southern trailhead on **Highway 430** near Rocky Harbour. ∎

APRÈS HIKE

• **L'Anse Aux Meadows National Historic Site:** Perched at Newfoundland's northern tip, this history-shifting archaeological site preserves the remains of an early 11th-century Viking settlement.

• **Theatre Newfoundland Labrador:** TNL organizes the annual Gros Morne Theatre Festival, which stages six to eight plays and more than 150 total performances each summer at the Warehouse Theatre in Cow Head.

• **Humber River Off Grid Tours:** Glamping tents and guided kayak

tours on the Humber River are the forte of this outdoor adventure crew based in Deer Lake.

• **The Tablelands:** This windswept highlands on the southwest side of Gros Morne National Park offer a rare chance to walk on Earth's mantle where two continental plates collide.

• **Anchor Pub:** Groove to the traditional sounds of Newfoundland—and quaff a few Quidi Vidi beers—during Anchors Aweigh concerts or Kitchen Parties at this musical pub in Rocky Harbour.

Sentier Les Caps

Québec

A three-hour drive north of Québec City, this wilderness route offers an adventurous journey through a landscape more redolent of Norway than typical Canadian countryside.

Saguenay Fjord, which leads into the St. Lawrence River in Québec, isn't just the southernmost navigable fjord in the Northern Hemisphere. It's also one of Canada's most astonishing natural landmarks, a massive sea-filled valley framed by 980-foot (300-m) walls and stretching more than 65 miles (105 km) from east to west.

The **Sentier Les Caps** (Capes Trail) wanders among the granite heights, deep woods, and glacial lakes on the south side of **Saguenay Fjord National Park.** With deep-blue bays anchoring both ends, the route normally takes three days to walk. Wooden huts provide rustic but warm indoor accommodations along the way. Trekkers can also overnight at three primitive campsites.

The trail is most often trekked from west to east, with a scenic pre-hike overnight at the national park campground along the shore of **Baie-Éternité** (Eternity Bay). The nearby **Fjord du Saguenay**

THE BIG PICTURE

Distance: 17 or 19.5 miles (27 or 32 km)

Elevation Change: approx. 3,700 feet (1,130 m)

Time: 3 days

Difficulty: Moderate to strenuous

Best Time: Summer or early fall

More Info: sepaq.com/pq/sag

Discovery and Visitors Centre offers exhibits on the fjord's geology and marine life, as well as the latest trail conditions, which makes it the perfect stopping point before making your way onto the route.

In addition to providing the western trailhead, Baie-Éternité is actually a pretty cool place to linger for a few days before or after the trek. Hikers can purchase Saguenay swag at the **Boutique Nature,** snack at **Le Béluga café,** hike to the **Notre-Dame-du-Saguenay** (Madonna of Saguenay) statue at the tip of **Cap Trinité** (Cape Trinity), and maybe even take a dip in the chilly fjord.

Day one of the hike is far and away the toughest, an unrelenting rise of 1,115 feet (340 m) to **Point de vue du Géant** (Giant's Viewpoint) and its astounding aerial perspective. Looking down at the fjord from such a height, the forces that shaped it are more obvious. Glacial scouring during the ice ages caused the classic U shape. Yet the bedrock you're standing on is much older, created around 200 million years ago during a tectonic event that formed a deep rift valley later invaded by glaciers. The trek continues upward to **Refuge du Lac de la Chute,** tucked into the trees beside a small lake.

Day two kicks off in spectacular

Take a ferry ride to Île aux Coudres, which didn't connect to the mainland until 1930.

Snowshoe to the clouds along the peaks of Sentier Les Caps in the Charlevoix region.

fashion with a short hike to **Cap Éternité** and its views across the water to the fjord's north shore. The trail dances across the cliff tops to **Lac de la Goutte** campground. Veering away from the precipice, it heads for **Lac du Kalmia** campground and the **Refuge du Lac du Marais.**

Early on day three, hikers have a choice of tramping two routes to the end: via **Montagne Blanche** (7.6 miles/12.3 km) or **Tabatière** (5.1 miles/8.2 km). Although it's longer, the former ascends the highest point along the Sentier Les Caps—the bald granite summit of 1,854-foot (565-m) "White Mountain" with its spectacular views across the park—making it well worth your effort.

Both forks end up near lovely **L'Anse-Saint-Jean,** a bayside village with cafés, campground, cabins, and B&Bs. Hikers can reserve a shuttle back to Baie-Éternité with **OrganisAction**. ∎

APRÈS HIKE

• **Pyramide des Ha! Ha!:** Fashioned from 3,000 aluminum "yield" signs, this towering red pyramid in La Baie commemorates a 1996 flood; guided tours are offered during summer.

• **Musée du Fjord:** A vivarium with amphibians and insects, local history exhibits, and a 20-minute multimedia presentation on Saguenay Fjord are part of the mix at this excellent regional museum.

• **Marine Mammal Interpretation Centre (CIMM):** Check out whale videos, sound recordings, skeletons, and a chance to view real-life belugas, minkes, and other whales that hang out near the confluence of Saguenay Fjord and the St. Lawrence Estuary.

• **Fjord en Kayak:** Explore the waterway on guided paddles from two hours to six days with an outfitter based in L'Anse-Saint-Jean.

• **Navettes Maritimes du Fjord:** Scenic cruises along the fjord in modern riverboats depart from La Baie and L'Anse-Saint-Jean.

Mantario Trail
Manitoba

Dive deep into the boreal forest and across some of the planet's oldest rock on a wilderness trek along the Manitoba-Ontario frontier.

THE BIG PICTURE

Distance: 37.5 miles (60 km)

Elevation Change: approx. 4,100 feet (1,250 m)

Time: 3–5 days

Difficulty: Strenuous

Best Time: Summer or early fall

More Info: wildernesssupply.ca/mantario-trail-hiking-guide

Despite its name, nearly all of this wilderness route through Whiteshell Provincial Park rambles through Manitoba, rather than Ontario. The park and its iconic trail are a 20-hour drive from **Toronto** in the best of weather, so it's better to stage the hike from **Winnipeg,** which lies about 90 minutes from the north and south trailheads of the **Mantario Trail**.

Although the pristine boreal forest and abundant wildlife are the route's main attractions, the region's geology is also fascinating. It's part of the **Canadian Shield,** a vast horseshoe-shaped outcrop of Precambrian rock formed 2.5 to 4.2 billion years ago. Anyone trekking the Mantario Trail is stepping on some of the oldest rock on planet Earth.

Much more recently, glaciers and ice caps smoothed and shaped the ancient terrain into a lake-filled landscape reminiscent of northern Minnesota that makes for great canoe trips. That's how the French voyageurs and British trappers crossed the Whiteshell.

Poor soils dissuaded farmers, and extreme remoteness kept loggers at bay, resulting in a region that remains refreshingly pristine, with old-growth spruce, poplar, aspen, and fir trees. It's classic moose country, but hikers should also be on the lookout for beavers, river otters, and black bears.

Fourteen primitive campsites with picnic tables, fire pits, "garden throne" toilets, and bear boxes are scattered along the trail. Before setting off, hikers should be well aware that this is true wilderness. There are no stores, ranger stations, or other amenities at any point, and cell phone reception is sketchy throughout.

The route's **South Trailhead** is on Provincial Road 312 between **McDougall's Landing** on West Hawk Lake and the **Green Bay Resort** on Caddy Lake. Perched on the western shore, **Caddy Lake Campground** is a great place to crash for the night before you start or end the trek.

Hikers generally make for Caribou Lake on the first day along a route that crosses the **Whiteshell River,** Canadian Pacific Railway tracks, and an abandoned airfield. Day two starts with a hike around the east end of **Caribou Lake** and a

Sunsets don't get any more peaceful than they are in the wild.

Experienced backpackers will need about four days to complete the challenging 37.5-mile (60-km) Mantario Trail.

very brief interlude in Ontario. Snaking along the east shore of **Marion Lake,** the trail passes beneath power lines into a designated wilderness area.

Those huge electric pylons are the last human-made thing you're going to see for several days, because the middle section of the route is all water and woods as the trail weaves between **Doreen, Moosehead, Mantario,** and **Ritchey Lakes.** There's quite a bit of stream fording, which can be dodgy earlier in the year when the water runs high. The trail peters out on the north shore of **Big Whiteshell Lake,** not far from lodges and campgrounds that cater to tired, hungry, and dirty hikers. ■

OTHER GREAT TRAILS

• **Winnipeg Riverwalk:** The city's waterfront redevelopment includes a paved trail along the Red and Assiniboine Rivers between Forks National Historic Site and the Manitoba Legislative Building.

• **Crow Wing Trail:** Meandering 124 miles (200 km) down the Red River Valley between Winnipeg's southern outskirts and the Canada-U.S. border, the Crow Wing traces the path of a 19th-century frontier route.

• **Oxbow Nature Trail:** A bison pen, swinging bridge, and Little Saskatchewan River feature in this easy 1.9-mile (3.1-km) walk that starts from the Museum and Heritage Village in Minnedosa.

• **Elk Island:** One of Manitoba's more unusual hikes entails a wade across a submerged sandbar from Victoria Beach and then a loop around the wooded isle in Lake Winnipeg; total distance is around 10 miles (16 km).

• **Grey Owl Trail:** It's around nine miles (14.5 km) out and back to the remote log cabin where renowned British-born Canadian naturalist Archibald Belaney (aka Grey Owl) lived in 1931.

Meewasin Trail
Saskatchewan

A blend of nature and nurture, this meandering riverside route through the heart of Saskatoon reveals all that's cool about the big Canadian prairie city.

THE BIG PICTURE

Distance: approx. 55 miles (90 km)

Elevation Change: Negligible (other than bridges)

Time: 1 day

Difficulty: Easy

Best Time: Year-round

More Info: meewasin.com/locations

Canadian rock legends the Guess Who once sang that "nothing much ever happens" in **Saskatoon.** But they had obviously never trekked the **Meewasin Trail.** Snaking its way for more than 55 miles (90 km) down both sides of the **South Saskatchewan River,** the route offers one of Canada's best urban hiking adventures.

In making its way from north to south across the Saskatchewan metropolis, the trail rambles through riverside parks and nature reserves, patches of prairie and forest, dog runs and boat launches, vintage neighborhoods and newbie suburbs.

Meewasin means "beautiful" in the language of the Cree people, testimony to the trail's visual appeal, especially during spring and fall when the riverside foliage bursts with color.

Much of the route is paved, especially in the city center, with dirt and gravel segments on the pastoral outskirts of Saskatoon.

A bona fide multiuse trail, the Meewasin is open to hikers, bikers, joggers, skaters, cross-country skiers, and snowshoers.

The trail's longest continuous section runs 8.3 miles (13.3 km) along the river's west bank between **Silverwood Heights** and the **Holiday Park** neighborhood. Starting from the north, the trail makes its way along a waterfront golf course on the spot where a utopian industrial town called **Factoria** once stood until falling during World War I.

One of the city's favorite green spaces, **Meewasin Park** carries the trail around leafy Lawson Heights to sandy **Spadina Beach,** one of the best places to take a dip in the South Saskatchewan. Up ahead is **Circle Drive Bridge,** the first of eight spans trail users can cross to the **Meewasin Trail East** on the opposite bank.

Edging closer to the city center, the trail passes the **Archibald Arena** ice-skating rink, the historic **Canadian Pacific Railway Bridge** (opened in 1908), and the **Weir,** constructed as a back-to-work project during the Great Depression and now used as a way station by migrating pelicans. Eclectic **Kinsmen Park** offers old-timey carnival rides, the **Nutrien Wonderhub** children's museum, cruises on the

Hike the Meewasin Trail for a skyline view of Saskatoon.

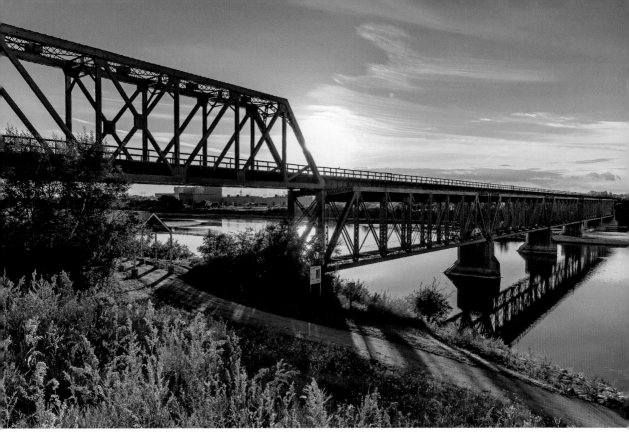

The Meewasin Trail skirts the South Saskatchewan River in Saskatoon.

Prairie Lily riverboat, and summer performances of **Shakespeare on the Saskatchewan.**

Reaching downtown, the route passes the **Ukrainian Museum of Canada** and the redbrick facades of **St. John's Cathedral** (completed in 1912) and **St. Paul's Cathedral** (completed in 1911) before slipping between the river and the castle-like **Bessborough Hotel,** which reigned as the city's tallest building until 1966. The past soon gives way to **River Landing,** a modern waterfront development that harbors restaurants, the **Remai Modern** museum of contemporary art, and stage plays at the **Persephone Theatre.**

South of city center, the Meewasin Trail runs through **Victoria Park** and its little Chinese pagoda; the former site of the **Saskatoon Sanatorium** for patients with tuberculosis, which has been transformed into a nature reserve; and municipal **Gordon Howe Campground,** named after the legendary ice hockey player who was born nearby and raised in Saskatoon. ■

LAY YOUR HEAD

• **The James Hotel:** Located along Saskatoon's riverfront cathedral row—and recently listed as one of the five best hotels in Canada—this chic boutique earns kudos for its simple yet elegant design and river-view rooms; from C$269; thejameshotel.ca.

• **Delta Hotels Bessborough:** Restaurants and a cocktail lounge, indoor pool, spa, and riverside garden are among the features of a historic grand railway hotel inspired by European chateaus and opened in 1935; from C$159; marriott.com.

• **Alt Hotel Saskatoon:** Floor-to-ceiling windows offer panoramic views of the river, bridges, and downtown at a new River Landing hotel with quick and easy access to the Meewasin Trail and nearby cultural landmarks; from C$129; germainhotels.com/en/alt-hotel/saskatoon.

• **The Inn on College:** Simple, friendly digs along the Meewasin Trail East near University of Saskatchewan offer a common kitchen area, free breakfast, and nearby bike rentals; from C$65; innoncollege.com.

Plain of Six Glaciers Trail
Alberta

Hikers can pause for hot tea and scones—and incredible views—along a path in Banff National Park that blends nature, nutrition, and architecture.

THE BIG PICTURE

Distance: 8.8 miles (14.2 km)

Elevation Gain: approx. 1,900 feet (580 m)

Time: Half day

Difficulty: Moderate

Best Time: Summer or early fall

More Info: pc.gc.ca/en/pn-np/ab/Banff

Can a single hike encompass everything that makes **Banff National Park** such an incredible place to visit? Only if it's along the **Plain of Six Glaciers Trail,** which rises from a picture-perfect lake through thick forest to rocky talus slopes and a huge natural amphitheater draped in ice and snow.

Above and beyond the awesome natural setting, the moderately challenging trail also features the park's most iconic architecture and more than a century of Banff history.

Founded in the 1890s by the Canadian Pacific Railway, the **Chateau Lake Louise** hovers above the route's waterfront starting point. From the lawn and terrace behind the huge hotel, hikers can gaze across the lake at the glacier-filled cirque they will eventually reach.

The first leg runs along the north shore of **Lake Louise,** quickly transforming from pavement to gravel just past the sign warning hikers to beware of bears. Called Ho-run-num-nay (Lake of Little Fishes) by the Stoney Nakoda people who once inhabited the valley, the lake morphs from frozen over in winter to milky turquoise in the spring to crystal clear in late summer and fall. The lakeshore trail is a relatively easy stroll—but one that is also rewarding and breathtakingly scenic.

Beyond the lake, the trail rises through the forest along a natural path carved by **Upper Louise Creek,** constantly fed by melt from the nearby snowfields and glaciers. Towering pyramid-shaped peaks now flank the valley—**Mount Aberdeen** on one side (10,358 feet/3,157 m) and **Mount Whyte** on the other (9,787 feet/2,983 m).

About a mile (1.6 km) past an intersection with the **Highline Trail** is a stone terrace with brawny log benches where hikers can gaze into the massive amphitheater and a side trail leading to a most remarkable sight: the **Plain of Six Glaciers Teahouse.** Built in 1927, the two-story stone and log structure serves drinks, meals, and a "treat of the day" during warmer months. Find your seat at one of the outdoor picnic tables, thoughtfully placed near a burbling mountain stream. Or take in the views—and enjoy your refreshments—from the teahouse's covered porch.

The Plain of Six Glaciers Teahouse offers warm drinks alongside a stellar view of the Canadian Rocky Mountains in Banff National Park.

Start the Plain of Six Glaciers Trail hike at the stunning Lake Louise before ascending into the mountains.

After tea and scones, continue on the trail's upward march through a stand of larch trees that emerges onto the rocky scree of the **Plain of Six Glaciers.** There really are six of them arrayed around the cirque: **Upper** and **Lower Victoria, Upper** and **Lower Lefroy, Popes,** and **Aberdeen.** Keep an eye out for pikas and marmots popping out from rocks along the final stretch of trail leading to **Abbot Pass Viewpoint.**

Looming high above is **Mount Victoria,** a gargantuan mass of Cambrian-era sedimentary rock formed on the bottom of an ancient inland sea and pushed 11,365 feet (3,464 m) into the sky when the Rockies were formed 70 to 80 million years ago. Named after the 19th-century British monarch, Victoria rides the border between Alberta and British Columbia.

On the return journey to Lake Louise, hikers can veer left on the Highline Trail to **Lake Agnes** along a route that slides between rocky outcrops called the **Devil's Thumb** and the **Big Beehive.** This detour totals around four miles (6.4 km), including one very steep ascent. ■

OTHER GREAT TRAILS

• **Sulphur Mountain:** Ride the gondola to the top or hike 3.4 miles (5.5 km) of switchbacks to a summit that offers a breathtaking boardwalk trail, panoramic restaurant, and the historic Cosmic Ray Station.

• **Lake Minnewanka:** Backpack the north shore of the park's largest lake along a 35-mile (56-km) trail with half a dozen wilderness campsites.

• **Johnston Canyon:** Follow the elevated boardwalk to the Lower Falls and then a forest-flanked path to the Upper Falls and thermal Ink Pots.

• **Cory Pass:** This steep but visually stunning hike northwest of Banff town can be done as a 5.6-mile (9-km) out-and-back or an 8.1-mile (13-km) loop when combined with Edith Pass.

• **Sunshine Meadows:** Ride the Standish Chairlift to a scenic mountaintop that offers guided hikes or 6.3 miles (10 km) of trails to explore on your own.

Start the hike to Larch Valley at Moraine Lake for views of alpine valleys and larch meadows.

Trans Canada Trail
Multiple Provinces

From sea to shining seas, the world's longest trail network reaches all the way from the Atlantic Ocean to Pacific and Arctic shores, calling on every major Canadian city and provincial capital, as well as the nation's iconic rivers, lakes, mountain ranges, and national parks.

By no stretch of the imagination is the **Trans Canada Trail** (TCT) ordinary. It's actually a network of more than 500 local and regional trails that stretches 17,400 miles (28,000 km) across the whole of Canada, from the Maritimes on the Atlantic coast to Vancouver Island on the Pacific, with a branch that reaches all the way up to the Arctic Ocean. That's around twice as long as the Appalachian, Pacific Crest, and Continental Divide Trails combined. But that's not the only thing that sets it apart from other epic, long-distance routes.

The world's longest multiuse recreational trail network, the TCT earns kudos for the fact that it connects more than 15,000 communities and lies within a 30-minute drive of places where 80 percent of Canadians live. But it's also earned its fair share of criticism, focused on the fact that so much of the route is neither off-road nor dry land. "How the dream of the Trans Canada Trail soars—and falls short," screamed a headline in *Maclean's* magazine.

Although the percentage of true trail grows year by year, only around a third of the TCT is nonmotorized. Hikers, bikers, horseback riders, skaters, and cross-country skiers share another third of the right-of-way with cars, trucks, tractors, and RVs. The remaining third is divided between water-only paddle portions and segments that are also open to snowmobiles, ATVs, and other all-terrain vehicles.

Even so, the TCT is worth sharing the route for any serious thru-hiker looking to tackle epic distances—and remarkable views. Given its extreme distance and fractionalization, the Trans Canada is a quixotic undertaking. Even though the route coalesced in the 1990s, the first thru-hike didn't make the record book until 2018. It took British Columbia–born hiker Dana Meise a decade—trekking an average of six months a year—to finish his quest.

But that doesn't mean you shouldn't try. The shortest route from the Atlantic to the Pacific is more than 5,000 miles (8,050 km)

The Trans Canada Trail stretches 17,400 miles (28,000 km) from coast to coast.

Douglas fir and western red cedar tower over visitors to Capilano River Regional Park in North Vancouver.

from start to finish. Even at a crisp pace, without weather delays and having figured out ahead of time how to skirt the water-only portions, that's nearly a full year's worth of walking.

Kilometer zero at the Atlantic end was originally beside the **Railway Coastal Museum** in **St. John's.** But it was later moved down the coast to **Cape Spear,** the easternmost point in North America (if you don't count Greenland) and a much more inspiring start than a city sidewalk.

Bidding adieu to the historic **Cape Spear Lighthouse** (built in 1836), the trail follows the rugged

OTHER GREAT TRAILS

Paddle Routes

The Trans Canada Trail features more than 20 water-only sections that require passage by canoe or kayak. Four of them are epic adventures all on their own, requiring advanced paddling skills and meticulous planning and preparation.

The **Lake Superior State Water Trail** stretches nearly 600 miles (1,000 km) across the northern shore of the largest Great Lake between Sault Ste. Marie and Thunder Bay. National and provincial parks provide campsites and access points.

Path of the Paddle drifts through 690 miles (1,110 km) of lakes and

rivers in western Ontario along wilderness routes that First Nations people and French voyageurs pioneered centuries ago.

The only water segment that treads open ocean, the **Salish Sea Marine Trail** links Vancouver and Victoria via 166 miles (267 km) of salt water through the Gulf Islands with a chance to spot orca, humpback, and minke whales, and other marine mammals along the way.

Toughest of them all, the **Mackenzie River Trail** passes through 1,030 miles (1,660 km) of the remote Northwest Territories between Great Slave Lake and Tuktoyaktuk on the Arctic coast.

Newfoundland coast 11 miles (18 km) into St. John's. Those already in need of a break can hit the pubs along **George Street,** former haunt of sailors and fishermen but nowadays renowned for craft beers and live music.

Otherwise, keep on truckin' down the TCT. In one of the longest unbroken segments along the entire route, the 548-mile (883-km) **Newfoundland T'Railway** rail trail takes hikers all the way across the island to **Port aux Basques** via **Terra Nova National Park.** Trekkers board a big **Marine Atlantic ferry** for a seven-hour passage across the **Cabot Strait** to **Nova Scotia.**

Disembarking in **North Sydney** on **Cape Breton Island,** trekkers are confronted with the first of the water segments that makes thru-hiking such a tough proposition for landlubbers. Unless you're going to paddle across sprawling **Bras d'Or Lake,** the only ways to reach the next terra firma segment are public transport or traversing country roads to **Whycocomagh Provincial Park.**

Brilliant autumn colors shade the Shubie Park Greenway Corridor section of the Trans Canada Trail in Nova Scotia.

Officially opened in 2000, the Trans Canada Trail incorporates a mix of multiuse trails and environments that span the country.

From there, a series of three backwoods trails takes the route to Port Hastings and the Canso Causeway to the Nova Scotia mainland.

Another sequence of footpaths, including the **Guysborough Nature Trail,** carries the route into **New Brunswick** past the mega-high tides of **Fundy National Park** and into the cities of St. John and Fredericton. A walk up the **St. John River Valley** into **Québec Province** ends

on the east bank of the **St. Lawrence River** in **Rivière-du-Loup.**

After a ferry to the west bank, the TCT follows the river upstream to the cobblestone streets of **Québec City** before a long dogleg to **Sherbrooke** and **Mont-Orford National Park** plunks hikers in downtown **Montreal.** Having had their fill of the bright lights and big city, they can resume walking along another long, nonmotorized segment: the

---

SHORT CIRCUITS

These sections of the TCT are ideal for day hikes:

• **River Valley Trail (Alberta):** Follow the North Saskatchewan River through Edmonton on a 21.5-mile (35-km) paved trail via waterfront parks, leafy neighborhoods, historic sights, and six bridges.

• **Wascana Centre Trails (Saskatchewan):** Circumnavigate Regina's Wascana Lake on paths that wander past the imposing Legislative Building,

Royal Saskatchewan Museum, MacKenzie Art Gallery, University of Regina, and Saskatchewan Science Centre.

• **Martin Goodman Trail (Ontario):** Explore 10 miles (16 km) of the Lake Ontario waterfront on a paved trail that features sandy beaches, water sport rentals, and the repurposed Port Lands docks.

• **Capital Pathway (Ontario):** Meandering along the south bank of the Ottawa River, this paved, multiuse

urban trail runs past the majestic Parliament Buildings, the Confederation Building, the Supreme Court of Canada, and other historic structures.

• **Harbour Passage (New Brunswick):** Follow a cranberry-colored trail from the oddball Reversing Falls Rapids to Fort La Tour, the New Brunswick Museum, and Market Square in Uptown, St. John.

145-mile (234-km) **P'tit Train du Nord** rail trail through the fetching **Laurentian Mountains.**

Turning south, the trail makes its way through the **Gatineau River** corridor to **Ottawa** and then a sequence of old railway routes like the **Ottawa Carleton Trailway, Frontenac K&P Trail,** and **Northumberland Rail Trail** to tumble down to **Toronto.**

The popular **Great Lakes Waterfront Trail** hugs the shore of **Lake Ontario** to **Hamilton,** where the route turns inland again for a long transit via various trails across central and western Ontario. One of the most intriguing sections is 50-mile (80-km) **Nipissing Road,** also called the **Ontario Ghost Trail**

because it runs through many pioneer-era farms and hamlets abandoned long ago. More waterfront hiking and biking awaits west of **Sudbury** along the 230-mile (370-km) **Huron Shores Trail** to **Sault Ste. Marie,** where giant Great Lakes bulk carriers pass through the historic canal locks.

Beyond Sault Ste. Marie, TCT users face another conundrum. Rather than dry land, the Trans Canada creators decided a canoe/kayak trail was the best way to advance almost 600 miles (1,000 km) across the top of **Lake Superior. Pukaskwa National Park, Rainbow Falls Provincial Park,** and a few other spots along the shore offer short land paths. Otherwise,

it's time to hire a boat or hit the road, Jack.

Beyond **Thunder Bay,** the **Pigeon River Trail** offers 28 miles (45 km) of dry-land hiking. But then you'll need to canoe or kayak through the vast **Boundary Waters** and **Lake of the Woods** regions in far western Ontario. For hikers and bikers, the busy **Trans-Canada Highway** between Sault Ste. Marie and **Whiteshell Provincial Park** in **Manitoba** is the only option.

But up ahead are the sprawling **Canadian Prairies,** a revelation for land-based travelers. Other than two relatively short water portions—the **Qu'Appelle River** and **Chief Whitecap Waterway** in **Saskatchewan**—the entire route from **Lake**

A crystal clear day in which to embrace the magic of the Trans Canada Trail

Winnipeg to the Rocky Mountains is road, gravel, dirt, or sidewalk.

Most of the trek across the prairies is through ranches and farmland. But the route also runs through major cities: **Winnipeg, Regina, Moose Jaw, Edmonton, Red Deer,** and **Calgary,** respectively. Each metropolis offers a chance to rest up and restock.

Moseying west from Stampede City, the TCT follows the **Bow Valley** into the **Canadian Rockies.** The trail loops through **Banff** village before an incredibly scenic transit through Kananaskis Country along the **High Rockies Trail.** Climbing over 6,250-foot (1,905-m) the **Elk Pass,** the route crosses the Continental Divide and into British Columbia. It also changes names, morphing into the **Elk Valley Trail** and taking hikers down to the **Kootenay River.**

West of climbing-crazy **Cranbrook,** the TCT follows **Gray Creek Pass** through the **Purcell Range** and the **Columbia and Western Rail Trail.** It then goes on through the **Monashee Mountains** to the old copper mining town of **Grand Forks** on the U.S.-Canada border. The final leg to the Pacific coast is a 310-mile (500-km) journey along the **Kettle Valley Rail Trail** through the **Okanagan Valley, Cascade Range,** and along the **Fraser River** to **Vancouver.**

The official route features passage from downtown Vancouver to the **North Shore** aboard the **Seabus** catamaran ferry. But it's much cooler to stroll through **Stanley Park** and across the fabled **Lions Gate Bridge** to reach the ferry terminal at **Horseshoe Bay.** A 90-minute sail across the **Salish Sea** on a big **BC Ferry** transports trekkers to **Nanaimo** on the eastern side of huge **Vancouver Island.**

"Greeting Figures," by Squamish Nation artist Darren Yelton, welcomes guests to the Trans Canada Trail pavilion.

Knowing the end of their winding trek across Canada is near, hikers and bikers make their way along the **Cowichan Valley Rail Trail** to the island's bottom end and a long-awaited rendezvous with **Victoria.** Slipping beneath the imposing colonial-era buildings flanking the harbor, the TCT finally peters out at **Clover Point** on the **Strait of Juan de Fuca.** ∎

OTHER GREAT TRAILS

Hiking or Biking to the Arctic

The northern leg of the Trans Canada reaches from Edmonton to Tuktoyaktuk, a remote Inuvialuit village on the Arctic Ocean. The 2,000-mile (3,200-km) trek runs through northern Alberta and British Columbia, and the Yukon and Northwest Territories.

"Rough-and-tumble" is an apt description of a route that runs through boreal forest, tundra, and the very top end of the Rocky Mountains, terrain inhabited by grizzlies, moose, caribou, and even polar bears as you approach the Arctic coast.

The caveat is the fact that almost the entire Arctic route is via roads rather than nonmotorized paths. This includes legendary lanes like the Alaska Highway and Dempster Highway (the only Canadian road that crosses the Arctic Circle). Although that's fine for long-distance biking, hiking that many miles along highways is an arduous undertaking.

Among the only nonmotorized sections are the Athabasca Landing Trail, Peace River Trail, and Lesser Slave Lake Trail in Alberta, and the Whitehorse Copper Trail and Dawson Overland Trail in the Yukon Territory.

Chilkoot Trail
Yukon, British Columbia & Alaska

Follow in the footsteps of author Jack London and the other Klondike gold seekers on a trail that links Alaska's Pacific shore and the remote Yukon wilderness.

THE BIG PICTURE

Distance: 33 miles (53 km)

Elevation Gain: approx. 6,040 feet (1,840 m)

Time: 3–5 days

Difficulty: Strenuous

Best Time: Summer

More Info: pc.gc.ca/en/lhn-nhs/yt/chilkoot and nps.gov/klgo/planyourvisit/chilkoottrail.htm

After gold was discovered in the Yukon's Klondike region in 1896, prospectors jumped at the rare but real chance to make their fortunes. But how to get there? Trekking across western Canada or the Alaskan heartland would take months, not to mention the dangers involved. But there was an alternative: a relatively short route from the Alaska Panhandle over the Chilkoot Pass that 100,000-some "stampeders" eventually followed to the Klondike goldfields.

Nowadays, the **Chilkoot Trail** takes thousands of backpackers each summer along the same route, a 33-mile (53-km) hike almost equally split between Alaska and British Columbia. Jointly maintained by Parks Canada and the U.S. National Park Service, the trail runs through 3,759-foot (1,146-m) Chilkoot Pass, where modern hikers traverse the international boundary just like those bygone fortune seekers.

Authorities limit the number of people who can set off along the Chilkoot during the summer high season (June 1 to September 13), when hikers must obtain a permit through the Parks Canada telephone reservation system.

Given the fact that the Canadian end of the trail is not accessible by road, hikers must also figure out how to travel onward from the British Columbia wilderness. The most popular choice is the **White Pass and Yukon Route railway** between **Skagway,** Alaska, and **Carcross** in the Yukon Territory, with connections to **Whitehorse.** Reservations for the train should be made well in advance. Alternatively, hikers who don't have to ask the price can charter a helicopter, floatplane, or speedboat for crossing Lake Bennett after the hike.

Before striking out, hikers must pick up their permits and backpack tags—and attend a mandatory orientation session that includes bear awareness training—at either **S.S. Klondike National Historic site** in Whitehorse or the **Chilkoot Trail Center** in Skagway.

The historic Chilkoot Pass was one of only three routes through the Coast Mountains that could be accessed year-round. The trail was placed on the historic registry in 1975.

Hikers now travel the same routes through the Chilkoot Pass that the Tlingit people once guarded and that prospectors later depended on during the gold rush.

The trail starts at **Dyea,** a national historic landmark that preserves the remains of a town that boomed during the Klondike gold rush. The three town cemeteries bear witness to the deadly nature of trekking the Chilkoot Trail in those days.

From there, a fairly easy walk through the temperate rainforest of the **Taiya River Valley** leads to the campgrounds at **Finnegan's Point** and **Canyon City** ghost town. A short loop trail at Canyon City features gold rush artifacts and interpretive panels.

Past Canyon City, the ever rising Taiya Valley takes the route to **Pleasant Camp** and **Sheep Camp** in the sparse forest below the alpine zone. Then it really starts to get tough: 2,700 feet (820 m) in elevation gain over the next three miles (4.8 km) as the trail climbs to the **Chilkoot Pass.** It's rocky and cold, vegetation almost nonexistent as hikers breach the legendary pass. But the view of the snowy peaks and deep, green valleys is awesome.

Chilkoot Pass marks the trail's halfway point. But from there it's mostly downhill to aptly named **Happy Camp** (trekkers who make it that far are definitely cheerful) and through boreal forest to **Lindeman City,** where Parks Canada maintains a ranger post and interpretive tent. A final seven-mile (11-km) stretch takes the Chilkoot Trail down to **Lake Bennett** and a train ride back to civilization. ∎

OTHER GREAT TRAILS

Jack London's Chilkoot Trek

At the age of 21, struggling writer Jack London decided that Klondike gold rather than books was his path to fame and fortune. With four companions, London hiked the Chilkoot Pass route in August 1897.

It took 20 days to complete the task, with each hiker hauling 150 pounds (68 kg) of gear. London never struck gold and later complained that "I brought nothing back from the Klondike but my scurvy"—if you don't count the adventures that he spun into *The Call of the Wild,* the book that made him famous.

The White Pass and Yukon Route Railroad curves around the mountainside on its way to Skagway, Alaska.

Stanley Park Seawall Path

British Columbia

A mosaic of woods, water, and wondrous views makes this Vancouver loop one of the world's best and most diverse urban trails.

THE BIG PICTURE

Distance: approx. 6 miles (10 km)

Elevation Gain: approx. 330 feet (100 m)

Time: 3–4 hours

Difficulty: Easy

Best Time: Year-round

More Info: vancouver.ca/parks-recreation-culture/stanley-park-seawall.aspx

It's not often that humankind can improve on what nature has already created. But the promenade around **Stanley Park** in Vancouver may just be one of those rare exceptions.

The six-mile (10-km) hiking, biking, skating, and jogging **Seawall Path** was the brainchild of park superintendent William Stanley Rawlings, who, in pitching the seawall, declared that "personally I doubt if there exists anywhere on this continent such possibilities of a combined park and marine walk as we have in Stanley Park."

Rawlings also emphasized that a sturdy seawall would protect the city's foreshore from storms and erosion. Municipal leaders agreed, ponied up the funds, and construction started in 1918. Although most of the seawall was finished by the 1930s, various extensions and enhancements stretched over the next 60 years.

More than a century after he first floated the idea, Rawlings' dream remains one of Vancouver's leading attractions for residents and visitors alike. They come for the exercise, of course, as well as panoramic views of the skyline, snowy mountains to the north, and Strait of Georgia. There are also plenty of attractions and activities along the way.

Another thing that makes the Seawall Path unique is the fact that nearly all of it is navigated in a counterclockwise direction, a traffic flow that is especially welcome on sunny summer weekends when the trail is packed.

There are dozens of places to join the trail. But mile/kilometer zero is a pedestrian roundabout on the southern edge of the park between **Coal Harbour** and **Lost Lagoon.** From there the route makes its way along the harbor's north shore past the **Queen Victoria Fountain,** the official **Stanley Park Information Booth,** and a stand for **horse-drawn carriage rides.**

Past the **Brockton Oval** for rugby and cricket, the trail passes a collection of **totem poles** and **ceremonial gateways** that honor the fact that First Nations people, including the Coast Salish, Musqueam, Squamish, Tsleil-Waututh, and Haida, occupied Stanley Park's location for thousands of years before the arrival of the first

The life-size "Girl in a Wetsuit" statue by Elek Imredy looks out over the waters of north Stanley Park, Vancouver.

The six-mile (10-km) seawall in Vancouver is the world's longest uninterrupted waterfront path, granting walkers, joggers, and cyclists a breathtaking route along the coastline.

Europeans. Mounted on **Brockton Point** is the historic **Nine O'Clock Gun,** a naval cannon fired at nine in the evening since 1898 to help mariners set their timepieces.

Tacking northwest along the narrow **Lions Gate** channel, the trail passes the offshore **Girl in a Wetsuit** statue (Vancouver's answer to "The Little Mermaid" in Denmark) and a children's splash area called the **Fox's Den.** The trail eventually ducks beneath the iconic **Lions Gate Bridge,** a massive suspension span (opened in 1938) that connects Vancouver and its northern suburbs.

Past the bridge and **Prospect Point,** the Seawall Path hunkers beneath steep cliffs on its way to a photogenic sea stack called **Siwash Rock** and sandy **Third Beach,**

where trekkers can catch a few rays, watch sunset over the Salish Sea, or even take a dip in the almost always chilly water.

Reaching **English Bay,** the trail sidles up to **Second Beach** and its popular heated seaside swimming

pool. With a **golf course, tennis courts,** and **lawn bowls,** this southwest corner is the park's competitive sports hub. Hanging a sharp left, the route continues along the south shore of Lost Lagoon to its starting point. ■

APRÈS HIKE

• **Vancouver Aquarium:** From sea otters and rescued sea lions to jellies and clownfish, Canada's largest aquarium is home to more than 70,000 creatures.

• **Malkin Bowl:** This open-air theater hosts big-name concerts and a summer "Theatre Under the Stars" stage series.

• **Stanley Park Railway:** Miniature trains take passengers on a

narrow-gauge journey through dense urban forest.

• **Harbour Cruises:** One-hour narrated boat rides and sunset dinner cruises depart from a pier at the end of Denman Street near Lost Lagoon.

• **Food and Drink:** Park eateries include Stanley's Bar & Grill, Stanley Park Brewing, Prospect Point Bar & Grill, and the Teahouse at Stanley Park.

La Boucle de la Diable

Québec

Channel the spirit of the Algonquin people on a wilderness trail through Mont-Tremblant National Park in the gorgeous Laurentian Mountains north of Montréal.

THE BIG PICTURE

Distance: 29.3 miles (47.2 km)

Elevation Change: approx. 2,400 feet (730 m)

Time: 3 days

Difficulty: Moderate

Best Time: Year-round

More Info: sepaq.com/pq/mot/index.dot?language_id=1

The Algonquin people who once inhabited the rugged highlands of what is now south-central Québec believed that an evil spirit made the mountains tremble whenever he was angered. Arriving much later, French trappers and settlers named many of the region's geographical features after the legend: Mont-Tremblant (Trembling Peak), Rivière du Diable (Devil's River), and Chute du Diable (Devil's Falls).

In modern times, the most popular multiday hike in **Mont-Tremblant National Park** is **La Boucle de la Diable,** or Devil's Loop, a 29.3-mile (47.2-km) circuit through the wooded hills and valleys in the park's westside **Secteur de la Diable.**

Ideal for hiking in summer and cross-country skiing come winter, the path is well marked and often quite wide, much of the trail along old logging roads cut in the 19th century when timber extraction was the region's primary industry. Logging in the area ended in 1895, when Mont-Tremblant first became a park. So the forest has had more than a century to recover its former grandeur.

Dispersed camping is allowed on multiday paddle trips and on treks through the backcountry, but not on central trails like the Devil's Loop. Hikers and skiers overnight in two wilderness huts along the loop that can each sleep a dozen people. Power hikers doing the route as a two-day trek also have the option of overnighting at a campground beside Lac Cache.

About a 10-minute drive along the main road from the park entrance station, **Lac Monroe Visitor Center** marks the official start of the trail. Open from May to October, the lakeside center offers the latest news on weather and trail conditions, as well as a general store, ice and firewood, bike and watercraft rentals, hot showers, and coin-operated washers and dryers.

Between October and May, the nearby **Centre de Découvertes** (Discovery Center) offers similar information as well as snacks, showers, and snowshoe/Nordic ski rentals.

With 102 ski trails from expert to beginner, the snow-blanketed Mont-Tremblant resort is a perfect winter escape for skiers and snowshoers alike.

Visit Mont-Tremblant National Park in the fall for golden views of La Pimbina Valley.

Traveling counterclockwise, the loop starts with a scenic trek along the western shore of **Lac Monroe** to **Chutes Croches** (Quavering Falls), where it veers west and follows a stream into the mountains. Up ahead, **Refuge Le Liteau** overnight hut looms along the edge of **Lac Croche.**

Day two kicks off with a meander through a landscape spangled with glacial lakes to **Chute-aux-Mûres** (Blackberry Falls). The route soon turns south onto a dirt road along the shore of **Lac Cache** to a waterfront campground with a sandy beach and **Refuge La Cache.**

On the final day, hikers have a short walk to the **Petite Rivière Cachée** before a steep climb back into the mountains to **Lac du Brochet.** Returning to the park's main corridor, the final leg runs beneath cliffs that frame the western edge of the valley and along **Petit Lac Monroe** to the visitors center. ∎

OTHER GREAT TRAILS

• **Lachine Canal Path:** A 19th-century canal that carried St. Lawrence shipping around the Lachine Rapids is the focus of an 8.4-mile (13.5-km) national historic site hiking/biking trail in Montréal.

• **Pingualuit Crater:** Reach this giant, flooded, almost perfectly round crater from a meteor that hit Earth around 1.4 million years ago via a short but spectacular trail in the Nunavik region of far northern Québec.

• **L'Acropole des Draveurs:** A 6.5-mile (10.4-km) trail rises to three peaks and spectacular views on the Acropolis of Loggers in Hautes-Gorges-de-la-Rivière-Malbaie National Park.

• **Grande île Loop:** Whimsical rock outcrops like the Château and the Zoo feature in a 14-mile (22.5-km) coastal walk around the largest island in Mingan Archipelago National Park Reserve in the Gulf of St. Lawrence.

• **Québec City:** Hike through 500 years of history on a 2.5-mile (4-km) trail along the ramparts and palisades between the Château Frontenac and the Plains of Abraham.

International Appalachian Trail
Multiple Provinces

The Appalachian Trail may end on Maine's Mount Katahdin, but the range keeps going. And so does the hiking, along an awesome route through northern Maine and five Canadian provinces.

THE BIG PICTURE

Distance: approx. 1,580 miles (2,540 km)

Elevation Gain: Unknown

Time: 3–4 months

Difficulty: Strenuous

Best Time: Late spring, summer, or early fall

More Info: iat-sia.org

Divided into four sections by the Gulf of St. Lawrence, the **International Appalachian Trail** (IAT) hops back and forth from the North American mainland to several large islands on a route that takes hikers from dense forest and deep-blue lakes to rocky shores and wind-blown tundra.

It's a relatively new trail, blazed in the 1990s and early 21st century after the route was first proposed. The Newfoundland section opened in 2006, and plans are in the works to extend the IAT along the rugged Labrador shore.

Because it stretches so far north, the IAT has a shorter season than its older, longer cousin. Yet starting from the southern end in late spring or very early summer should give thru-hikers enough time to reach the northern tip of Newfoundland before winter arrives.

No matter which way they trek, hikers need to pack their passports for the international border crossing between Maine and New Brunswick. And because the IAT isn't contiguous, they need to figure two ferry trips and one multi-segment bus ride into their planning.

From the southern end, the trail kicks off in **Katahdin Woods and Waters National Monument** with an amble along the East Branch of the **Penobscot River,** a waterway with a rich literary heritage ranging from Henry David Thoreau to Stephen King. Rural roads take the route across the potato fields of **Aroostook County** before a dead-straight section along the U.S.-Canada border to the **Fort Fairfield** port of entry.

Cutting across the northwest corner of **New Brunswick,** the IAT calls on **Mount Carleton Provincial Park** before slipping across the **Restigouche River** into **Québec Province**. Hanging a right onto the **Gaspé Peninsula,** the route climbs into the **Chic-Choc Mountains** and a remote wilderness that nurtures

An adult male moose in Cape Breton Highlands National Park

Visit L'Anse aux Meadows National Historic Site to scope out a striking 11th-century Viking settlement.

Canada's southernmost woodland caribou herd.

The IAT reaches its highest point atop **Mount Jacques Cartier** (4,160 feet/1,268 m) before a gorgeous stretch along the **St. Lawrence River** and a rendezvous with coastal **Forillon National Park.**

Until the trail is extended along the **Gulf of St. Lawrence** coast, hopping a bus via **Moncton** is the best way for hikers to reach **Prince Edward Island.** From the island end of **Confederation Bridge,** the PEI segment runs through a picture-perfect landscape of forest and farms to the **Wood Islands** waterfront and a 75-minute ferry to **Caribou,** Nova Scotia.

Crossing the **Strait of Canso** on a rocky causeway, the IAT rambles across **Cape Breton Island** to **Sydney** and a seven-hour ferry ride on the open Atlantic to **Channel-**

Port aux Basques on the isle of Newfoundland.

Newfoundland boasts the IAT's longest segment, a 462-mile (744-km) walk up the island's west coast that includes the spectacular fjords of **Gros Morne National Park** and the Viking settlement at **L'Anse aux Meadows.** PAL regional airline offers flights from the small airport at **St. Anthony** to Montréal, Halifax, and other international hubs. ∎

LOCAL FLAVOR

• **Courtyard Café:** Seafood chowder, crab quiche, fresh haddock, and baked sole are some of the New England–style maritime meals at this Aroostook County eatery near the IAT; 61 Main Street, Houlton, ME; thecourtyardcafe.biz.

• **Salmon Lodge:** Overlooking the Restigouche River, this cozy restaurant has been serving fresh salmon, lobster, and other iconic Canadian dishes since the early 20th century; 33716 Route 11, Flatlands, NB; (506) 753-8004.

• **Le Brise Bise:** Live music, craft beers, and French Canadian dishes like shrimp poutine, bouillabaisse *gaspésienne,* and smoked salmon bagels are the allures of this Gaspé Peninsula bistro bar; 135 Rue de la Reine, Gaspé, QC; brisebise.ca.

• **Governor's Pub & Eatery:** Relish the waterfront view from the upper deck and select from a menu heavy on surf and turf at a public house that opened in 1867; 233 Esplanade, Sydney, NS; governorseatery.com.

Global Trails

Cross the River Marsyangdi to reach the village of Chame on the
186-mile (300-km) Annapurna Circuit in western Nepal.

Mexico, Central America & the Caribbean

From breathtaking ravines to ancient ruins, oceanic wonders to sandy shores, discover the best hiking and walking in these warm-weather destinations.

COPPER CANYON RIM TO RIM TO RIM, Mexico

The Barrancas del Cobre in north-west Mexico is a series of six deep ravines rather than just one. There are dozens of trekking choices, but the classic hike is a challenging 38-mile (61-km) loop between Divisadero and Pamachi via the Rio Urique Canyon, a journey that takes around a week to complete.

More Info: *coppercanyontrails.org*

LOWER MAYAN TRAIL, Guatemala

Four Indigenous villages along the north shore of Lake Atitlán are the focus of an easy five-mile (8-km) hike that starts and ends with a water taxi ride across the photogenic water body in the highlands of northern Guatemala.

More Info: *adventuresguatemala.com*

MONTEVERDE LOOP, Costa Rica

One of the earliest attempts to preserve primary tropical forest, the Monteverde Cloud Forest Biological Reserve is best explored along a 2.3-mile (3.7-km) loop that includes the Sendero Bosque Nuboso, Sendero Wilford Guindon, and Sendero Camino. Along the way are several viewpoints, a suspension bridge, and a chance to see iconic species like the resplendent quetzal bird.

More Info: *cloudforestmonteverde.com*

Take in the sweeping views of the town of Soufrière from the Pitons UNESCO World Heritage site in St. Lucia.

BLACK HOLE DROP, Belize

Rather than schlepping up a mountainside and reaching the peak via a technical climb, this hike involves a short but challenging jungle trek punctuated by a rappel into Actun Loch Tunich, a 500-foot-deep (150-m) limestone sinkhole in the Maya Mountains. Several local outfitters offer guided trips with all the gear.

More Info: *cavesbranch.com*

LOST WATERFALLS TRAIL, Panama

The Sendero de las Tres Cascadas takes hikers on a short but steep trek to three towering cascades—and cool swimming holes—hidden in the thick jungle of western Panama.

More Info: *thelostwaterfalls.com*

WAITUKUBULI NATIONAL TRAIL, Dominica

The Caribbean's first marked long-distance hiking trail extends all the way across the island. Among the highlights of the 115-mile (185-km) trek are the Emerald Pool and Valley of Desolation volcanic field in Morne Trois Pitons National Park and the Carib Territory Indigenous reservation.

More Info: *waitukubulitrail.dm*

MOUNT PELÉE, Martinique

The "Paris of the Caribbean" was destroyed by a massive 1902 eruption. Hikers can summit this still active volcano via several trails, including the Aileron Route, which reaches the eastern edge of the caldera in just a mile (1.6 km).

More Info: *summitpost.org/ la-montagne-pel-e/920283*

GROS PITON, St. Lucia

This iconic peak hovering above the island's southwest shore is reached via a precipitous jungle trail that

A resplendent quetzal in the Curi-Cancha Reserve in Monteverde, Costa Rica

rises 1,800 feet (550 m) in half a mile (1.6 km) on what seems more like a mountain climb than a hike. Hiring a guide is strongly recommended.

More Info: *grospiton.com*

SHETE BOKA NATIONAL PARK, Curaçao

This 3.4-mile (5.5-km) double out-and-back along the island's north shore leads to a cove with a natural bridge (Boka Wandomi) and another where sea turtles lay their eggs (Boka Kalki). Hikers questing for more of a challenge can climb nearby Christoffelberg (1,220 feet/ 372 m), the highest peak on the Dutch isle.

More Info: *shetebokapark.org*

PICO DUARTE, Dominican Republic

Conquer the highest peak in the Caribbean (10,127 feet/3,087 m) via several routes in Armando Bermúdez National Park. The trek normally takes three to seven days depending on the route. Guides, camping gear, and mules are available at the park office.

More Info: *visitdominican republic.com/things-to-do/pico-duarte*

Catch the last rays of sunset cliffside while camping at the Trigo Overlook on Copper Canyon, Chihuahua state, Mexico.

South America

These Southern Hemisphere treks feature some of the most beloved world wonders, from the natural kind (Torres del Paine) to the human-made (Machu Picchu).

Trek the O Circuit for a view of the granite peaks of Torres del Paine, Patagonia, Chile.

"W" CIRCUIT, Chile

One of the globe's most spectacular trails traces a W-shaped route around the base of Patagonia's soaring Torres del Paine: glacier-topped granite peaks that rise more than 6,500 feet (2,000 m) straight up from the surrounding pampas and lakes. The 50-mile (80-km) path features campsites, mountain huts, and the Hotel Las Torres.

More Info: *fantasticosur.com*

SALKANTAY AND INCA TRAILS, Peru

Two popular hiking routes traverse the Peruvian Andes to the ruins of Machu Picchu. The legendary (two- to four-day) Inca Trail now features a daily quota system to reduce human impact from damaging the path. The longer (five-day) Salkantay Trail is more strenuous, and reaches a higher altitude (15,190 feet/4,630 m).

More Info: *machu-picchu.org/hikes*

MOUNT RORAIMA, Venezuela, Guyana, and Brazil

Inspiration for the 1912 sci-fi novel *Lost World,* this gigantic flat-topped *tepui* rising along the northern edge of the Amazon Basin requires a weeklong trek through virgin rainforest and should only be attempted with an experienced local guide. Waiting at the top are rare plants and animals and vertigo-inducing views.

More Info: *hike-venezuela.com/en*

FITZ ROY LOOP, Argentina

Starting and ending in the village of El Chaltén in Los Glaciares National Park, this jaunt through the Patagonian wilderness offers glaciers, granite peaks, and dazzling alpine lakes.

More Info: *elchalten.com*

The ancient Lost City in the Sierra Nevada de Santa Marta, Colombia, is thought to have been founded around 800 B.C.

CHIMBORAZO CIRCUIT, Ecuador

A massive snowcapped stratovolcano—the highest mountain on Earth when measured from the planet's core—forms the heart of this scenic multiday trek through the Ecuadorian Andes. The loop around the mountain is relatively easy; toss in another full day to reach the 20,548-foot (6,263-m) summit.

More Info: *goandestrek.com*

CHAPADA DIAMANTINA CIRCUIT, Brazil

The deep canyons, ruddy cliffs, caverns, and waterfalls of Brazil's dazzling "Diamond Highlands" provide a stunning backdrop for hikes through the wilderness of the northern Bahia state. Trekking the national park's Pati Valley end to end takes five days.

More Info: *diamantinamountains.com*

CIUDAD PERDIDA, Colombia

Discover your inner Indiana Jones on this trek to the "Lost City" of Teyuna in the Sierra Nevada de Santa Marta mountains along Colombia's Caribbean coast. The ruins are reached via four days of trekking through thick tropical rainforest.

More Info: *baquianos.com/en*

COLCA CANYON, Peru

Located on the cusp of the Andes Mountains and Atacama Desert, South America's largest chasm offers opportunities to visit Indigenous villages and natural hot springs, and a chance to view condors and vicuña in the wild. Three different routes depart from Cabanaconde village on the south rim.

More Info: *colcaperu.gob.pe*

KAIETEUR FALLS TREK, Guyana

Five days of canoeing and trekking through the Guyana rainforest culminate in the world's highest single-drop waterfall: 741-foot (226-m) Kaieteur, the centerpiece of Guyana's only national park. Hikers normally fly back to Georgetown from the national park airstrip.

More Info: *rftoursgy.com*

ACONCAGUA, Chile to Argentina

No technical climbing skills are necessary to summit South America's highest mountain (22,837 feet/6,960 m), but the upward path is long and literally breathtaking. Guided hiking trips to/from Mendoza take around three weeks total with plenty of time to acclimatize along the way.

More Info: *aconcaguamountainguides.com*

Europe

The geothermic wonders, relics from the Middle Ages, and beloved pilgrimages on these classic trails across the Atlantic are worth traveling for.

BRÈCHE DE ROLAND,
Spain and France

The epic route takes hikers over the crest of the Pyrenees between the deep Ordesa Valley in northern Spain and the spectacular Cirque de Gavarnie in southern France. The brèche ("breach") is a giant U-shaped gap on the international border that legendary French knight Roland allegedly leaped across on horseback while fleeing the Moors.

More Info: *us.france.fr/en/occitanie-south-of-france* and *spain.info/en/nature/ordesa-monte-perdido-national-park*

WEST HIGHLAND WAY,
Scotland

The biggest challenge of hiking this ultra-scenic trail through the moors, lochs, and vales of the Scottish Highlands is learning how to pronounce its Gaelic name: Slighe na Gàidhealtachd an Iar. The 96-mile (155-km) route between Glasgow and Fort William includes eight sections that can be easily done as day hikes.

More Info: *westhighlandway.org*

KUNGSLEDEN, Sweden

The "King's Trail" across northern Sweden renders an extraordinary adventure in one of Europe's wildest corners. Although it's tempting to look for gnomes, trolls, and other folk creatures along the way, trekkers are more likely to encounter reindeer and Sami people along a 270-mile (440-km) route through four national parks.

More Info: *swedishtourist association.com/areas/kungsleden*

CAMINO DE SANTIAGO,
Spain

Pilgrims first started trekking this route across northern Spain, stretching nearly 800 miles (1,300 km) between the Basque Country and Santiago de Compostela, in the Middle Ages, a practice that both devout Catholics and others seeking an outdoor and cultural adventure revived in the late 20th century.

More Info: *santiago.forwalk.org/en*

LAUGAVEGURINN, Iceland

Glacial lakes, lava deserts, snowfields, and geothermal wonders highlight the popular "Hot Springs Route" of southwest Iceland. Stretching 34 miles (55 km)

The Pindos Mountains look out over rolling greenery and flowering meadows in Epirus, Greece.

Hike one of the least populated regions in all of Europe on the Kungsleden Trail (King's Trail) in Swedish Lapland.

between lakeside Thórsmörk and mountaintop Landmannalaugar, the route features six overnight huts.

More Info: *laugavegur.is*

COASTAL HIKING TRAIL, Baltic States

The shorelines of Estonia, Latvia, and Lithuania are the backdrop to an 880-mile (1,420-km) route that features bays, beaches, and fishing villages between Tallinn and Nida at the eastern end of the Baltic Sea.

More Info: *baltictrails.eu/en/ coastal*

TOUR DU MONT BLANC, France, Italy, and Switzerland

Set aside at least 12 days for this circumnavigation of western Europe's highest peak. The TMB meanders through three Alpine nations—France, Italy, and Switzerland—on a 110-mile (170-km) trek through forests, snowfields, and flower-filled Alpine meadows.

More Info: *autourdumontblanc .com/en*

PINDUS MOUNTAINS HORSESHOE, Greece

Leave the crowds on the islands behind for a 36-mile (58-km) hike through the rugged Pindus Mountains of northern Greece. Starting from Vitsa village in the remote Zagori region, the trail traverses pine and beech forest and rocky highlands on a route through Vikos Gorge and the Tymfi Massif of Vikos–Aoös National Park.

More Info: *mountaingoat.gr*

E3 EAST, Poland, Slovakia, and the Czech Republic

One of 12 long-distance hiking routes the European Ramblers Association endorses, the E3 ends with a spectacular eastern section that features the wild and rugged Carpathian Mountains.

More Info: *era-ewv-ferp.org/e-paths*

RHEINSTEIG, Germany

Romantic castles, Riesling wines, and bird's-eye views of the famous river are the hallmarks of a 200-mile (320-km) trail along the eastern bank of the Rhine between Bonn and Wiesbaden. Trekkers can make it a loop by returning via the Rheinburgenweg on the opposite side of Germany's fabled waterway.

More Info: *rheinsteig.de/en/ rheinsteig*

Africa

National parks, volcanoes, desert oases, and remarkable wildlife are the features of these 10 hikes throughout the continent.

JEBEL TOUBKAL, Morocco

Hiking to the top of Morocco's highest peak (13,671 feet/4,167 m) offers a chance to visit remote Berber villages in the Atlas Mountains and the possibility of looking out over the endless Sahara desert while standing in snow. Located 41 miles (66 km) south of Marrakech, Imlil village marks the start of the two-day trek.

More Info: *trekkinginmorocco.com*

PICO DO FOGO, Cape Verde Islands

Extra-sturdy boots and hiking poles are musts for the jagged, lava-laden trail to the caldera of a 9,281-foot (2,829-m) volcano on Fogo Island. The one-day hike starts from Chã Das Caldeiras village, many of its homes still eerily buried in lava from the last eruption in 2014–15.

More Info: *capeverdeislands.org/pico-do-fogo*

SIMIEN MOUNTAINS, Ethiopia

Rare and endangered animals like the Ethiopian wolf, scimitar-horned walia ibex, and gelada are the allures of a trek through the secluded highlands of northern Ethiopia. That's not to say the scenery isn't just as stunning, a warren of grassy plateaus tilted at odd angles and deep gorges framed by sheer cliffs.

More Info: *simienpark.org*

RWENZORI CENTRAL CIRCUIT, Uganda

Explore the fabled Mountains of the Moon along a rigorous route that passes equatorial glaciers at the base of Mount Stanley and Margherita Peak. Guided treks include English-speaking guides, porters, meals, and overnights in mountain camps located as high as 15,000 feet (4,540 m) along a route blazed in 1906 by an Italian team led by the Duke of Abruzzi.

More Info: *rwenzorimountaineeringservices.com*

MOUNT KILIMANJARO, Tanzania

Reaching the fabled snows of Kilimanjaro requires three or four days of steady upward trekking through tropical rainforest, rare alpine vegetation, a barren high-altitude desert, and a final push up killer switchbacks to the glacier-crowned highest point in Africa

Although short, the Umbwe Route on Mount Kilimanjaro is a real challenge without stages to acclimatize to the changes in altitude.

(19,341 feet/5,895 m). Hemingway never made it that far, but you can.

More Info: *ultimatekilimanjaro
.com*

MULANJE MASSIF, Malawi

One of the world's largest monadnocks (isolated rock outcrops) towers more than 9,800 feet (3,000 m) over southern Malawi. Rising from savanna to woodland to bare rock, several routes lead to a summit offering views of national capital Blantyre in the west and Mozambique to the east. Hiring a guide is highly recommended.

More Info: *mcm.org.mw*

FISH RIVER CANYON, Namibia

Plunging 1,800 feet (550 m) into the desert of southern Namibia, Africa's version of the Grand Canyon is conquered via a five-day trek between Hobas and the Ais-Ais hot springs oasis. But those 53 miles (85 km) can be brutal, especially in summer when temperatures on the canyon floor can rise as high as 118°F (48°C).

More Info: *fishriverlodge-namibia
.com*

BLYDE RIVER CANYON, South Africa

It's not South Africa's longest hiking route, but it's certainly one of the most spectacular, a 37-mile (60-km) trek along the west rim of a scenic gorge between Johannesburg and Kruger National Park. Along the way are lofty waterfalls, vintage gold-mining towns, and geological wanders like God's Window, Bourke's Luck Potholes, and the Three Rondavels.

More Info: *www.nature-reserve
.co.za/blyde-river-canyon-natural
-preserve.html*

The Mulanje Massif in Malawi rises more than 9,800 feet (3,000 m), towering over neighboring Mozambique.

MONT-AUX-SOURCES, South Africa and Lesotho

Royal Natal National Park is the starting point for a 27-mile

A quiver tree in Fish River Canyon, Namibia

(45-km) out-and-back to a flat-topped summit in the Drakensberg range shared by South Africa and Lesotho. Those who reach the summit via multiple switchbacks and a chain ladder can peer down into the Amphitheatre and 3,106-foot (947-m) Tugela Falls.

More Info: *www.nature-reserve
.co.za/royal-natal-national-park.html*

TSITSIKAMMA TRAIL, South Africa

Avoid the crowds on the coastal Otter Trail in favor of an inland route through the lush forest- and grass-covered mountains of Tsitsikamma National Park. Hikers overnight in mountain huts with bunk beds, bathrooms, and outdoor cooking areas. Crossing streams in waist-high water is part of the fun.

More Info: *mto.group/eco-tourism/
tsitsikamma-trail/hikes*

Asia

From world wonders to a 17th-century monastery on the edge of a cliff, behold thousands of years of history—and natural wonder—on these trails.

LYCIAN WAY, Turkey

Curling 335 miles (540 km) around Turkey's Mediterranean coast, this year-round route swings between turquoise coves and snow-covered peaks like Mount Olympus. Along the way are coastal campgrounds, golden beaches, tasty taverna food, crusader castles, and two dozen ancient Greco-Roman archaeological sites, including Xanthos.

More Info: *lycianturkey.com/lycian-way.htm*

ISRAEL NATIONAL TRAIL, Israel

Hike the entire length of Israel on a 680-mile (1,100-km) footpath that stretches between the Golan Heights and the Red Sea. The route includes a lengthy segment along the Mediterranean coast between Haifa and Tel Aviv, a brief trek through Jerusalem, and then a long walk across the Negev desert to Eilat.

More Info: *israeltrail.net*

TIGER'S NEST, Bhutan

This short but classic Himalayan hike is less than four miles (6.4 km) round-trip but rises nearly 2,000 feet (610 m) to Paro Taktsang Monastery. Poised on a narrow rock ledge, the 17th-century monastery is embellished with vibrant thangka paintings. Those who cannot make the trek on foot can opt for horseback.

More Info: *bhutan.travel*

WORLD'S END TRAIL, Sri Lanka

A 2,890-foot (880-m) drop awaits hikers who reach World's End in Horton Plains National Park. The shortest route to the top of the escarpment is just 2.3 miles (3.7 km) from the park headquarters and campgrounds, but involves substantial elevation gain. Your reward? A panorama of misty mountains, tea plantations, and the far-off Indian Ocean.

More Info: *srilanka.travel*

MANASLU CIRCUIT, Nepal

Wrapping around the base of the world's eighth highest mountain—26,781-foot (8,163-m) Manaslu—this 105-mile (170-km) hiking trail in central Nepal features glaciers, snowfields, alpine lakes, and overnights in local teahouses. Reaching an elevation of 16,847 feet (5,135 m) at Larkya La Pass, altitude can

This 196-foot (60-m) waterfall lies just outside the village of Bhulebule along the Annapurna Circuit in Nepal.

The moonlike surface of Mount Kinabalu, Malaysia

challenge even the fittest trekkers.

More Info: *trekroute.com/ manaslu-circuit-trek*

COAST-TO-COAST TRAIL, Singapore

Leaping from park to park across the middle of the island—with urban sidewalks as connectors—the 22-mile (35-km) Coast-to-Coast passes through or beside major natural attractions like Jurong Lake Gardens, Bukit Batok Nature Park, the world-renowned Singapore Botanic Gardens, and the Central Catchment Nature Reserve with its myriad lakes and jungle trails.

More Info: *nparks.gov.sg/gardens -parks-and-nature/parks-and-nature -reserves/coast-to-coast*

MOUNT KINABALU, Malaysia

The highest point between the Himalaya and New Guinea, Kinabalu rises 13,435 feet (4,095 m) above the island of Borneo. The 11-mile (18-km) trail to the summit doesn't require any technical climbing skill but is normally done as a two-day trek with an overnight at Laban Rata Resthouse.

More Info: *mountkinabalu.com*

MACLEHOSE TRAIL, Hong Kong

Aptly shaped like a giant dragon, this 62-mile (100-km) route between Sai Kung and Tuen Mun rambles across lofty peaks and ridges above the city's ultra-crowded Kowloon (Nine Dragons) Peninsula.

More Info: *thruhikinghk.com/ the-maclehose-trail.html*

GREAT WALL OF CHINA, China

Although not officially a trail, the Great Wall lures a handful of hikers determined to walk its entire length each year. At 5,500 miles (8,851 km), distance is the biggest challenge. Even the speediest hikers take at least three months to complete a route fraught with extreme weather and rugged terrain.

More Info: *www.travelchinaguide .com/how-to-hike-the-great-wall-of -china.htm*

SHIN-ETSU TRAIL, Japan

The beech tree forests of the Sekida Mountains provide a leafy setting for a 68-mile (110-km) route through the highlands of Nagano and Niigata Prefectures. The route dips through passes used for more than a thousand years by traders and warriors moving between the Sea of Japan and cities along the Pacific coast.

More Info: *s-trail.net/english*

Oceania & the South Pacific

Find reason to lace up your boots on trails from Australia's outback to tropical island destinations.

MILFORD TRACK,
New Zealand

Dubbed the "finest walk in the world," this 33-mile (53-km) trail on the South Island was originally blazed by Maori before guides started leading recreational hikers along the route in the late 1800s. Only 40 hikers a day are allowed on a trail that scales the heights of Fiordland National Park between Glade Wharf and Milford Sound.

More Info: *milfordtrack.net* and *doc.govt.nz/milfordtrack*

Discover white- and black-sand beaches, a jungle paradise, and waterfalls along the Lavena Coastal Walk on Taveuni, Fiji's third largest island.

MUNDA BIDDI TRAIL,
Australia

The world's longest continuous off-road bike trail stretches for more than 620 miles (1,000 km) between Mundaring and Albany in Western Australia. Along the way are wildlife-rich eucalyptus forests, remote beaches, and half a dozen national parks—but not a single vehicle. Hikers are also welcome, but cyclists have the right-of-way.

More Info: *mundabiddi.org.au*

CROSS ISLAND TREK,
Cook Islands

Don't let the shortness (3.7 miles/ 6 km) fool you: This hike across the Rarotonga highlands is tougher than many longer trails. In addition to stream crossings and thick jungle, the route includes an ascent of Te Rua Manga (aka the Needle), a towering volcanic monolith with spectacular views of the island.

More Info: *cookislands.travel/ hiking-on-rarotonga*

HANGA ROA-ANAKENA HIKE, Rapa Nui

Started from the edge of Hanga Roa town, the 12-mile (19-km) hike saunters along sea cliffs to half a dozen sacred sites along the island's west and north coasts. Among the highlights are the giant stone heads *(moai)* of Ahu Tahai, Ana Kakenga, and Anakena Beach.

More Info: *chile.travel/en/where -to-go/macrozone/rapa-nui*

SYDNEY GREAT COASTAL WALK, Australia

Bondi Beach, Sydney Opera House, Manly, Botany Bay, and Ku-ring-gai Chase National Park are just a few of the stops on an epic 61-mile (100-km) adventure along the coast of the down under continent's largest urban area. The

A moss-lined path glows almost fluorescent in Fiordland National Park near Milford Sound, New Zealand.

route's eight sections are easily done as day hikes.

More Info: *www.australia.com/ en/places/sydney-and-surrounds/great -coastal-walk.html*

GRAND RANDONNÉE NC1, New Caledonia

Inspired by France's famous long-distance hiking route, this South Pacific version is divided into seven sections that tramp the island's red-earth highlands between seaside Prony village and Dumbéa Gorge. Hikers crash at campgrounds or mountain huts along a passage that spans three nature reserves and Parc Provincial de la Rivière Bleue.

More Info: *newcaledonia.travel/au/ great-south/yate/trail-grr1*

THE LONG PATHWAY, New Zealand

Trek the entire length of New Zealand—from the subtropical beaches that fringe the Bay of Islands to the golden plains near Invercargill—on the Te Araroa (Long Pathway). The 1,900-mile (3,000-km) route takes about four months to thru-hike, almost equally split between the North and South Islands.

More Info: *teararoa.org.nz*

SIGATOKA SAND DUNES, Fiji

Set along the south coast of Viti Levu, these rolling coastal dunes are protected within the confines of Fiji's oldest national park. Clamber up sand hills that reach nearly 200 feet (60 m) along the Yatole Kaleka Walk and Yatobalavu Scenery trail. The park also safeguards an ancient burial site and archaeological digs.

More Info: *nationaltrust.org.fj/ssd*

GATOKAE WEATHER COAST, Solomon Islands

This three-day journey along the windward shore of remote Nggatokae Island features pristine South Pacific wilderness and the possibility of over-nights and meals at village homestays along the route. Hiring a guide with knowledge of local nature and culture is highly recommended. Access via a two-hour speedboat trip from a dock near Seghe Airport.

More Info: *flysolomons.com/ destination-guide/trek*

TASMANIAN TRAIL, Australia

The rocky alpine highlands of Australia's southernmost state are the focus of a six-day trek through the wilds of Cradle Mountain–Lake St. Clair National Park. Reservations are required and hikers should be prepared for subfreezing temperatures and even snow at a latitude similar to Patagonia (42°).

More Info: *parks.tas.gov.au/ explore-our-parks/cradle-mountain/ overland-track*

Hiking Conservation

As hikers, we have the good fortune of seeing the world's most magnificent corners. Majestic mountain peaks, dormant volcanoes, highland meadows, desert dunes, and lush marshlands are our oasis—the scenes and wonders that draw us back to the trail time and time again. It is our responsibility to protect these wild places and the wildlife that lives within them before they're lost forever.

Hikers should be leading the charge to protect our wilderness because we are in the privileged position to see the changes taking place. It's our backyard and our responsibility.

Not sure where to begin? Here are eight conservation guidelines to get you started:

VOTE

This is an easy—and important—one. Vote for politicians who champion conservation and let them (and their opponents) know why. Be vocal. Sign petitions. For as much good as we're doing individually, we need lawmakers to back it up on a global level.

SUPPORT SCIENCE

Misinformation and choked-off funding are making scientific research difficult, right when we need it most. Whether with local grassroots projects in your community, organizations looking at the larger picture, or solution-focused companies, you can provide support by donating your time, volunteering your individual expertise (be it graphic design or social media know-how), or backing them financially. Hikers should also consider becoming citizen scientists by monitoring and documenting your surroundings on hikes and making note of climate conditions.

DRIVE LESS

Get to your next trailhead via carpool or public transportation. According to the Environmental Protection Agency (EPA), America's transportation sector was responsible for 29 percent of greenhouse gas emissions in 2019. Ride the bus where you can, carpool when you can't, and use resources and apps to find car-free options to reach outdoor destinations.

LOOK BUT DON'T TOUCH

This should be a no-brainer, but in the age of Instagram, we could all use another reminder: Let wildlife choose the interaction. Give animals space, and *never* touch or feed wildlife. Avoid (and report) any operation that doesn't apply good practice.

PLANT TREES

We're not strangers to getting dirty, but instead of muddying up those boots, get a little dirt on your hands. Plants help absorb carbon dioxide from the atmosphere and offset carbon emissions. In 2019, the EPA reported the land use and forestry sector offset 12 percent of greenhouse gas emissions. Plant your own trees, or donate to organizations that do the work for you.

VOLUNTEER

Hiking trails don't maintain themselves. Help preserve the routes you love the most by volunteering as a trail steward. Bring friends—of any age—to help clean debris, mark routes, restore plants, and more. Come June, participate in the American Hiking Society's National Trails Day to give back to the places you love the most.

SUPPORT THE PARKS

Donate. Volunteer. Supporting our national parks, forests, waterways, nature reserves, and more helps sustain the wild places.

REMEMBER THAT PLASTIC IS NOT SO FANTASTIC

In May 2018 National Geographic launched its Planet or Plastic? campaign, a multiyear effort to raise awareness about the global plastic crisis. A few fast plastic facts for you:

More than 40 percent of plastic is used once and then discarded, with 6.3 billion tons (5.7 billion metric tons) of plastic in our landfills, landscapes, and oceans.

Nearly a million plastic bottles are sold every minute around the world.

Plastic takes nearly 400 years to degrade; a 2018 study found that only 9 percent of plastics are recycled.

Be mindful of the amount of plastic you use in your everyday life and take active steps to reduce it. You can do this while hiking and backpacking by bringing reusable water bottles with you, as well as multiuse utensils that you can pull out instead of the plastic stuff. Oh, and skip the plastic straws, please. It's that simple. And that effective.

ILLUSTRATIONS CREDITS

Cover

Front cover, (BACKGROUND), Christian Kober 1/Alamy Stock Photo; (UP LE), Kyle Ledeboer/Ascent Xmedia/Getty Images; (UP RT), Menno Schaefer/Shutterstock; (LO LE), Mumemories/Shutterstock; (LO CTR), Elyse Butler/Cavan Images; (LO RT), Peathegee Inc/Getty Images; spine, Bill Stevenson/Alamy Stock Photo; back cover, Lisa Seaman/Cavan Images/Alamy Stock Photo.

Front Matter

2-3, Matt Hage; 4, Travelvolo/Shutterstock; 6, © Parks Canada/Scott Munn.

West Coast

8-9, Michael DeYoung/TandemStock; 10, Bennett Barthelemy/TandemStock; 11, Melissa Goodwin; 12, Matt Hage; 13, Melissa Goodwin; 14, Rachid Dahnoun/TandemStock; 15, Ron Karpel/Getty Images; 16, George Ostertag/agefotostock/Alamy Stock Photo; 17, artran/Getty Images; 18-9, Atan Chua/Getty Images; 20, Jim Hargan/blogPacifica/Alamy Stock Photo; 21, Brown W Cannon III/Alamy Stock Photo; 22, Ryan Heffernan/Cavan Images; 23, Howie Shultz; 24, Robert Holmes/Alamy Stock Photo; 25, Adam Joseph Wells; 26, David Wall/Alamy Stock Photo; 27, Tim Walker/Marin Outdoor Images; 28, MakenaStockMedia/Design Pics/National Geographic Image Collection; 29, Christian Kober/robertharding; 30-1, maximkabb/

Getty Images; 32, Michael Jones/Design Pics/National Geographic Image Collection; 33, Matt Hage; 34, Zachary Krahmer; 35, Matthew Kuhns/TandemStock; 36, Zachary Krahmer; 37, 7713 Photography/Shutterstock; 38, perezoo/Shutterstock; 39, Tracy + David, Tracy Boulian and David Ahntholz; 40, Max Waugh; 41, NASHCO; 42, Michael Jones/Design Pics/National Geographic Image Collection; 43, Kevin G. Smith/Design Pics/National Geographic Image Collection; 44-7, Melissa Goodwin; 48, Adrian J Paul; 49, Adam Mowery/TandemStock; 50, Carrie Yuan Images/Shutterstock; 51, John Trax/Alamy Stock Photo; 52, Jon Hicks/Getty Images; 54, AutumnSkyPhotography/Getty Images; 55, ZUMA Press/Alamy Stock Photo; 56, Amanda Joy Meyers; 57, Matt Hage; 58, Raphael Rivest/Shutterstock; 59, John Hoover/Photo Resource Hawaii/Alamy Stock Photo; 60-1, KoTotoro/Shutterstock; 62, IM_photo/Shutterstock; 63, miroslav_1/Getty Images.

Rocky Mountains & Southwest

64-5, Alan Majchrowicz/Getty Images; 66, Ben Herndon/TandemStock; 67, Lee Rentz/Alamy Stock Photo; 68, Michael Hanson/National Geographic Image Collection; 69, Tracy + David, Tracy Boulian and David Ahntholz; 70, Suzanne Stroeer/Aurora Photos/Getty Images; 71, Amanda Joy Meyers; 72-3, Cory Marshall/TandemStock; 74,

Louis Arevalo/TandemStock; 75, Dane Cronin/TandemStock; 76, Andrew Coleman/National Geographic Image Collection; 78, Markus Thomenius/Alamy Stock Photo; 79, Scott Smith/Getty Images; 80, Dianne Leeth/Alamy Stock Photo; 81, Phil Degginger/Alamy Stock Photo; 82, Kirk Anderson-Photo; 83, jdiddy23/Getty Images; 84, Ben Herndon/TandemStock; 85, Justin Bailie/TandemStock; 86-7, Ben Herndon/TandemStock; 88, Matt Hage; 89, Matt Hage; 90, Nick Lake/TandemStock; 92, Helen H. Richardson/MediaNews Group/The Denver Post via Getty Images; 93, melissamn/Shutterstock; 94, Michael DeYoung/TandemStock; 95, Ian G Dagnall/Alamy Stock Photo; 96-7, Matt Hage; 98, Ian Shive/TandemStock; 99, Daniel Kieslinger Photo/mauritius images GmbH/Alamy Stock Photo; 100, Dave Stamboulis/agefotostock/Alamy Stock Photo; 101, Matt Hage; 102, raquelmogado/Adobe Stock; 103, Wildnerdpix/Getty Images; 104, Larry N Young/Getty Images; 105, Mike Cavaroc/TandemStock; 106-7, Matt Hage; 108, Nelson Kenter; 109, Dan Oldenburg/Alamy Stock Photo; 110, © Adolphe Pierre-Louis/Albuquerque Journal/ZUMA/Alamy Stock Photo; 111, Greg Meland/Adobe Stock; 112, Dan Holz/TandemStock; 113, Jeff Goulden/Getty Images; 114, Dave Stamboulis/Alamy Stock Photo; 115, Celin Serbo/TandemStock; 116, Robb Kendrick/National Geographic Image

Collection; 117, Different_Brian/ Getty Images; 118, Amanda Joy Meyers; 119, Babak Tafreshi/ National Geographic Image Collection.

Midwest

120-1, Michael Szonyi/Getty Images; 122, PapaBear/Getty Images; 123, Kenneth Keifer/500px/Getty Images; 124, South Dakota Dept. of Tourism; 125, Mike Kline (notkalvin)/ Getty Images; 126, Bruce Leighty/Alamy Stock Photo; 127, Adam Welz/Alamy Stock Photo; 128, GeoStills/Alamy Stock Photo; 129, Gregory Holmgren/ Alamy Stock Photo; 130-1, Dawid Swierczek/Alamy Stock Photo; 132, Jim West/Alamy Stock Photo; 133, Arin Yoon; 134, Indiana Department of Natural Resources; 135, Indiana Department of Natural Resources; 136, Nebraskaland Magazine/Nebraska Game and Parks Commission; 137, marekuliasz/Getty Images; 138-9, Chuck Haney/DanitaDelimont/ Alamy Stock Photo; 140, Jeffrey Phelps/Cavan Images; 141, MarynaG/Shutterstock; 142, Timothy Mulholland/Alamy Stock Photo; 144, marekuliasz/ Getty Images; 145, Carol Bock/ Getty Images; 146, Dominique Braud/Dembinsky Photo Associates/Alamy Stock Photo; 147, Richard Cummins/robertharding/Alamy Stock Photo; 148-9, Chuck Haney/DanitaDelimont/ Alamy Stock Photo; 150, Brian Cahn/ZUMA Press/Alamy Stock Photo; 151, Kenneth Keifer/ Getty Images; 152, Suzanne Danyluk/Alamy Stock Photo;

153, Aaron Black-Schmidt/ TandemStock; 154, Daniel Borzynski/Alamy Stock Photo; 155, Posnov/Getty Images; 156, Aaron Peterson; 157, Aaron Peterson; 158, Bill Gozansky/ Alamy Stock Photo; 159, Jason Lindsey/Alamy Stock Photo; 160-1, Daniel Ripplinger/DansPhotoArt/Getty Images; 162, Ackerman + Gruber; 163, Franck Fotos/Alamy Stock Photo; 164, Iowa Great Lakes Spine Trail, Dickinson County Trails; 165, dosecreative/Getty Images.

South

166-7, Skip Brown/robertharding/Alamy Stock Photo; 168, Cyndi Monaghan/Getty Images; 169, Jim West/Alamy Stock Photo; 170, Courtesy of the Alabama Forestry Commission; 171, Jim Vallee/Shutterstock; 172, mtnmichelle/Getty Images; 173, Tim Fitzharris/Minden Pictures; 174-5, Andrew R. Slaton/TandemStock; 176, Rory Doyle; 177, Clint Farlinger/Alamy Stock Photo; 178, Tom Till/Alamy Stock Photo; 179, Ryan Maum/ Shutterstock; 180, Melissa Goodwin; 181, Amanda Joy Meyers; 182, Pete Muller/National Geographic Image Collection; 184, Melissa Goodwin; 185, Melissa Goodwin; 186, Danielsen_Photography/Shutterstock; 187, Patrick Jennings/Adobe Stock; 188-9, Patrick Jennings/Adobe Stock; 190, Michael W. Harding; 191, USDA Forest Service/Stacy Blomquist; 192, South Carolina Department of Parks, Recreation & Tourism; 193, Alexander Kreher/Ost Haus; 194, Buddy Mays/Alamy Stock Photo; 195,

Gunnar Rathbun/Shutterstock; 196, Ian Shive/TandemStock; 197, dszc/Getty Images; 198, Allen Creative/Steve Allen/Alamy Stock Photo; 199, Sean Pavone/ Getty Images; 200-1, Sean Pavone/Getty Images; 202, Frances Gallogly/TandemStock; 203, Adam Mowery/TandemStock; 204, Lori Kincaid; 206, Darrell Uruski; 207, Rob Hainer/Shutterstock; 208, samray/Shutterstock; 209, Byron Jorjorian/ Alamy Stock Photo; 210, M. Timothy O'Keefe/Alamy Stock Photo; 211, Jim West/Alamy Stock Photo; 212, Thomas Levine Photography/Alamy Stock Photo; 214-5, Amanda Joy Meyers; 216, Brent Martin; 217, W. Drew Senter, Longleaf Photography/Getty Images; 218, Ian Dagnall/Alamy Stock Photo; 219, Stephen Frink/RGB Ventures/ SuperStock/Alamy Stock Photo; 220, Lekali Studio/Shutterstock; 221, Creative Dog Media.

Northeast

222-3, Melissa Goodwin; 224, Edwin Remsberg/VWPics/Alamy Stock Photo; 225, Edwin Remsberg/VWPics/Alamy Stock Photo; 226, Patrick Tappe/Shutterstock; 227, PTZ Pictures/ Shutterstock; 228, Cliedy Bersola Sta. Ana; 229, Bridget Likely © Appalachian Mountain Club; 230, Richard Levine/Alamy Stock Photo; 231, Melissa Goodwin; 232-3, Kike Calvo/Alamy Stock Photo; 234, Babak Tafreshi/National Geographic Image Collection; 235, William Perry/DanitaDelimont/Alamy Stock Photo; 236, Kate Warren; 238, Raun Kercher/Shutterstock;

239, H. Mark Weidman Photography/Alamy Stock Photo; 240, Toni L. Sandys/The Washington Post via Getty Images; 241, Jeffrey Isaac Greenberg 12+/Alamy Stock Photo; 242-3, DNREC/Delaware State Parks; 244, Stan Tess/Alamy Stock Photo; 245, Ed Schernau; 246, Peter Steiner/Alamy Stock Photo; 247, Jonathan Duda, Parks & Trails New York; 248, Vespasian/Alamy Stock Photo; 249, Randy Duchaine/Alamy Stock Photo; 250-3, Melissa Goodwin; 254, Ian Dagnall/Alamy Stock Photo; 255, Sarah Jones Decker; 256, Stillman Rogers/Alamy Stock Photo; 257, Melissa Goodwin; 258, Denise LeBlanc/Shutterstock; 259, Kindra Clineff/Alamy Stock Photo; 260-1, Chuck Blackley/Alamy Stock Photo; 262-5, Melissa Goodwin; 266, Jakub Zajic/Shutterstock; 267, Fahmid Swaikat/Getty Images; 268, Mark Henninger/Getty Images; 269, Jumping Rocks/UCG/Universal Images Group via Getty Images.

Canada

270-1, Tracy + David, Tracy Boulian and David Ahntholz; 272, MJ Photography/Alamy Stock Photo; 273, Marc Guitard/Getty Images; 274, Darlyne A. Murawski/National Geographic Image Collection; 275, aprott/Getty Images; 276-7, Rasvan Iliescu/Alamy Stock Photo; 278, Walter Bibikow/mauritius images GmbH/Alamy Stock Photo; 279, Barrett & MacKay/All Canada Photos/Alamy Stock Photo; 280, PerfectDayToPlay/Shutterstock; 281, Ron Yue/Alamy Stock

Photo; 282, © Parks Canada/Josh McCulloch; 283, © Parks Canada; 284-5, © Parks Canada/Josh McCulloch; 286, Gaertner/Alamy Stock Photo; 287, GROGL/Getty Images; 288, Mark Heine/500px/Getty Images; 290, Rob Crandall/Alamy Stock Photo; 291, Marc Guitard/Getty Images; 292, Charlevoix © TQ/G.Leroyer; 293, Jean Robert; 294, Buddy409/Shutterstock; 295, Shayne Thiessen; 296, Dougall Photography/Getty Images; 297, sprokop/Getty Images; 298, Witold Skrypczak/Alamy Stock Photo; 299, © Parks Canada/Zoya Lynch; 300-1, Tracy + David, Tracy Boulian and David Ahntholz; 302, Destination Ontario; 303, The Heist; 304, Paul de Burger; 305, Destination Ontario; 306, Sam and Brian/Shutterstock; 307, Michael Wheatley/Alamy Stock Photo; 308, Stefan Wackerhagen/Getty Images; 309, Stefan Wackerhagen/imageBROKER/Alamy Stock Photo; 310-1, Rocky Grimes/Alamy Stock Photo; 312, Bandersnatch/Shutterstock; 313, Michael Wheatley/Alamy Stock Photo; 314, Maridav/Getty Images; 315, RnDmS/Adobe Stock; 316, Manuel Romaris/Getty Images; 317, Robert Chiasson/All Canada Photos/Alamy Stock Photo.

Global Trails

318-9, Matt Hage; 320, Alan Copson/Jon Arnold Images/Alamy Stock Photo; 321 (UP), Praveen P.N/Getty Images; 321 (LO), House Light Gallery—Steven House Photography/Getty

Images; 322, Austin Trigg/TandemStock; 323, Joerg Steber/Shutterstock; 324, Maya Karkalicheva/Getty Images; 325, Jens Ottoson/Shutterstock; 326, Maya Karkalicheva/Getty Images; 327 (UP), Radek Borovka/Shutterstock; 327 (LO), Jorge Fernandez/Alamy Stock Photo; 328, Matt Hage; 329, Adrian Samiro See/EyeEm/Getty Images; 330, Don Mammoser/Shutterstock; 331, Thomas Garcia/Alamy Stock Photo.

INDEX

Boldface indicates illustrations.

ACKNOWLEDGMENTS

Like any undertaking of this magnitude—and every book I've ever worked on—it takes a village. In this case comprising friends, family, and the publishing team at National Geographic.

My wife, Julia, was invaluable as a researcher, proofreader, sounding board, and hiking companion. My daughters, Chelsea and Shannon, both of whom are avid hikers, also lent a hand by suggesting trails in New England and the Far West. Time-tripping to my youth, scout master Joe Allen is the one who got me started hiking on trails in the mountains of southern California.

With editor Allyson Johnson leading the way, the *100 Trails* team at National Geographic included Ashley Leath (editorial project manager), Kay Hankins (designer), Jill Foley (senior photo editor), Elisa Gibson (creative director), Adrian Coakley (director of photography), and Michael O'Connor (senior production editor).

Once the book was rolling off the presses, Ann Day at Disney Publishing Worldwide got the word out and organized my radio, television, and podcast interviews with help from Christie Damato and Marisa Papa at Litzky Public Relations and Anna Gartaganis at Core Four Media.

It also behooves me to thank AllTrails, the extraordinary hiking app that made so many of the hikes for this book easier to plan and execute—especially that time when my daughters found themselves hiking in the dark on a remote cliff-top trail in southern Utah.

ABOUT THE AUTHOR

During three decades as an editor, writer, and photographer, Joe Yogerst has lived and worked in Asia, Africa, Europe, and North America. His writing has appeared in *Condé Nast Traveler,* CNN Travel, *Islands* magazine, the *International New York Times* (Paris), *Washington Post, Los Angeles Times,* and *National Geographic Traveler.* He has written for 34 National Geographic books, including the best-selling *50 States, 5,000 Ideas* and the sequel, *100 Parks, 5,000 Ideas.* His first U.S. novel, a murder mystery titled *Nemesis,* was published in 2018. Yogerst is the host of a National Geographic/Great Courses video series on America's state parks.

100 TRAILS 5000 IDEAS

Since 1888, the National Geographic Society has funded more than 14,000 research, conservation, education, and storytelling projects around the world. National Geographic Partners distributes a portion of the funds it receives from your purchase to National Geographic Society to support programs including the conservation of animals and their habitats.

Get closer to National Geographic Explorers and photographers, and connect with our global community. Join us today at nationalgeographic.org/joinus

For rights or permissions inquiries, please contact National Geographic Books Subsidiary Rights: bookrights@natgeo.com

Library of Congress Cataloging-in-Publication Data
Names: Yogerst, Joseph R., author.
Title: 100 trails, 5,000 ideas : where to go, when to go, what to see, what to do / Joe Yogerst.
Other titles: One hundred trails, five thousand ideas
Description: Washington, DC : National Geographic, [2023] | Includes index.
| Summary: "This authoritative travel guide takes you on a series of epic hiking and walking adventures on 100 trails around all 50 states and Canada"– Provided by publisher.
Identifiers: LCCN 2022021513 | ISBN 9781426222566 (Trade Paperback)
Subjects: LCSH: Hiking–United States–Guidebooks. |
    Hiking–Canada–Guidebooks. | Walking–United States–Guidebooks. |
    Walking–Canada–Guidebooks. | Trails–United States–Guidebooks. |
    Trails–Canada–Guidebooks.
Classification: LCC GV199.4 .Y64 2023 | DDC 796.51097–dc23/eng/20220708
LC record available at https://lccn.loc.gov/2022021513

ISBN: 978-1-4262-2256-6

Printed in South Korea

22/SPSK/1

The information in this book has been carefully checked and to the best of our knowledge is accurate. However, details are subject to change, and the publisher cannot be responsible for such changes, or for errors or omissions. Assessments of sites, hotels, and restaurants are based on the author's subjective opinions, which do not necessarily reflect the publisher's opinion.

I A LIFETIME OF PURSUITS

PACK YOUR GEAR AND LACE YOUR BOOTS!

This ultimate hiker's bucket list treks through 100 energizing experiences for all levels. Filled with beautiful National Geographic photography, wisdom from expert hikers, travel information, and practical wildlife-spotting tips, this inspirational guide offers the planet's best experiences for hikers and sightseers. From short day hikes to multiday excursions and multiweek treks, you'll find a hike that matches your interests and skill level.

AVAILABLE WHEREVER BOOKS ARE SOLD

 NatGeoBooks   @NatGeoBooks